BOUNDARIES

Resources by Henry Cloud and John Townsend

BOUNDARIES

When to Say YES
When to Say NO
To Take Control
of Your Life

Dr. Henry Cloud
Dr. John Townsend

ZONDERVAN™

GRAND RAPIDS, MICHIGAN 49530 USA

ZONDERVAN.COM/

AUTHORTRACKER

We want to hear from you. Please send your comments about this
book to us in care of the address below. Thank you.

Boundaries
Copyright © 1992 by Henry Cloud and John Townsend

This title is also available as a Zondervan ebook product.
Visit www.zondervan.com/ebooks for more information.

This title is also available as a Zondervan audio product.
Visit www.zondervan.com/audiopages for more information.

Requests for information should be addressed to:
Zondervan, *Grand Rapids, Michigan 49530*

Library of Congress Cataloging-in-Publication Data
Cloud, Henry.
    Boundaries: When to say yes, when to say no to take control of your life / Henry
Cloud and John Townsend.
       p. cm.
    ISBN-10: 0-310-24745-4 (softcover)
    ISBN-13: 978-0-310-24745-6 (softcover)
    1. Conduct of life. 2. Christian life—1960– 3. Interpersonal relations—Religious
aspects—Christianity. I. Townsend, John Sims, 1952–. II. Title.
    BJ1581.2.C52 1992
    248.4—dc20

                                      92–5503

All Scripture quotations, unless otherwise noted, are taken from the HOLY BIBLE: NEW
INTERNATIONAL VERSION® (North American Edition). Copyright © 1973, 1978, 1984
by International Bible Society. Used by permission of Zondervan. All rights reserved.

Verses marked nasb are taken from the New American Standard Bible, © 1960 by the Lock-
man Foundation; verses marked nrsv are taken from the New Revised Standard Version, ©
1989 by the Division of Christian Education of the National Council of the Churches of
Christ in the United States of America.

Since the case studies in this book are composites from Dr. Henry Cloud's and Dr. John
Townsend's practices, we have not attempted to identify which author is counseling which
client. All names and circumstances have been fictionalized to protect privacy.

Published in association with Yates & Yates, LLP, Attorneys and Counselors, Suite 1000,
Literary Agent, Orange, CA

Edited by Sandra L. Vander Zicht   *Interior designed by Bob Hudson*
Cover designed by John M. Lucas   *Cover illustration by Michael McGovern*

Printed in the United States of America

06 07 08 • 50 49 48 47 46 45 44 43 42 41 40 39 38 37 36 35 34 33 32 31 30

To Henry and Louise Cloud
and
John and Rebecca Townsend,

whose training in boundaries
made a difference in our lives

Contents

Acknowledgments

S cott Bolinder and Bruce Ryskamp caught the vision for this book from the very beginning. They arranged for a retreat on Lake Michigan, where we passed this vision on to other Zondervan staff members.

Sandy Vander Zicht directed the editorial process and, with Lori Walburg, fine-tuned the manuscript into a book that is more graceful, more precise, and easier to read and understand. Dan Runyon cut the book down to a manageable size.

Dave Anderson translated this book into a video curriculum.

Sealy Yates encouraged and supported us throughout the whole process, from contract to finished book.

PART ONE

WHAT ARE BOUNDARIES?

1

A Day in a Boundaryless Life

6:00 A.M.

T he alarm jangled. Bleary-eyed from too little sleep, Sherrie shut off the noisy intruder, turned on the bedside lamp, and sat up in bed. Looking blankly at the wall, she tried to get her bearings.

Why am I dreading this day? Lord, didn't you promise me a life of joy?

Then, as the cobwebs left her mind, Sherrie remembered the reason for her dread: the four-o'clock meeting with Todd's third-grade teacher. The phone call returned to her memory: "Sherrie, this is Jean Russell. I wonder if we could meet about Todd's performance and his . . . behavior."

Todd couldn't keep still and listen to his teachers. He didn't even listen to Sherrie and Walt. Todd was such a strong-willed child, and she didn't want to quench his spirit. Wasn't that more important?

"Well, no time to worry about all that," Sherrie said to herself, raising her thirty-five-year-old body off the bed and padding to the shower. "I've got enough troubles to keep me busy all day."

Under the shower, Sherrie's mind moved out of first gear. She began mentally ticking off the day's schedule. Todd, nine, and Amy, six, would have been a handful even if she *weren't* a working mother.

"Let's see . . . fix breakfast, pack two lunches, and finish sewing Amy's costume for the school play. That will be a trick—finishing sewing the costume before the car pool picks her up at 7:45 A.M."

Sherrie thought regretfully about last night. She'd planned to work on Amy's costume then, using her talents to make a special day for her little girl. But her mother had dropped over unexpectedly. Good manners dictated that she play hostess, and another evening was shot. The memories of her attempts to salvage the time weren't pretty.

Trying to be diplomatic, Sherrie artfully told her mother, "You can't imagine how much I enjoy your surprise visits, Mom! But I was wondering, would you mind if I sew Amy's costume while we talk?" Sherrie cringed inwardly, correctly anticipating her mother's response.

"Sherrie, you know I'd be the last to intrude on your time with your family." Sherrie's mother, widowed for twelve years, had elevated her widowhood to the status of martyrdom. "I mean, since your father died, it's been such an empty time. I still miss our family. How could I deprive you of that for yourself?"

I'll bet I find out how, Sherrie thought to herself.

"That's why I can understand why you don't bring Walt and the children to see me much anymore. How could I be entertaining? I'm just a lonely old lady who gave her entire life to her children. Who would want to spend any time with me?"

"No, Mom, no, no, no!" Sherrie quickly joined the emotional minuet she and her mom had been dancing for decades. "That's not what I meant at all! I mean, it's so special having you over. Goodness knows, with our schedule, we'd like to visit more, but we just haven't been able to. That's why I'm so glad you took the initiative!" *Lord, don't strike me dead for this little lie,* she prayed silently.

"In fact, I can do the costume any old time," Sherrie said. *Forgive me for this lie, too.* "Now, why don't I make us some coffee?"

Her mother sighed. "All right, if you insist. But I'd just hate to think I'm intruding."

The visit lasted well into the night. By the time her mother left, Sherrie felt absolutely crazy, but she justified it to herself. *At least I've helped make her lonely day a little brighter.* Then a pesky voice piped up. *If you helped so much, why was she still talking about her loneliness when she left?* Trying to ignore the thought, Sherrie went to bed.

6:45 A.M.

Sherrie returned to the present. "No use crying over spilt time, I guess," she mumbled to herself as she struggled to close the zipper of her black linen skirt. Her favorite suit had become, as many others had, too tight. *Middle-age spread so soon?* she thought. *This week, I really have to go on a diet and start exercising.*

The next hour was, as usual, a disaster. The kids whined about getting out of bed, and Walt complained, "Can't you get the kids to the table on time?"

7:45 A.M.

Miraculously, the kids made it to their rides, Walt left for work in his car, and Sherrie went out and locked the front door after her. Taking a deep breath, she prayed silently, *Lord, I'm not looking forward to this day. Give me something to hope for.* In her car on the freeway, she finished applying her makeup. *Thank the Lord for traffic jams.*

8:45 A.M.

Rushing into McAllister Enterprises where she worked as a fashion consultant, Sherrie glanced at her watch. Only a few minutes late. Maybe by now her colleagues understood that being late was a way of life for her and did not expect her to be on time.

She was wrong. They'd started the weekly executive meeting without her. Sherrie tried to tiptoe in without being noticed, but every eye was on her as she struggled into her seat. Glancing around, she gave a fleeting smile and muttered something about "that crazy traffic."

11:59 A.M.

The rest of Sherrie's morning proceeded fairly well. A talented fashion designer, Sherrie had an unerring eye for attractive clothing and was a valuable asset to McAllister. The only hitch came just before lunch.

Her extension rang. "Sherrie Phillips."

"Sherrie, thank goodness you're there! I don't know what I'd have done if you'd been at lunch!" There was no mistaking this voice. Sherrie had known Lois Thompson since grade school. A high-strung woman, Lois was always in crisis. Sherrie had always tried to make herself available to Lois, to "be there for her." But Lois never asked Sherrie how she was doing, and when Sherrie mentioned her struggles, Lois either changed the subject or had to leave.

Sherrie genuinely loved Lois and was concerned about her problems, but Lois seemed more like a client than a friend. Sherrie resented the imbalance in their friendship. As always, Sherrie felt guilty when she thought about her anger at Lois. As a Christian, she knew the value the Bible placed on loving and helping others. *There I go again,* she would say to herself. *Thinking of myself before others. Please, Lord, let me give to Lois freely and not be so self-centered.*

Sherrie asked, "What's the matter, Lois?"

"It's horrible, just horrible," Lois said. "Anne was sent home from school today, Tom was denied his promotion, and my car gave out on the freeway!"

This is what my life's like every day! Sherrie thought to herself, feeling the resentment rising. However, she merely said, "Lois, you poor thing! How are you coping with all of this?"

Lois was happy to answer Sherrie's question in great detail—so much detail that Sherrie missed half her lunch break consoling her friend. *Well,* she thought, *fast food's better than no food.*

Sitting at the drive-through waiting for her chicken burger, Sherrie thought about Lois. *If all my listening, consoling, and advice had made any difference over the years, maybe it would be worth it. But Lois makes the same mistakes now that she made twenty years ago. Why do I do this to myself?*

4:00 P.M.

Sherrie's afternoon passed uneventfully. She was on the way out of the office to the teacher's meeting when her boss, Jeff Moreland, flagged her down.

"Glad I caught up with you, Sherrie," he said. A successful figure at MacAllister Enterprises, Jeff made things happen. Trouble was, Jeff often used other people to "make things happen." Sherrie could sense the hundredth verse of the same old song tuning up again. "Listen, I'm in a time crunch," he said, handing her a large sheaf of papers. "This is the data for the final recommendations for the Kimbrough account. All it needs is a little writing and editing. And it's due tomorrow. But I'm sure it'll be no problem for you." He smiled ingratiatingly.

Sherrie panicked. Jeff's "editing" needs were legendary. Hefting the papers in her hands, Sherrie saw a minimum of five hours' work. *I had this data in to him three weeks ago!* she thought furiously. *Where does this man get off having me save his face for his deadline?*

Quickly she composed herself. "Sure, Jeff. It's no problem at all. Glad I can help. What time do you need it?"

"Nine o'clock would be fine. And . . . thanks, Sherrie. I always think of you first when I'm in a jam. You're so dependable." Jeff strolled away.

Dependable . . . faithful . . . reliable, Sherrie thought. *I've always been described this way by people who wanted something from me. Sounds like a description of a good mule.* Suddenly the guilt hit again. *There I am, getting resentful again. Lord, help me "bloom where I'm planted."* But secretly she found herself wishing she could be transplanted to another flowerpot.

4:30 P.M.

Jean Russell was a competent teacher, one of many in the profession who understood the complex factors beneath a child's problem behavior. The meeting with Todd's teacher began as so many before, minus Walt. Todd's father hadn't been able to get off work, so the two women talked alone.

"He's not a bad child, Sherrie," Mrs. Russell reassured her. "Todd is a bright, energetic boy. When he minds, he's one of the most enjoyable kids in the class."

Sherrie waited for the ax to fall. *Just get to the point, Jean. I have a "problem child," don't I? What's new? I have a "problem life" to go with it.*

Sensing Sherrie's discomfort, the teacher pressed ahead. "The problem is that Todd doesn't respond well to limits. For example, during our task period, when children work on assignments, Todd has great difficulty. He gets up from his desk, pesters other kids, and won't stop talking. When I mention to him that his behavior is inappropriate, he becomes enraged and obstinate."

Sherrie felt defensive about her only son. "Maybe Todd has an attention-deficit problem, or he's hyperactive?"

Mrs. Russell shook her head. "When Todd's second-grade teacher wondered about that last year, psychological testing ruled that out. Todd stays on task very well when he's interested in the subject. I'm no therapist, but it seems to me that he's just not used to responding to rules."

Now Sherrie's defensiveness turned from Todd to herself. "Are you saying this is some sort of home problem?"

Mrs. Russell looked uncomfortable. "As I said, I'm not a counselor. I just know that in third grade, most children resist rules. But Todd is off the scale. Any time I tell him to do something he doesn't want to it's World War III. And since all his intellectual and cognitive testing comes out normal, I was just wondering how things were at home?"

Sherrie no longer tried to hold back the tears. She buried her head in her hands and wept convulsively for a few minutes, feeling overwhelmed with everything.

Eventually, her crying subsided. "I'm sorry . . . I guess this just hit on a bad day." Sherrie rummaged in her purse for a tissue. "No, no, it's more than that. Jean, I need to be honest with you. Your problems with him are the same as mine. Walt and I have a real struggle making Todd mind at home. When we're playing or talking, Todd is the most wonderful son I could imagine. But any time I have to discipline him, the tantrums are more than I can handle. So I guess I don't have any solutions for you."

Jean nodded her head slowly. "It really helps me, Sherrie, to know that Todd's behavior is a problem at home, too. At least now we can put our heads together on a solution."

5:15 P.M.

Sherrie felt strangely grateful for the afternoon rush-hour traffic. *At least there's no one tugging on me here,* she thought. She used the time to plan around her next crises: kids, dinner, Jeff's project, church, . . . and Walt.

6:30 P.M.

"For the fourth and last time, dinner's ready!" Sherrie hated to scream, but what else worked? The kids and Walt always seemed to shuffle in whenever they felt like it. More often than not, dinner was cold by the time everyone was assembled.

Sherrie had no clue what the problem was. She knew it wasn't the food, because she was a good cook. Besides, once they got to the table, everyone inhaled it in seconds.

Everyone but Amy. Watching her daughter sit silently, picking distractedly at her food, Sherrie again felt uneasy. Amy was such a loveable, sensitive child. Why was she so reserved? Amy had never been outgoing. She preferred to spend her time reading, painting, or just sitting in her bedroom "thinking about stuff."

"Honey, what kind of stuff?" Sherrie would probe.

"Just stuff," would be the usual reply. Sherrie felt shut out of her daughter's life. She dreamed of mother-daughter talks, conversations for "just us girls," shopping trips. But Amy had a secret place deep inside where no one was ever invited. This unreachable part of her daughter's heart Sherrie ached to touch.

7:00 P.M.

Halfway through dinner, the phone rang. *We really need to get an answering machine to handle calls during dinner,* Sherrie thought. *There's precious little time for us to be together as a family anymore.* Then, as if on cue, another familiar thought struck her. *It might be someone who needs me.*

As always, Sherrie listened to the second voice in her head and jumped up from the table to answer the phone. Her heart sank as she recognized the voice on the other end.

"Hope I'm not disturbing anything," said Phyllis Renfrow, the women's ministries leader at church.

"Certainly you aren't disturbing anything," Sherrie lied again.

"Sherrie, I'm in deep water," Phyllis said. "Margie was going to be our activities coordinator at the retreat, and now she's cancelled. Something about "priorities at home." Any way you can pitch in?"

The retreat. Sherrie had almost forgotten that the annual gathering of church women was this weekend. She had actually been looking forward to leaving the kids and Walt behind and strolling around the beautiful mountainous area for two days, just herself and the Lord. In fact, the possibility of solitude felt better to her than the planned group activities. Taking on Margie's activities coordinator position would mean giving up her precious alone time. No, it wouldn't work. Sherrie would just have to say ...

Automatically, the second thought pattern intervened. *What a privilege to serve God and these women, Sherrie! By giving up a little portion of your life, by letting go of your selfishness, you can make a big difference in some lives. Think it over.*

Sherrie didn't have to think it over. She'd learned to respond unquestioningly to this familiar voice, just as she responded to her mother's, and Phyllis's, and maybe God's, too. Whoever it belonged to, it was too strong to be ignored. Habit won out.

"I'll be happy to help," Sherrie told Phyllis. "Just send me whatever Margie's done, and I'll get working on it."

Phyllis sighed, audibly relieved. "Sherrie, I know it's a sacrifice. Myself, I have to do it several times, every day. But that's the abundant Christian life, isn't it? Being living sacrifices."

If you say so, thought Sherrie. But she couldn't help wondering when the "abundant" part would come in.

7:45 P.M.

Dinner finally finished, Sherrie watched Walt position himself in front of the TV for the football game. Todd reached for the phone, asking if his friends could come over and play. Amy slipped unobserved to her room.

The dishes stayed on the table. The family hadn't quite gotten the hang of helping clean up yet. But maybe the kids were still a little young for that. Sherrie started clearing the dishes from the table.

11:30 P.M.

Years ago, Sherrie could have cleaned up after dinner, gotten the kids to bed on time, and performed Jeff's handed-off project with ease. A cup of coffee after dinner and the adrenaline rush that accompanied crises and deadlines galvanized Sherrie into superhuman feats of productivity. She wasn't called "Super Sherrie" for nothing!

But it was becoming noticeably harder these days. Stress didn't work like it used to. More and more, she was having trouble concentrating, forgetting dates and deadlines, and not even caring a great deal about it all.

At any rate, by sheer willpower, she had completed most of her tasks. Maybe Jeff's project had suffered a little in quality, but she felt too resentful to feel bad. *But I did say yes to Jeff*, Sherrie thought. *It's not his fault, it's mine. Why couldn't I tell him how unfair it was for him to lay this on me?*

No time for that now. She had to get on with her real task for the evening: her talk with Walt.

Her and Walt's courtship and early marriage had been pleasant. Where she'd been confused, Walt had been decisive. Where she'd felt insecure, he'd been strong. Not that Sherrie wasn't contributing to the marriage. She saw Walt's lack of emotional connectedness, and she had taken upon herself the job of providing the warmth and love the relationship lacked. *God has put together a good team,* she would tell herself. *Walt has the leadership, and I have the love.* This would help her get over the lonely times when he couldn't seem to understand her hurt feelings.

But over the years, Sherrie noted a shift in the relationship. It started off subtly, then became more pronounced. She could hear it in his sarcastic tone when she had a complaint. She saw it in the lack of respect in his eyes when she tried to tell him about her need for more support from him. She felt it in his increasingly insistent demands for her to do things his way.

And his temper. Maybe it was job stress, or having kids. Whatever it was, Sherrie never dreamed she'd ever hear the cutting, angry words she heard from the lips of the man she'd married. She didn't have to cross him much at all to be subjected to the anger—burnt toast, a checking overdraft, or forgetting to gas up the car—any of these seemed to be enough.

It all pointed to one conclusion: the marriage was no longer a team, if it ever had been one. It was a parent-child relationship, with Sherrie on the wrong end.

At first she thought she was imagining things. *There I go again, looking for trouble when I have a great life,* she told herself. That would help for a while—until Walt's next temper attack. Then her hurt and sadness would tell her the truth her mind wasn't willing to accept.

Finally realizing that Walt was a controlling person, Sherrie took the blame upon herself. *I'd be that way, too, if I had a basket case like me to live with,* she'd think. *I'm the reason he gets so critical and frustrated.*

These conclusions led Sherrie to a solution she had practiced for years: "Loving Walt Out of His Anger." This remedy went something like this: first, Sherrie learned to read Walt's emotions by watching his temper, body language, and speech. She became exquisitely aware of his moods, and especially sensitive to things that could set him off: lateness, disagreements, and her own anger. As long as she was quiet and agreeable, things went well. But let her preferences raise their ugly heads and she risked getting her head lopped off.

Sherrie learned to read Walt well, and quickly. After sensing that she was crossing an emotional line, she would employ Stage Two of "Loving Walt": She did an immediate backtrack. Coming around to his viewpoint (but not really), quietly holding her tongue, or even outrightly apologizing for being "hard to live with" all helped.

Stage Three of "Loving Walt" was doing special things for him to show that she was sincere. This might mean dressing more attractively at home. Or making his favorite meals several times a week. Didn't the Bible talk about being this kind of wife?

The three steps of "Loving Walt" worked for a time. But the peace never lasted. The problem with "Loving Walt Out of His Anger" was that Sherrie was dead tired of trying to soothe Walt out of his tantrums. Thus, he stayed angry longer, and his anger isolated her more from him.

Her love for her husband was eroding. She had felt that no matter how bad things were, God had joined them and that their love would get them through. But, in the past few years, it was more commitment than love. When she was honest, she admitted that many times she could feel nothing at all toward Walt but resentment and fear.

And that's what tonight was all about. Things needed to change. Somehow, they needed to rekindle the flames of their first love.

Sherrie walked into the family room. The late-night comedian on the television screen had just finished his monologue. "Honey, can we talk?" she asked tentatively.

There was no answer. Moving closer, she saw why. Walt had fallen asleep on the couch. Thinking about waking Walt up, she remembered his stinging words the last time she'd been so "insensitive." She turned off the television and lights and walked to the empty bedroom.

11:50 P.M.

Lying in bed, Sherrie couldn't tell which was greater, her loneliness or her exhaustion. Deciding it was the first, she picked up her Bible from the bedside table and opened it to the New Testament. *Give me something to hope for, Lord. Please,* she prayed silently. Her eyes fell to the words of Christ in Matthew 5:3–5:

> "Blessed are the poor in spirit, for theirs is the kingdom of heaven. Blessed are those who mourn, for they will be comforted. Blessed are the meek, for they will inherit the earth."

But Lord, I already feel like that! Sherrie protested. *I feel poor in spirit. I mourn over my life, my marriage, my children. I try to be gentle, but I just feel run over all the time. Where is your promise? Where is your hope? Where are you?*

Sherrie waited in the darkened room for an answer. None came. The only sound was the quiet pit-pat of tears running off her checks and onto the pages of her Bible.

What's the Problem?

Sherrie tries to live her life the right way. She tries to do a good job with her marriage, her children, her job, her relationships, and her Lord. Yet it's obvious that something isn't right. Life isn't working. Sherrie's in deep spiritual and emotional pain.

Woman or man, we can all identify with Sherrie's dilemma—her isolation, her helplessness, her confusion, her guilt. And, above all, her sense that her life is out of control.

Look closely at Sherrie's circumstances. Parts of Sherrie's life may be remarkably similar to your own. Understanding her struggle may shed light on yours. You can immediately see a few answers that *don't* work for Sherrie.

First, *trying harder isn't working.* Sherrie expends lots of energy trying to have a successful life. She isn't lazy. Second, *being nice out of fear isn't working.* Sherrie's people-pleasing efforts don't seem to bring her the intimacy she needs.

Third, *taking responsibility for others isn't working.* A master of taking care of the feelings and problems of others, Sherrie feels like her life is a miserable failure. Sherrie's unproductive energy, fearful niceness, and overresponsibility point to the core problem: *Sherrie suffers from severe difficulties in taking ownership of her life.*

Back in the Garden of Eden, God told Adam and Eve about ownership: " 'Be fruitful and increase in number; fill the earth and subdue it. Rule over the fish of the sea and the birds of the air and over every living creature that moves on the ground' " (Gen. 1:28).

Made in the image of God, we were created to take responsibility for certain tasks. Part of taking responsibility, or ownership, is knowing what *is* our job, and what *isn't*. Workers who continually take on duties that aren't theirs will eventually burn out. It takes wisdom to know what we should be doing and what we shouldn't. We can't do everything.

Sherrie has great difficulty in knowing what things *are* her responsibility and what *aren't*. In her desire to do the right thing, or to avoid conflict, she ends up taking on problems that God never intended her to take on: her mother's chronic loneliness, her boss's irresponsibility, her friend's unending crises, her church leader's guilt-ridden message of self-sacrifice, and her husband's immaturity.

And her problems don't end there. Sherrie's inability to say no has significantly affected her son's ability to delay gratification and behave himself in school, and, in some way, this inability may be driving her daughter to withdraw.

Any confusion of responsibility and ownership in our lives is a problem of *boundaries.* Just as homeowners set physical property lines around their land, we need to set mental, physical, emotional, and spiritual boundaries for our lives to help us distinguish what is our responsibility and what isn't. As we see in Sherrie's many struggles, the inability to set appropriate boundaries at appropriate times with the appropriate people can be very destructive.

And this is one of the most serious problems facing Christians today. Many sincere, dedicated believers struggle with tremendous confusion about when it is biblically appropriate to set limits. When confronted with their lack of boundaries, they raise good questions:

1. Can I set limits and still be a loving person?
2. What are legitimate boundaries?
3. What if someone is upset or hurt by my boundaries?
4. How do I answer someone who wants my time, love, energy, or money?
5. Why do I feel guilty or afraid when I consider setting boundaries?
6. How do boundaries relate to submission?
7. Aren't boundaries selfish?

Misinformation about the Bible's answers to these issues has led to much wrong teaching about boundaries. Not only that, but many clinical psychological symptoms, such as depression, anxiety disorders, eating disorders, addictions, impulsive disorders, guilt problems, shame issues, panic disorders, and marital and relational struggles, find their root in conflicts with boundaries.

This book presents a biblical view of boundaries: what they are, what they protect, how they are developed, how they are injured, how to repair them, and how to use them. This book will answer the above questions and more. Our goal is to help you use biblical boundaries appropriately to achieve the relationships and purposes that God intends for you as his child.

Sherrie's knowledge of the Scriptures seems to support her lack of boundaries. This book aims to help you see the deeply biblical nature of boundaries as they operate in the character of God, his universe, and his people.

2

What Does a Boundary Look Like?

T he parents of a twenty-five-year-old man came to see me with a common request: they wanted me to "fix" their son, Bill. When I asked where Bill was, they answered, "Oh, he didn't want to come."

"Why?" I asked.

"Well, he doesn't think he has a problem," they replied.

"Maybe he's right," I said, to their surprise. "Tell me about it."

They recited a history of problems that had begun at a very young age. Bill had never been "quite up to snuff" in their eyes. In recent years he had exhibited problems with drugs and an inability to stay in school and find a career.

It was apparent that they loved their son very much and were heartbroken over the way he was living. They had tried everything they knew to get him to change and live a responsible life, but all had failed. He was still using drugs, avoiding responsibility, and keeping questionable company.

They told me that they had always given him everything he needed. He had plenty of money at school so "he wouldn't have to work and he would have plenty of time for study and a social life." When he flunked out of one school, or stopped going to classes, they were more than happy to do everything they could to get him into another school, "where it might be better for him."

After they had talked for a while, I responded: "I think your son is right. He doesn't have a problem."

You could have mistaken their expression for a snapshot; they stared at me in disbelief for a full minute. Finally the

27

father said, "Did I hear you right? You don't think he has a problem?"

"That's correct," I said. "He doesn't have a problem. You do. He can do pretty much whatever he wants, no problem. You pay, you fret, you worry, you plan, you exert energy to keep him going. He doesn't have a problem because you have taken it from him. Those things *should* be his problem, but as it now stands, they are yours. *Would you like for me to help you help him to have some problems?*"

They looked at me like I was crazy, but some lights were beginning to go on in their heads. "What do you mean, 'help him to have some problems'?" his mother asked.

"Well," I explained, "I think that the solution to this problem would be to clarify some boundaries so that his actions cause *him* problems and not you."

"What do you mean, 'boundaries'?" the father asked.

"Look at it this way. It is as if he's your neighbor, who never waters his lawn. But, whenever you turn on your sprinkler system, the water falls on his lawn. Your grass is turning brown and dying, but Bill looks down at his green grass and thinks to himself, 'My yard is doing fine.' That is how your son's life is. He doesn't study, or plan, or work, yet he has a nice place to live, plenty of money, and all the rights of a family member who is doing his part.

"If you would define the property lines a little better, if you would fix the sprinkler system so that the water would fall on your lawn, and if he didn't water his own lawn, he would have to live in dirt. He might not like that after a while.

"As it stands now, he is *irresponsible and happy,* and you are *responsible and miserable.* A little boundary clarification would do the trick. You need some fences to keep his problems out of your yard and in his, where they belong."

"Isn't that a bit cruel, just to stop helping like that?" the father asked.

"Has helping him helped?" I asked.

His look told me that he was beginning to understand.

Invisible Property Lines and Responsibility

In the physical world, boundaries are easy to see. Fences, signs, walls, moats with alligators, manicured lawns, or hedges are all physical boundaries. In their differing appearances, they give the same message: THIS IS WHERE MY PROPERTY BEGINS. The owner of the property is legally responsible for what happens on his or her property. Nonowners are not responsible for the property.

Physical boundaries mark a visible property line that *someone holds the deed to.* You can go to the county courthouse and find out exactly where those boundaries of responsibility are and whom to call if you have business there.

In the spiritual world, boundaries are just as real, but often harder to see. The goal of this chapter is to help you define your intangible boundaries and to recognize them as an everpresent reality that can increase your love and save your life. In reality, these boundaries define your soul, and they help you to guard it and maintain it (Prov. 4:23).

Me and Not Me

Boundaries define us. They define *what is me* and *what is not me.* A boundary shows me where I end and someone else begins, leading me to a sense of ownership.

Knowing what I am to own and take responsibility for gives me freedom. If I know where my yard begins and ends, I am free to do with it what I like. Taking responsibility for my life opens up many different options. However, if I do not "own" my life, my choices and options become very limited.

Think how confusing it would be if someone told you to "guard this property diligently, because I will hold you responsible for what happens here," and then did not tell you the boundaries of the property. Or they did not give you the means with which to protect the property? This would be not only confusing but also potentially dangerous.

This is exactly what happens to us emotionally and spiritually, however. God designed a world where we all live "within" ourselves; that is, we inhabit our own souls, and we are responsible for the things that make up "us." "The heart knows its own bitterness, and no one shares its joy" (Prov. 14:10). We have to deal with what is in our soul, and boundaries help us to define what that is. If we are not shown the parameters, or are taught wrong parameters, we are in for much pain.

The Bible tells us clearly what our parameters are and how to protect them, but often our family, or other past relationships, confuses us about our parameters.

In addition to showing us what we are responsible for, boundaries help us to define what is *not* on our property and what we are *not* responsible for. We are not, for example, responsible for other people. Nowhere are we commanded to have "other-control," although we spend a lot of time and energy trying to get it!

To and For

We are responsible *to* others and *for* ourselves. "Carry each other's burdens," says Galatians 6:2, "and in this way you will fulfill the law of Christ." This verse shows our responsibility *to* one another.

Many times others have "burdens" that are too big to bear. They do not have enough strength, resources, or knowledge to carry the load, and they need help. Denying ourselves to do for others what they *cannot* do for themselves is showing the sacrificial love of Christ. This is what Christ did for us. He did what we could not do for ourselves; he saved us. This is being responsible "to."

On the other hand, verse 5 says that "each one should carry his own load." Everyone has responsibilities that only he or she can carry. These things are our own particular "load" that we need to take daily responsibility for and work out. No one can do certain things *for* us. We have to take ownership of certain aspects of life that are our own "load."

The Greek words for *burden* and *load* give us insight into the meaning of these texts. The Greek word for *burden* means "excess burdens," or burdens that are so heavy that they weigh us down. These burdens are like boulders. They can crush us. We shouldn't be expected to carry a boulder by ourselves! It would break our backs. We need help with the boulders—those times of crisis and tragedy in our lives.

In contrast, the Greek word for *load* means "cargo," or "the burden of daily toil." This word describes the everyday things we all need to do. These loads are like knapsacks. Knapsacks are possible to carry. We are expected to carry our own. We are expected to deal with our own feelings, attitudes, and behaviors, as well as the responsibilities God has given to each one of us, even though it takes effort.

Problems arise when people act as if their "boulders" are daily loads, and refuse help, or as if their "daily loads" are boulders they shouldn't have to carry. The results of these two instances are either perpetual pain or irresponsibility.

Lest we stay in pain or become irresponsible, it is very important to determine what "me" is, where my boundary of responsibility is and where someone else's begins. We will define what we are responsible for later in this chapter. For now let's look more closely at the nature of boundaries.

Good In, Bad Out

Boundaries help us to distinguish our property so that we can take care of it. They help us to "guard our heart with all diligence." We need to keep things that will nurture us inside our fences and keep things that will harm us outside. In short, *boundaries help us keep the good in and the bad out.* They guard our treasures (Matt. 7:6) so that people will not steal them. They keep the pearls inside, and the pigs outside.

Sometimes, we have bad on the inside and good on the outside. In these instances, we need to be able to open up our boundaries to let the good in and the bad out. In other words, our *fences need gates in them.* For example, if I find that I have some pain or sin within, I need to open up and communicate it to God and others, so that I can be healed. Confessing pain and sin helps to "get it out" so that it does not continue to poison me on the inside (1 John 1:9; James 5:16; Mark 7:21–23).

And when the good is on the outside, we need to open

our gates and "let it in." Jesus speaks of this phenomenon in "receiving" him and his truth (Rev. 3:20; John 1:12). Other people have good things to give us, and we need to "open up to them" (2 Cor. 6:11–13). Often we will close our boundaries to good things from others, staying in a state of deprivation.

In short, *boundaries are not walls.* The Bible does not say that we are to be "walled off" from others; in fact, it says that we are to be "one" with them (John 17:11). We are to be in community with them. But in every community, all members have their own space and property. The important thing is that property lines be permeable enough to allow passing and strong enough to keep out danger.

Often, when people are abused while growing up, they reverse the function of boundaries and keep the *bad in* and the *good out.* When Mary was growing up she suffered abuse from her father. She was not encouraged to develop good boundaries. As a result, she would close herself off, holding the pain inside; she would not open up to express her hurt and get it out of her soul. She also would not open up to let support from the outside in to heal her. In addition, she would continually allow others to "dump" more pain into her soul. Consequently, when she came in for help, she was carrying a lot of pain, still being abused, and "walled off" from support from the outside.

She had to reverse the ways her boundaries worked. She needed fences that were strong enough to keep the bad out and gates in those fences to let out the bad already in her soul and let in the good she desperately needed.

God and Boundaries

The concept of boundaries comes from the very nature of God. God defines himself as a distinct, separate being, and he is responsible for himself. He defines and takes responsibility for his personality by telling us what he thinks, feels, plans, allows, will not allow, likes, and dislikes.

He also defines himself as separate from his creation and from us. He differentiates himself from others. He tells us who he is and who he is not. For example, he says that he is love and that he is not darkness (1 John 4:16; 1:6).

In addition, he has boundaries within the Trinity. The Father, the Son, and the Spirit are one, but at the same time they are distinct persons with their own boundaries. Each one has his own personhood and responsibilities, as well as a connection and love for one another (John 17:24).

God also limits what he will allow in his yard. He confronts sin and allows consequences for behavior. He guards his house and will not allow evil things to go on there. He invites people in who will love him, and he lets his love flow outward to them at the same time. The "gates" of his boundaries open and close appropriately.

In the same way he gave us his "likeness" (Gen. 1:26), he gave us personal responsibility within limits. He wants us to "rule and subdue" the earth and to be responsible stewards over the life he has given us. To do that, we need to develop boundaries like God's.

Examples of Boundaries

Boundaries are anything that helps to differentiate you from someone else, or shows where you begin and end. Here are some examples of boundaries.

Skin

The most basic boundary that defines you is your physical skin. People often use this boundary as a metaphor for saying that their personal boundaries have been violated: "He really gets under my skin." Your physical self is the first way that you learn that you are separate from others. As an infant, you slowly learn that you are different from the mother or father who cuddles you.

The skin boundary keeps the good in and the bad out. It protects your blood and bones, holding them on the inside and all together. It also keeps germs outside, protecting you from infection. At the same time skin has openings that let the "good" in, like food, and the "bad" out, like waste products.

Victims of physical and sexual abuse often have a poor sense of boundaries. Early in life they were taught that their property did not really begin at their skin. Others could invade their property and do whatever they wanted. As a result, they have difficulty establishing boundaries later in life.

Words

In the physical world a fence or some other kind of structure usually delineates a boundary. In the spiritual world, fences are invisible. Nevertheless, you can create good protective fences with your words.

The most basic boundary-setting word is *no*. It lets others know that you exist apart from them and that you are in control of you. Being clear about your no—and your yes—is a theme that runs throughout the Bible (Matt. 5:37; James 5:12).

No is a confrontational word. The Bible says that we are to confront people we love, saying, "No, that behavior is not okay. I will not participate in that." The word *no* is also important in setting limits on abuse. Many passages of Scripture urge us to say no to others' sinful treatment of us (Matt. 18:15–20).

The Bible also warns us against giving to others "reluctantly or under compulsion" (2 Cor. 9:7). People with poor boundaries struggle with saying no to the control, pressure, demands, and sometimes the real needs of others. They feel that if they say no to someone, they will endanger their relationship with that person, so they passively comply but inwardly resent. Sometimes a person is pressuring you to do something; other times the pressure comes from your own sense of what you "should" do. If you cannot say no to this external or internal pressure, you have lost control of your property and are not enjoying the fruit of "self-control."

Your words also define your property for others as you communicate your feelings, intentions, or dislikes. It is difficult for people to know where you stand when you do not use words to define your property. God does this when he says, "I like this and I hate that." Or, "I will do this, and I will not do that." Your words let people know where you stand and thus give them a sense of the "edges" that help identify you. "I don't like it when you yell at me!" gives people a clear message about how you conduct relationships and lets them know the "rules" of your yard.

Truth

Knowing the truth about God and his property puts limits on you and shows you his boundaries. Realizing the truth of his unchangeable reality helps you to define yourself in relation to him. When he says that you will reap what you sow (Gal. 6:7), for example, you either define yourself in relation to that reality, or continue to get injured if you try to go against it. To be in touch with God's truth is to be in touch with reality, and to live in accord with that reality makes for a better life (Ps. 119:2, 45).

Satan is the great distorter of reality. Recall in the garden when he tempted Eve to question God's boundaries and his truth. The consequences were disastrous.

There is always safety in the truth, whether it be knowing God's truth or knowing the truth about yourself. Many people live scattered and tumultuous lives trying to live outside of their own boundaries, not accepting and expressing the truth of who they are. Honesty about who you are gives you the biblical value of integrity, or oneness.

Geographical Distance

Proverbs 22:3 says that "the prudent man sees the evil and hides himself." Sometimes physically removing yourself from a situation will help maintain boundaries. You can do this to replenish yourself physically, emotionally, and spiritually after you have given to your limit, as Jesus often did.

Or, you can remove yourself to get away from danger and put limits on evil. The Bible urges us to separate from those who continue to hurt us and to create a safe place for ourselves. Removing yourself from the situation will also cause the one who is left behind to experience a loss of fellowship that may lead to changed behavior (Matt. 18:17–18; 1 Cor. 5:11–13).

When a relationship is abusive, many times the only way to finally show the other person that your boundaries are real is to create space until they are ready to deal with the problem. The Bible supports the idea of limiting togetherness for the sake of "binding evil."

Time

Taking time off from a person, or a project, can be a way of regaining ownership over some out-of-control aspect of your life where boundaries need to be set.

Adult children who have never spiritually and emotionally separated from their parents often need time away. They have spent their whole lives embracing and keeping (Eccl. 3:5–6) and have been afraid to refrain from embracing and to throw away some of their outgrown ways of relating. They need to spend some time building boundaries against the old ways and creating new ways of relating that for a while may feel alienating to their parents. This time apart usually improves their relationship with their parents.

Emotional Distance

Emotional distance is a temporary boundary to give your heart the space it needs to be safe; it is never a permanent way of living. People who have been in abusive relationships need to find a safe place to begin to "thaw out" emotionally. Sometimes in abusive marriages the abused spouse needs to keep emotional distance until the abusive partner begins to face his or her problems and become trustworthy.

You should not continue to set yourself up for hurt and disappointment. If you have been in an abusive relationship, you should wait until it is safe and until real patterns of change have been demonstrated before you go back. Many people are too quick to trust someone in the name of forgiveness and not make sure that the other is producing "fruit in keeping with repentance" (Luke 3:8). To continue to open yourself up emotionally to an abusive or addicted person without seeing true change is foolish. Forgive, but guard your heart until you see sustained change.

Other People

You need to depend on others to help you set and keep boundaries. People subject to another person's addictions, control, or abuse are finding that after years and years of "loving too much," they can find the ability to create boundaries only through a support group. Their support system is giving them the strength to say no to abuse and control for the first time in their lives.

There are two reasons why you need others to help with boundaries. The first is that *your most basic need in life is for relationship*. People suffer much to have relationships, and many put up with abuse because they fear their partners will leave them and they will be alone if they stand up to them. Fear of being alone keeps many in hurtful patterns for years. They are afraid that if they set boundaries they will not have any love in their life.

When they open themselves up to support from others, however, they find that the abusive person is not the only source of love in the world and that they can find the strength through their support system to set the limits they need to set. They are no longer alone. The church of Christ is there to give strength to ward off the blows against them.

The other reason we need others is because *we need new input and teaching*. Many people have been taught by their church or their family that boundaries are unbiblical, mean, or selfish. These people need good biblical support systems to help them stand against the guilt that comes from the old "tapes" inside that tell them lies to keep them in bondage. They need supportive others to stand against the old messages and the guilt involved in change. In Part II we will be discussing in greater detail how to build boundaries in all the primary relationships in your life. Our point for now is that boundaries are not built in a vacuum; *creating boundaries always involves a support network*.

Consequences

Trespassing on other people's property carries consequences. "No Trespasssing" signs usually carry a threat of
prosecution if someone steps over the boundaries. The Bible
teaches this principle over and over, saying that if we walk
one way, this will happen, and if we walk another way,
something else will happen.

Just as the Bible sets consequences for certain behaviors,
we need to back up our boundaries with consequences. How
many marriages could have been saved if one spouse had
followed through with the threat of "if you don't stop
drinking" (or "coming home at midnight," or "hitting me,"
or "yelling at the kids"), I will leave until you get some
treatment!" Or how many young adults' lives would have
been turned around if their parents had followed through
with their threat of "no more money if you quit another job
without having further employment" or "no bed if you
continue to smoke marijuana in my house."

Paul is not kidding in 2 Thessalonians 3:10 when he says
that if anyone will not work, don't let him or her eat. God
does not enable irresponsible behavior. Hunger is a consequence of laziness (Prov. 16:26).

Consequences give some good "barbs" to fences. They
let people know the seriousness of the trespass and the
seriousness of our respect for ourselves. This teaches them
that our commitment to living according to helpful values is
something we hold dear and will fight to protect and guard.

What's Within My Boundaries?

The story of the Good Samaritan is a model of correct
behavior in many dimensions. It is a good illustration of
boundaries—when they should be both observed and violated. Imagine for a moment how the story might read if the
Samaritan were a boundaryless person.

You know the story. A man traveling from Jerusalem to
Jericho was mugged. The robbers stripped him and beat
him, leaving him half dead. A priest and Levite passed by on
the other side of the road, ignoring the hurt man, but a

Samaritan took pity on him, bandaged his wounds, brought him to an inn, and took care of him. The next day the Samaritan gave the innkeeper some money and said, "Look after him. When I return, I will reimburse you for any extra expense you may have."

Let's depart from the familiar story here. Suppose the injured man wakes up at this point in the story and says: "What? You're leaving?"

"Yes, I am. I have some business in Jericho I have to attend to," the Samaritan replies.

"Don't you think you're being selfish? I'm in pretty bad shape here. I'm going to need someone to talk to. How is Jesus going to use you as an example? You're not even acting like a Christian, abandoning me like this in my time of need! Whatever happened to 'Deny yourself'?"

"Why, I guess you're right," the Samaritan says. "That would be uncaring of me to leave you here alone. I should do more. I will postpone my trip for a few days."

So he stays with the man for three days, talking to him and making sure that he is happy and content. On the afternoon of the third day, there's a knock at the door and a messenger comes in. He hands the Samaritan a message from his business contacts in Jericho: "Waited as long as we could. Have decided to sell camels to another party. Our next herd will be here in six months."

"How could you do this to me?" the Samaritan screams at the recovering man, waving the message in the air. "Look what you've done now! You've caused me to lose those camels that I needed for my business. Now I can't deliver my goods. This may put me out of business! How could you do this to me?"

At some level this story may be familiar to all of us. We may be moved with compassion to give to someone in need, but then this person manipulates us into giving more than we want to give. We end up resentful and angry, having missed something we needed in our own life. Or, we may want more from someone else, and we pressure them until they give in. They give not out of their heart and free will, but out of compliance, and they resent us for what they give. Neither one of us comes out ahead.

To avoid these scenarios, we need to look at what falls within our boundaries, what we are responsible for.

Feelings

Feelings have gotten a bad rap in the Christian world. They have been called everything from unimportant to fleshly. At the same time, example after example shows how our feelings play an enormous role in our motivation and behavior. How many times have you seen people do ungodly things to one another because of hurt feelings? Or how many times has someone had to be hospitalized for depression after years and years of trying to ignore the way they felt until they became suicidal?

Feelings should neither be ignored nor placed in charge. The Bible says to "own" your feelings and be aware of them. They can often motivate you to do much good. The Good Samaritan's pity moved him to go to the injured Israelite (Luke 10:33). The father was filled with compassion for his lost son and threw his arms around him (Luke 15:20). Many times Jesus "had compassion" for the people to whom he ministered (Matt. 9:36; 15:32).

Feelings come from your heart and can tell you the state of your relationships. They can tell you if things are going well, or if there is a problem. If you feel close and loving, things are probably going well. If you feel angry, you have a problem that needs to be addressed. But the point is, your feelings are *your* responsibility and you must own them and see them as your problem so you can begin to find an answer to whatever issue they are pointing to.

Attitudes and Beliefs

Attitudes have to do with your orientation toward something, the stance you take toward others, God, life, work, and relationships. Beliefs are anything that you accept as true. Often we do not see an attitude, or belief, as the source of discomfort in our life. We blame other people as did our first parents, Adam and Eve. We need to *own* our attitudes and convictions because they fall within our property line. We are the ones who feel their effect, *and* the only ones who can change them.

The tough thing about attitudes is that we learn them very early in life. They play a big part in the map of who we are and how we operate. People who have never questioned their attitudes and beliefs can fall prey to the dynamic that Jesus referred to when he described people holding on to the "traditions of men," instead of the commands of God (Mark 7:8; Matt. 15:3).

People with boundary problems usually have distorted attitudes about responsibility. They feel that to hold people responsible for their feelings, choices, and behaviors is *mean*. However, Proverbs repeatedly says that setting limits and accepting responsibility will save lives (Prov. 13:18, 24).

Behaviors

Behaviors have consequences. As Paul says, "A man reaps what he sows" (Gal. 6:7–8). If we study, we will reap good grades. If we go to work, we will get a paycheck. If we exercise, we will be in better health. If we act lovingly toward others, we will have closer relationships. On the negative side, if we sow idleness, irresponsibility, or out-of-control behavior, we can expect to reap poverty, failure, and the effects of loose living. These are natural consequences of our behavior.

The problem comes when someone interrupts the law of sowing and reaping in another's life. A person's drinking or abuse *should* have consequences for the drinker or the abuser. "Stern discipline awaits him who leaves the path" (Prov. 15:10). To rescue people from the natural consequences of their behavior is to render them powerless.

This happens a lot with parents and children. Parents often yell and nag, instead of allowing their children to reap the natural consequences of their behavior. Parenting with love and limits, with warmth and consequences, produces confident children who have a sense of control over their lives.

Choices

We need to take responsibility for our choices. This leads to the fruit of "self-control" (Gal. 5:23). A common boundary problem is disowning our choices and trying to lay the responsibility for them on someone else. Think for a moment how often we use the phrases, "I had to" or "She (he) made me" when explaining why we did or did not do something. These phrases betray our basic illusion that we are not active agents in many of our dealings. We think someone else is in control, thus relieving us of our basic responsibility.

We need to realize that we *are* in control of our choices, no matter how we feel. This keeps us from making choices to give "reluctantly or under compulsion," as 2 Corinthians 9:7 says. Paul would not even accept a gift that he felt was given because the giver felt he "had to" give it. He once sent a gift back so "that any favor you do will be spontaneous and not forced" (Philem. 1:14). Joshua said the same thing to the people in his famous "choice" verse: "But if serving the Lord *seems undesirable to you,* then *choose for yourselves* this day whom you will serve" (Josh. 24:15).

Jesus said a similar thing to the worker who was angry about the wage for which he had agreed to work: "Friend, I am not being unfair to you. Didn't you agree to work for a denarius?" (Matt. 20:13). The man had made a free choice to work for a certain amount and was angry because someone who had worked fewer hours had gotten the same wage.

Another example is the prodigal son's brother, who had chosen to stay home and serve and then was resentful. Not satisfied with his choice, he needed to be reminded that he made a choice to stay home.

Throughout the Scriptures, people are reminded of their choices and asked to take responsibility for them. Like Paul says, if we choose to live by the Spirit, we will live; if we choose to follow our sinful nature, we will die (Rom. 8:13). Making decisions based on others' approval or on guilt breeds resentment, a product of our sinful nature. We have been so trained by others on what we "should" do that we think we are being loving when we do things out of compulsion.

Setting boundaries inevitably involves taking responsibility for your choices. You are the one who makes them. You are the one who must live with their consequences. And you are the one who may be keeping yourself from making the choices you could be happy with.

Values

What we value is what we love and assign importance to. Often we do not take responsibility for what we value. We are caught up in valuing the approval of men rather than the approval of God (John 12:43); because of this misplaced value, we miss out on life. We think that power, riches, and pleasure will satisfy our deepest longing, which is really for love.

When we take responsibility for out-of-control behavior caused by loving the wrong things, or valuing things that have no lasting value, when we confess that we have *a heart that values things that will not satisfy,* we can receive help from God and his people to "create a new heart" within us. Boundaries help us not to deny but to own our old hurtful values so God can change them.

Limits

Two aspects of limits stand out when it comes to creating better boundaries. The first is *setting limits on others.* This is the component that we most often hear about when we talk about boundaries. In reality, setting limits on others is a misnomer. We can't do that. What we *can* do is set limits on our own exposure to people who are behaving poorly; we can't change them or make them behave right.

Our model is God. He does not really "set limits" on people to "make them" behave. God sets standards, but he lets people be who they are and then separates himself from them when they misbehave, saying in effect, "You can be that way if you choose, but you cannot come into my house." Heaven is a place for the repentant, and all are welcome.

But God limits his exposure to evil, unrepentant people, as should we. Scripture is full of admonitions to separate

ourselves from people who act in destructive ways (Matt.
18:15–17; 1 Cor. 5:9–13). We are not being unloving.
Separating ourselves protects love, because we are taking a
stand against things that destroy love.

The other aspect of limits that is helpful when talking
about boundaries is *setting our own internal limits*. We need
to have spaces inside ourselves where we can have a feeling,
an impulse, or a desire, without acting it out. *We need self-
control without repression.*

We need to be able to say no to ourselves. This includes
both our destructive desires and some good ones that are not
wise to pursue at a given time. Internal structure is a very
important component of boundaries and identity, as well as
ownership, responsibility, and self-control.

Talents

Contrast these two responses:

"Well done, good and faithful servant! You have been
faithful with a few things; I will put you in charge of many
things. Come and share your master's happiness!"

"You wicked, lazy servant! So you knew that I harvest
where I have not sown and gather where I have not
scattered seed? Well then, you should have put my money
on deposit with the bankers, so that when I returned I
would have received it back with interest. Take the talent
from him and give it to the one who has the ten talents."
(Matt. 25:23, 26–28)

No other passage better illustrates God-ordained responsibility for ownership and use of talents. Although the
example is of money, it also applies to internal talents and
gifts. Our talents are clearly within our boundaries and are
our responsibility. Yet taking ownership of them is often
frightening and always risky.

The parable of the talents says that we are accountable—
not to mention much happier—when we are exercising our
gifts and being productive. It takes work, practice, learning,
prayer, resources, and grace to overcome the fear of failure
that the "wicked and lazy" servant gave in to. He was not

chastised for being afraid; we are all afraid when trying something new and difficult. He was chastised for not confronting his fear and trying the best he could. Not confronting our fear denies the grace of God and insults both his giving of the gift and his grace to sustain us as we are learning.

Thoughts

Our minds and thoughts are important reflections of the image of God. No other creature on earth has our thinking ability. We are the only creatures who are called to love God with all our mind (Mark 12:30). And Paul wrote that he was taking "captive every thought to make it obedient to Christ" (2 Cor. 10:5). Establishing boundaries in thinking involves three things.

1. *We must own our own thoughts.* Many people have not taken ownership of their own thinking processes. They are mechanically thinking the thoughts of others without ever examining them. They swallow others' opinions and reasonings, never questioning and "thinking about their thinking." Certainly we should listen to the thoughts of others and weigh them; but we should never "give our minds" over to anyone. We are to weigh things for ourselves in the context of relationship, "sharpening" each other as iron, but remaining separate thinkers.

2. *We must grow in knowledge and expand our minds.* One area in which we need to grow is in knowledge of God and his Word. David said of knowing God's Word, "My soul is consumed with longing for your laws at all times. Your statutes are my delight; they are my counselors" (Ps. 119:20, 24). We also learn much about God by studying his creation and his work. In learning about his world, we obey the commandment to "rule and subdue" the earth and all that is within it. We must learn about the world that he has given us to become wise stewards. Whether we are doing brain surgery, balancing our checkbook, or raising children, we are to use our brains to have better lives and glorify God.

3. *We must clarify distorted thinking.* We all have a tendency to not see things clearly, to think and perceive in

distorted ways. Probably the easiest distortions to notice are in personal relationships. We rarely see people as they really are; our perceptions are distorted by past relationships and our own preconceptions of who we think they are, even the people we know best. We do not see clearly because of the "logs" in our eyes (Matt. 7:3–5).

Taking ownership of our thinking in relationships requires being active in checking out where we may be wrong. As we assimilate new information, our thinking adapts and grows closer to reality.

Also we need to make sure that we are communicating our thoughts to others. Many people think that others should be able to read their minds and know what they want. This leads to frustration. Even Paul says, "For who among men knows the thoughts of a man except the man's spirit within him?" (1 Cor. 2:11). What a great statement about boundaries! We have our own thoughts, and if we want others to know them, we must tell them.

Desires

Our desires lie within our boundaries. Each of us has different desires and wants, dreams and wishes, goals and plans, hungers and thirsts. We all want to satisfy "me." But why are there so few satisfied "me's" around?

Part of the problem lies in the lack of structured boundaries within our personality. We can't define who the real "me" is and what we truly desire. Many desires masquerade as the real thing. They are lusts that come out of not owning our real desires. For example, many sex addicts are looking for sexual experiences, but what they really desire is love and affection.

James writes about this problem of not owning and seeking our real desires with pure motives: "You want something but don't get it. You kill and covet, but you cannot have what you want. You quarrel and fight. You do not have, because you do not ask God. When you ask, you do not receive, because you ask with wrong motives, that you may spend what you get on your pleasures" (James 4:2–3).

We often do not actively seek our desires from God, and

those desires are mixed up with things that we do not really need. God is truly interested in our desires; he made them. Consider the following: "You have granted him the desire of his heart and have not withheld the request of his lips. You welcomed him with rich blessings and placed a crown of pure gold on his head" (Ps. 21:2–3). "Delight yourself in the LORD and he will give you the desires of your heart" (Ps. 37:4). "He fulfills the desires of those who fear him" (Ps. 145:19).

God loves to give gifts to his children, but he is a wise parent. He wants to make sure his gifts are right for us. To know what to ask for, we have to be in touch with who we really are and what are our real motives. If we are wanting something to feed our pride or to enhance our ego, I doubt that God is interested in giving it to us. But if it would be good for us, he's very interested.

We are also commanded to play an active role in seeking our desires (Phil. 2:12–13; Ecc. 11:9; Matt. 7:7–11). We need to own our desires and pursue them to find fulfillment in life. "A desire accomplished is sweet to the soul" (Prov. 13:19 KJV), but it sure is a lot of work!

Love

Our ability to give and respond to love is our greatest gift. The heart that God has fashioned in his image is the center of our being. Its abilities to open up to love and to allow love to flow outward are crucial to life.

Many people have difficulty giving and receiving love because of hurt and fear. Having closed their heart to others, they feel empty and meaningless. The Bible is clear about both functions of the heart: the receiving of grace and love inward and the flow outward.

Listen to how the Bible tells how we should love: "Love the Lord your God with all your heart and with all your soul and with all your mind. . . . Love your neighbor as yourself" (Matt. 22:37, 39). And how we should receive love: "We have spoken freely to you, Corinthians, and opened wide our hearts to you. We are not withholding our affection from you, but you are withholding yours from us. As a fair exchange—I

speak as to my children—open wide your hearts also"
(2 Cor. 6:11–13).

Our loving heart, like our physical one, *needs an inflow
as well as an outflow of lifeblood.* And like its physical
counterpart, our heart is a muscle, a trust muscle. This trust
muscle needs to be used and exercised; if it is injured it will
slow down or weaken.

We need to take responsibility for this loving function of
ourselves and use it. Love concealed or love rejected can
both kill us.

Many people do not take ownership for how they resist
love. They have a lot of love around them, but do not realize
that their loneliness is a result of their own lack of respon-
siveness. Often they will say, "Others' love can not 'get in.'"
This statement negates their responsibility to respond. We
maneuver subtly to avoid responsibility in love; we need to
claim our hearts as our property and work on our weaknesses
in that area. It will open up life to us.

We need to take responsibility for all of the above areas
of our souls. These lie within our boundaries. But taking care
of what lies within our boundaries isn't easy; neither is
allowing other people to take care of what lies within their
boundaries. Setting boundaries and maintaining them is
hard work. But, as you'll see in the next chapter, boundary
problems take some very recognizable shapes.

3

Boundary Problems

F ollowing a day-long seminar that we were leading on biblical boundaries, a woman raised her hand and said, "I understand that I have boundary problems. But my estranged husband's the one who had an affair and took all our money. Doesn't he have a problem with boundaries?"

It's easy to misunderstand boundaries. At first glance, it seems as if the individual who has difficulty setting limits is the one who has the boundary problem; however, people who don't respect others' limits also have boundary problems. The woman above may have difficulty setting limits, but, in addition, her husband hasn't respected her limits.

In this chapter, we'll categorize the main types of boundary problems, providing you some pegs on which to hang your thoughts. You'll see that boundary conflicts are by no means limited to those who "can't say no."

Compliants: Saying "Yes" to the Bad

"May I tell you something embarrassing?" Robert asked me. A new client, Robert was trying to understand why he had so much difficulty refusing his wife's constant demands. He was going broke trying to keep up with the Joneses.

"I was the only boy in my family, the youngest of four children. There was a strange double standard in my house involving physical fighting." Robert cleared his throat, struggling to continue. "My sisters were three to seven years older than me. Until I was in sixth grade, they were a lot bigger and stronger. They'd take advantage of their size and strength and wale on me until I was bruised. I mean, they really hurt me.

"The strangest part of it all was my parents' attitude. They'd tell us, 'Robert is the boy. Boys don't hit girls. It's bad manners.' Bad manners! I was getting triple-teamed, and fighting back was bad manners?" Robert stopped. His shame kept him from continuing, but he'd said enough. He had unearthed part of the reason for his conflicts with his wife.

When parents teach children that setting boundaries or saying no is bad, they are teaching them that others can do with them as they wish. They are sending their children defenseless into a world that contains much evil. Evil in the form of controlling, manipulative, and exploitative people. Evil in the form of temptations.

To feel safe in such an evil world, children need to have the power to say things like:

- "No."
- "I disagree."
- "I will not."
- "I choose not to."
- "Stop that."
- "It hurts."
- "It's wrong."
- "That's bad."
- "I don't like it when you touch me there."

Blocking a child's ability to say no handicaps that child for life. Adults with handicaps like Robert's have this first boundary injury: they say yes to bad things.

This type of boundary conflict is called *compliance.* Compliant people have fuzzy and indistinct boundaries; they "melt" into the demands and needs of other people. They can't stand alone, distinct from people who want something from them. Compliants, for example, pretend to like the same restaurants and movies their friends do "just to get along." They minimize their differences with others so as not to rock the boat. Compliants are chameleons. After a while it's hard to distinguish them from their environment.

The inability to say no to the bad is pervasive. Not only

does it keep us from refusing evil in our lives, *it often keeps us from recognizing evil.* Many compliant people realize too late that they're in a dangerous or abusive relationship. Their spiritual and emotional "radar" is broken; they have no ability to guard their hearts (Prov. 4:23).

This type of boundary problem paralyzes people's no muscles. Whenever they need to protect themselves by saying no, the word catches in their throats. This happens for a number of different reasons:

- Fear of hurting the other person's feelings
- Fear of abandonment and separateness
- A wish to be totally dependent on another
- Fear of someone else's anger
- Fear of punishment
- Fear of being shamed
- Fear of being seen as bad or selfish
- Fear of being unspiritual
- Fear of one's overstrict, critical conscience

This last fear is actually experienced as guilt. People who have an overstrict, critical conscience will condemn themselves for things God himself doesn't condemn them for. As Paul says, "Since their conscience is weak, it is defiled" (1 Cor. 8:7). Afraid to confront their unbiblical and critical internal parent, they tighten appropriate boundaries.

When we give in to guilty feelings, we are complying with a harsh conscience. This fear of disobeying the harsh conscience translates into an inability to confront others—a saying yes to the bad—because it would cause more guilt.

Biblical compliance needs to be distinguished from this kind of compliance. Matthew 9:13 says that God desires "compassion, and not sacrifice" (NASB). In other words, God wants us to be compliant from the inside out (compassionate), not compliant on the outside and resentful on the inside (sacrificial). Compliants take on too many responsibilities and set too few boundaries, not by choice, but because they are afraid.

Avoidants: Saying "No" to the Good

The living room suddenly became very quiet. The Bible study group that had been meeting at the Craigs' house for six months had suddenly become more intimate. Tonight the five couples began to share real struggles in their lives, not just the usual "please pray for Aunt Sarah" requests. Tears were shed, and genuine support, not just well-meaning advice, was offered. Everyone, except the hostess, Rachel Henderson, had taken a turn talking.

Rachel had been the driving force behind the formation of the Bible study. She and her husband, Joe, had developed the format, invited the other couples, and opened up their home to the study. Caught up in her leadership role, however, Rachel never opened up about her struggles. She shied away from such opportunities, preferring instead to help draw out others. Tonight the others waited.

Rachel cleared her throat. Looking around the room, she finally spoke, "After hearing all the other problems in the room, I think the Lord's speaking to me. He seems to be saying that my issues are nothing compared to what you all deal with. It would be selfish to take up time with the little struggles I face. So . . . who'd like dessert?"

No one spoke. But disappointment was evident on each face. Rachel had again avoided an opportunity for others to love her as they'd been loved by her.

This boundary problem is called *avoidance:* saying no to the good. It's the inability to ask for help, to recognize one's own needs, to let others in. Avoidants withdraw when they are in need; they do not ask for the support of others.

Why is avoidance a boundary problem? At the heart of the struggle is a confusion of boundaries as walls. Boundaries are supposed to be able to "breathe," to be like fences with a gate that can let the good in and the bad out. Individuals with walls for boundaries can let in neither bad nor good. No one touches them.

God designed our personal boundaries to have gates. We should have the freedom to enjoy safe relationships and to avoid destructive ones. God even allows us the freedom to let him in or to close him off:

"Here I am! I stand at the door and knock. If anyone hears my voice and opens the door, I will come in and eat with him, and he with me." (Rev. 3:20)

God has no interest in violating our boundaries so that he can relate to us. He understands that this would cause injuries of trust. It is our responsibility to open up to him in need and repentance. Yet, for avoidants, opening up to both God and people is almost impossible.

The impermeable boundaries of avoidants cause a rigidity toward their God-given needs. They experience their problems and legitimate wants as something bad, destructive, or shameful.

Some people, like Marti, are both compliants and avoidants. In a recent session, Marti laughed ruefully at herself. "I'm beginning to see a pattern here. When someone needs four hours with me, I can't say no. When I need someone for ten minutes, I can't ask for it. Isn't there a transistor in my head that I can replace?"

Marti's dilemma is shared by many adults. She says "yes" to the bad (compliant) and says "no" to the good (avoidant). Individuals who have both boundary conflicts not only cannot refuse evil, they are unable to receive the support they so readily offer to others. They are stuck in a cycle of feeling drained, but with nothing to replace the lost energy.

Compliant avoidants suffer from what is called "reversed boundaries." They have no boundaries where they need them, and they have boundaries where they shouldn't have them.

Controllers: Not Respecting Others' Boundaries

"What do you mean, you're quitting? You can't leave now!" Steve looked across his desk at his administrative assistant. Frank had been working for Steve for several years and was finally fed up. He had given his all to the position, but Steve didn't know when to back off.

Time after time, Steve would insist on Frank's spending unpaid time at the office on important projects. Frank had even switched his vacation schedule twice at Steve's insistence. But the final straw was when Steve began calling Frank at home. An occasional call at home Frank could understand. But almost every day, during dinnertime, the family would wait while Frank had a telephone conference with his boss.

Several times Frank had tried to talk with Steve about the time violations. But Steve never really understood how burned out Frank was. After all, he needed Frank. Frank made him look successful. And it was so easy to get him to work harder.

Steve has a problem hearing and accepting others boundaries. To Steve, no is simply a challenge to change the other person's mind. This boundary problem is called *control*. Controllers can't respect others' limits. They resist taking responsibility for their own lives, so they need to control others.

Controllers believe the old jokes about training top sales people: no means maybe, and maybe means yes. While this may be productive in learning to sell a product, it can wreak havoc in a relationship. Controllers are perceived as bullies, manipulative and aggressive.

The primary problem of individuals *who can't hear no*— which is different from *not being able to say no*—is that they tend to project responsibility for their lives onto others. They use various means of control to motivate others to carry the load intended by God to be theirs alone.

Remember the "boulder and knapsack" illustration in chapter 2? Controllers look for someone to carry their knapsacks (individual responsibilities) in addition to their boulders (crises and crushing burdens). Had Steve shouldered the weight of his own job, Frank would have been happy to pitch in extra hours from time to time. But the pressure of covering for Steve's irresponsibility made a talented professional look elsewhere for work.

Controllers come in two types:

1. *Aggressive controllers.* These people clearly don't listen to others' boundaries. They run over other people's fences like a tank. They are sometimes verbally abusive, sometimes physically abusive. But most of the time they simply aren't aware that others even have boundaries. It's as

if they live in a world of yes. There's no place for someone else's no. They attempt to get others to change, to make the world fit their idea of the way life should be. They neglect their own responsibility to accept others as they are.

Peter is an example of an aggressive controller. Jesus was telling the disciples about his upcoming suffering, death, and resurrection. Peter took Jesus aside and began to rebuke him. But Jesus rebuked Peter, saying, "Get behind me, Satan! You do not have in mind the things of God, but the things of men" (Mark 8:33).

Peter didn't want to accept the Lord's boundaries. Jesus immediately confronted Peter's violation of his boundaries.

2. *Manipulative controllers.* Less honest than the aggressive controllers, manipulators try to persuade people out of their boundaries. They talk others into yes. They indirectly manipulate circumstances to get their way. They seduce others into carrying their burdens. They use guilt messages.

Remember how Tom Sawyer tricked his playmates into whitewashing the fence for him? He made it seem like such a privilege that kids were lined up to paint!

Isaac's son Jacob finagled his twin brother Esau into giving up his birthright (Gen. 25:29–34) and, with his mother's help, deceived his father into bestowing Esau's blessing on him (Gen. 27:1–29). In fact, Jacob's name means "deceiver." Numerous times he used his cleverness to avoid others' boundaries.

The event that helped Jacob work out of his manipulative boundarylessness was his confrontation with God in human form (Gen. 32:24–32). God "wrestled" with him all night long and then changed his name to Israel. The word *Israel* means "he who fights with God." God left Jacob with a dislocated thigh.

And Jacob changed. He became less deceitful and more honest. His aggressiveness was clearer, as evidenced by his new name. He was owning his feistiness. Only when the manipulative controller is confronted with his dishonesty can he take responsibility for it, repent of it, and accept his and others' limits.

Manipulators deny their desires to control others; they brush aside their own self-centeredness. They are like the adulterous woman in Proverbs: "She eats and wipes her mouth and says, 'I've done nothing wrong'" (30:20).

Believe it or not, compliants and avoidants can also be controllers. They tend, however, to be more manipulative than aggressive. When compliant avoidants need emotional support, for example, they may do a favor for a friend. They hope that by being loving, they'll receive love. So then they wait, anticipating the return of the favor. And sometimes they wait for years. Especially if they performed the favor for someone who can't read minds.

What's wrong with this picture? It's not a picture of love. The love that God talks about doesn't seek a return on its investment: "It is not self-seeking" (1 Cor. 13:5). Caring for someone so that they'll care back for us is simply an indirect means of controlling someone else. If you've ever been on the "receiving" end of that kind of maneuver, you'll understand. One minute you've taken the compliment, or favor— the next minute you've hurt someone's feelings by not figuring out the price tag attached.

Boundary Injuries

At this point, you might be saying to yourself, "Wait a minute. How can controllers be called 'injured'? They are the injurers, not the injured!" Indeed, controllers do lots of damage to others, but they also have boundary problems. Let's see what goes on underneath.

Controllers are undisciplined people. They have little ability to curb their impulses or desires. While it appears that they "get what they want in life," they are still slaves to their appetites. Delaying gratification is difficult for them. That's why they hate the word no from others. They desperately need to learn to listen to the boundaries of others to help them observe their own.

Controllers also are limited in their ability to take responsibility for owning their lives. Having relied on bullying or indirectness, they can't function on their own in the world. The only remedy is to let controllers experience the consequences of their irresponsibility.

Finally, controllers are isolated. People stay with them

out of fear, guilt, or dependency. If they're honest, controllers rarely feel loved. Why? Because in their heart of hearts, they know that the only reason people spend time with them is because they are pulling the strings. If they stopped threatening or manipulating, they would be abandoned. And, at some deep level, they are aware of their isolation. "There is no fear in love. But perfect love drives out fear" (1 John 4:18). We can't terrorize or make others feel guilty and be loved by them at the same time.

Nonresponsives: Not Hearing the Needs of Others

Brenda's hand trembled as she talked. "Usually I've got pretty thick skin with Mike. But I guess the past couple of weeks of kid problems and work stresses had me feeling very vulnerable. This time his response didn't make me angry. It just hurt. And it hurt bad."

Brenda was recounting a recent marital struggle. Overall, she thought her marriage to Mike was a good one. He was a good provider, an active Christian, and a competent father. Yet the relationship allowed no room for her hurts or needs.

The incident Brenda was discussing began in a fairly benign manner. She and Mike were talking in the bedroom after putting the kids to bed. Brenda began to unburden her fears about child rearing and her feelings of inadequacy at work.

Without warning, Mike turned to her and said, "If you don't like the way you feel, change your feelings. Life's tough. So just . . . just handle it, Brenda."

Brenda was devastated. She felt she should have expected the rebuff. It wasn't that easy to express her neediness in the first place, especially with Mike's coldness. Now she felt as if he had chopped her feelings to bits. He seemed to have no understanding whatsoever of her struggles—and didn't want to.

How could this be a boundary problem? Isn't it just basic insensitivity? Partially. But it's not quite that simple. Remember that boundaries are a way to describe our spheres of responsibility: what we are and are not responsible for. While we shouldn't take on the responsibility of others' feelings, attitudes, and behaviors, we do have certain responsibilities *to* each other.

Mike does have a responsibility to connect with Brenda, not only as a provider and as a parenting partner, but also as a loving husband. Connecting emotionally with Brenda is part of loving her as himself (Eph. 5:28, 33). He isn't responsible *for* her emotional well-being. *But he is responsible to her.* His inability to respond to her needs is a neglect of his responsibility.

Termed "nonresponsives" because of their lack of attention to the responsibilities of love, these individuals exhibit the opposite of the pattern exhorted in Proverbs 3:27 (NRSV): "Do not withhold good from those to whom it is due, when it is in your power to do it" (that last phrase, "in your power," has to do with our resources and availability). Another key Scripture here is "If it is possible, so far as it depends on you, live peaceably with all" (Rom. 12:18 NRSV). Again, note the condition: "so far as it depends on you": we can't bring peace to someone who doesn't accept it!

Both of the above verses indicate the same idea: we are responsible to care about and help, *within certain limits,* others whom God places in our lives. To refuse to do so when we have the appropriate resources can be a boundary conflict.

Nonresponsives fall into one of two groups:

1. Those with a critical spirit toward others' needs (a projection of our own hatred of our needs onto others, a problem Jesus addressed in Matthew 7:1–5). They hate being incomplete in themselves. As a result, they ignore the needs of others.

2. Those who are so absorbed in their own desires and needs they exclude others (a form of narcissism).

Don't confuse this self-absorption with a God-given sense of taking responsibility for one's own needs first so that one is able to love others: "Do not merely look out for your own personal interests, but also for the interests of others" (Phil. 2:4). God wants us to take care of ourselves so that we can help others without moving into a crisis ourselves.

Controllers and Nonresponsives

Controlling nonresponsives have a hard time looking past themselves. They see others as responsible for their struggles and are on the lookout for someone to take care of them. They gravitate toward someone with blurry boundaries, who will naturally take on too many responsibilities in the relationship and who won't complain about it. It's like the old joke about relationships: What happens when a rescuing, enabling person meets a controlling, insensitive person? Answer: they get married!

Actually, this makes sense. Compliant avoidants search for someone to repair. This keeps them saying yes and keeps them out of touch with their own needs. Who fits the bill better than a controlling nonresponsive? And controlling nonresponsives search for someone to keep them away from responsibility. Who better than a compliant avoidant?

Below is a chart of the four types of boundary problems.[1] It will help you see at a glance the kinds of problems with which you may struggle.

Summary of Boundary Problems

	CAN'T SAY	CAN'T HEAR
NO	The Compliant	The Controller
	Feels guilty and/or controlled by others; can't set boundaries	Aggressively or manipulatively violates boundaries of others
YES	The Nonresponsive	The Avoidant
	Sets boundaries against responsibility to love	Sets boundaries against receiving care of others

Functional and Relational Boundary Issues

A final boundary problem involves the distinction between functional and relational boundaries. *Functional boundaries* refers to a person's ability to complete a task, project, or job. It has to do with performance, discipline, initiative, and planning. *Relational boundaries* refers to the ability to speak truth to others with whom we are in relationship.

Another way of looking at it is that functional boundaries refer to our "Martha" parts, and relational, our "Mary" parts (Luke 10:38–42). Mary and Martha were friends of Jesus. Martha prepared dinner, while Mary sat at Jesus' feet. When Martha complained about Mary's not helping her, Jesus said: "Mary has chosen what is better" (v. 42). He didn't mean that Martha's busyness was bad; it was just the wrong thing at the wrong time.

Many people have good functional boundaries, but poor relational ones; that is, they can perform tasks at quite high levels of competence, but they may not be able to tell a friend that they don't like their chronic lateness. The reverse can also be true. Some people can be absolutely honest with others about their complaints and dislikes but be unable to get up for work in the morning!

We've taken a look at the different categories of boundaries. But how do you develop boundaries? Why do some people seem to have natural boundaries and others have no boundaries at all? As with many things, it has a lot to do with the family in which you grew up.

4

How Boundaries
Are Developed

J im had never been able say no to anyone, especially to
his supervisors at work. He'd moved up to the position
of operations manager in a large firm. His dependability had
earned him the reputation of "Mr. Can Do."

But his kids had another name for him: "The Phantom."
Jim was never home. Being "Mr. Can Do" meant late nights
at the office. It meant business dinners several nights a
week. It meant weekends on the road, even after he'd
promised the kids fishing trips and trips to the zoo.

Jim didn't like being absent so much, but he had justified
it to himself, saying, *This is my contribution to the kids, my
way of giving them the good life.* His wife, Alice, had
rationalized the "dadless dinners" by telling the children
(and herself), "This is Dad's way of telling us he loves us."
And she almost believed it.

Finally, however, Alice had had enough. One night she
sat Jim down on the couch in the family room and said, "I
feel like a single parent, Jim. I missed you for a while, but
now all I feel is nothing."

Jim avoided her eyes. "Honey, I know, I know," he
replied. "I'd really like to say no to people more, but it's just
so hard to—"

"I found someone you can say no to," Alice broke in.
"Me and the kids!"

That did it. Something broke deep within Jim. A sense of
pain, of guilt and shame, of helplessness and rage.

The words tumbled out of his mouth. "Do you think I
like being like this, always giving in to others? Do you think

I enjoy letting my family down?" Jim paused, struggling for composure. "All my life it's been this way, Alice. I've always feared letting people down. I hate this part of me. I hate my life. How did I get like this?"

How *did* Jim "get like this"? He loved his family. The last thing he wanted was to neglect his most precious relationships: his wife and children. Jim's problems didn't start the day he was married. They developed during his early significant relationships. They were already a part of his character structure.

How do boundary abilities develop? That's the purpose of this chapter. We hope you'll be able to gain some understanding of where your own boundaries started crumbling or became set in concrete—and how to repair them.

As you read this section, remember David's prayer to God about his life and development:

> Search me, O God, and know my heart; test me and know my anxious thoughts. See if there is any offensive way in me, and lead me in the way everlasting. (Ps. 139:23–24)

God's desire is for you to know where your injuries and deficits are, whether self-induced or other-induced. Ask him to shed light on the significant relationships and forces that have contributed to your own boundary struggles. The past is your ally in repairing your present and ensuring a better future.

Boundary Development

Remember the old saying, "Insanity is genetic. You inherit it from your kids"? Well, boundaries aren't inherited. They are built. To be the truth-telling, responsible, free, and loving people God wants us to be we need to learn limits from childhood on. Boundary development is an ongoing process, yet its most crucial stages are in our very early years, where our character is formed.

The Scriptures advise parents to "train a child in the way he should go, and when he is old he will not turn from it" (Prov. 22:6). Many parents misunderstand this passage. They think "the way he should go" means "the way *we, the parents* think he (or she) should go." Can you see the boundary conflicts already beginning?

The verse actually means "the way God has planned for him (or her) to go." In other words, good parenting isn't emotionally bludgeoning the child into some clone or ideal of the perfect child. It's being a partner in helping young ones discover what God intended for them to be and helping them reach that goal.

The Bible teaches that we pass through life in stages. John writes to "little children," "young men," and "fathers." Each group has distinct tasks to perform (1 John 2:12–13 KJV).

Boundaries also develop in specific, distinct phases that you can perceive. In fact, by noting infants and children in their early parental interactions, child development professionals have able to record the specific phases of boundary development.[1]

Bonding: The Foundation of Boundary Building

Wendy couldn't understand it. Something wasn't jelling. All those codependency books. All those assertiveness tapes. All that self-talk about being more confrontive. And yet, every time she talked to her mother on the phone, all the advice, all the self-help techniques melted away into vague, cloudy memories.

A typical conversation about Wendy's children would always conclude with her mom's analysis of Wendy's imperfect parenting style. "I've been a mother longer than you," Mom would say. "Just do it my way."

Wendy resented her advice. It wasn't that she wasn't open to guidance—Lord knows she could use it. It was just that her mom thought her way was the only way. Wendy wanted a new relationship with her mom. She wanted to be honest about her mom's control, her polite put-downs, and her inflexibility. Wendy wanted an adult-to-adult friendship with her mom.

But the words wouldn't pass her lips. She'd write letters explaining her feelings. She'd rehearse before telephoning.

Yet, when the time came, she panicked and remained silent. She well knew how to be compliant, appreciative, and childlike with her mom. It was only later, when she became angry, that she knew she'd been taken to task again. She was beginning to give up hope that things would ever change.

Wendy's struggle illustrates a basic need that we all have in boundary building. No matter how much you talk to yourself, read, study, or practice, *you can't develop or set boundaries apart from supportive relationships with God and others.* Don't even try to start setting limits until you have entered into deep, abiding attachments with people who will love you no matter what.

Our deepest need is to belong, to be in a relationship, to have a spiritual and emotional "home." The very nature of God is to be in relationship: "God is love," says 1 John 4:16. Love means relationship—the caring, committed connection of one individual to another.

Like God, our most central need is to be connected. When God said that even in his perfect new universe, it wasn't "good for the man to be alone" (Gen. 2:18), he wasn't talking about marriage. He was talking about relationship— other people outside ourselves to bond with, trust, and go to for support.

We are built for relationship. Attachment is the foundation of the soul's existence. When this foundation is cracked or faulty, boundaries become impossible to develop. Why? Because when we lack relationship, *we have nowhere to go in a conflict.* When we are not secure that we are loved, we are forced to choose between two bad options:

1. *We set limits and risk losing a relationship.* This was Wendy's fear. She was afraid her mother would reject her, and she would be isolated and alone. She still needed Mom's connection to feel secure.

2. *We don't set limits and remain a prisoner to the wishes of another.* By not setting limits on her mom, Wendy was a prisoner to her mom's wishes.

So the first developmental task of infants is to bond with their mom and dad. They need to learn that they are welcome and safe in the world. To bond with baby, Mom and Dad need to provide a consistent, warm, loving, and predictable emotional environment for him or her. During this stage, Mom's job is to woo the child into entering a relationship with the world—via attachment with her. (Most often, this is Mom's job, but Dad or a caregiver can do this as well.)

Bonding takes place when the mother responds to the needs of the child, the needs for closeness, for being held, for food, and for changing. As baby experiences needs and the mother's positive response to those needs, he or she begins to internalize, or take in, an emotional picture of a loving, constant mother.

Babies, at this stage, have no sense of self apart from Mother. They think, "Mommy and me are the same." It's sometimes called *symbiosis,* a sort of "swimming in closeness" with Mother. This symbiotic union is the reason babies panic when Mother isn't around. No one can comfort them but their mother.

The emotional picture developed by infants forms from thousands of experiences in the first few months of life. The ultimate goal of Mother's "being there" is a state called *emotional object constancy.* Object constancy refers to the child's having an internal sense of belonging and safety, even away from the presence of the mother. All those experiences of constant loving pay off in a child's inner sense of security. It's been built in.

Object constancy is referred to in the Bible as "being rooted and established in love" (Eph. 3:17) and as having been "rooted and built up in [Christ]" (Col. 2:7). It illustrates the principle that *God's plan for us is to be loved enough by him and others, to not feel isolated—even when we're alone.*[2]

Bonding is the prelude. As children learn to feel safe and at home with their primary relationships, they are building good foundations to withstand the separateness and conflict that comes with boundary development.

Separation and Individuation:
The Construction of a Soul

"It's like a switch was thrown," said Millie to the friends who made up her church Mom's Group. The Mom's Group provided activities and a place to talk for mothers of infants and toddlers. "On her first birthday—*to the very day*—my Hillary became the most difficult child I'd ever seen. This is the same baby who, the day before, had eaten her spinach like it was her last meal. The next day, though, it all ended up on the floor!"

Millie's exasperation was met with approving nods and smiles. The mothers all agreed—their babies had seemed to switch personalities around the same time. Gone were the agreeable, lovable infants. In their places were cranky, demanding toddlers.

What had happened? Any competent pediatrician or child therapist will attest to a shift that begins during the first year of life and continues until about three years. A shift which, though sometimes disruptive and chaotic, is completely normal. And part of God's plan for the child.

As infants gain a sense of internal safety and attachment, a second need arises. The baby's need for autonomy, or independence, starts to emerge. Child experts call this *separation and individuation.* "Separation" refers to the child's need to perceive him or herself as distinct from Mother, a "not-me" experience. "Individuation" describes the identity the child develops while separating from Mother. It's a "me" experience.

You can't have "me" until you first have a "not-me." It's like trying to build a house on a plot of land filled with trees and wild brush. You must first cut away some space, then begin building your home. You must first determine who you *aren't* before you discover the true, authentic aspects of your God-given identity.

The only recorded instance of Jesus' boyhood describes this principle. Remember when Jesus' mother and father left Jerusalem without him? When they went back and found him teaching in the temple, his mother admonished him. Jesus' words to his mother were, "Why were you searching for me? Didn't you know I had to be in my Father's house?" (Luke 2:49). Translation: I have values, thoughts, and opinions that are different from yours, Mother. Jesus knew who he was not, as well as who he was.

The separation-individuation process isn't a smooth transition into a person. Three phases are critical to developing healthy boundaries in childhood: hatching, practicing, and rapprochement.

Hatching: "Mommy and Me Aren't the Same"

"It's not fair," a mother of a five-month-old boy told me. "We had four months of bliss and closeness. I loved Eric's helplessness, his dependency. He needed me, and I was enough for him."

"All of a sudden it changed. He got—I don't know how to say it—more restless, wigglier. He didn't always want me to hold him. He became more interested in other people, even in brightly colored toys, than me!

"I'm beginning to get the picture," the woman concluded. "He needed me for four months. Now motherhood is spending the next seventeen and half years letting him leave me!"

In many ways, this mother got the picture. The first five to ten months of life mark a major shift in infants: from "Mommy and me are the same" to "Mommy and me aren't the same." During this period, babies begin moving out of their passive union with Mother into an active interest in the outside world. They become aware that there's a big, exciting world out there—and they want a piece of the action!

This period is called "hatching" or "differentiation" by child researchers. It's a time of exploration, of touching, of tasting and feeling new things. Though children in this phase are still dependent on Mother, they aren't wrapped up in closeness with her. The months of nurturing have paid off—the child feels safe enough to start taking risks. Watch crawlers in full tilt. They don't want to miss out. This is a geographical boundary in motion—away from Mother.

Look into the eyes of a baby in the "hatching" phase. You can see Adam's wide-eyed wonder at the flora, fauna, and majesty of the earth created for him by the Lord. You can see the desire to discover, the drive to learn hinted at in Job 11:7: "Can you discover the depths of God? Can you discover the limits of the Almighty?" No, we can't. But we are created to discover, to experience the Creation and to know the Creator.

This is a difficult period for new mothers. As the mom in the beginning of this section described, it can be a letdown. It's especially hard for women who have never really "hatched" themselves. They long for nothing but closeness, neediness, and dependency from their baby. These women often conceive lots of children, or find ways to spend time with very young infants. They often don't enjoy the "separating" part of mothering. They don't like the distance between themselves and baby. It's a painful boundary for Mother, but a necessary one for the child.

Practicing: "I Can Do Anything!"

"But what's wrong with wanting to have fun? Life wasn't meant to be boring," protested Derek. In his late forties, Derek dressed like a college student. His face had that tanned, unlined look that appears unnatural on a middle-aged man.

Something was out of place. Derek was talking to his pastor about switching his membership from the thirty-five-and-older singles group to the twenties and thirties group. "They're just not my speed. I like roller coasters, late nights out, and switching jobs. Keeps me young, you know?"

Derek's style describes someone still stuck in the second stage of separation-individuation: practicing. During this period, which usually lasts from age ten months to eighteen months (and then returns later), babies learn to walk and begin to use words.

The difference between hatching and practicing is radical. While the hatching baby is overwhelmed by this new world and still leans a great deal on Mother, the practicing child is trying to leave her behind! The newfound ability to walk opens up a sense of omnipotence. Toddlers feel exhilaration and energy. And they want to try everything, including walking down steep stairs, putting forks into electric sockets, and chasing cats' tails.

People like Derek who are stuck in this stage can be lots of fun. Except when you pop their bubble about their unrealistic grandiosity and their irresponsibility. Then you become a "wet blanket." It's revealing to talk to the "wet blanket" who is married to a practicing child. No job is more tiring.

Proverbs 7:7 describes the youth stuck in the practicing stage: "I saw among the simple, I noticed among the young men, a youth who lacked judgment."

This young man had energy, but no impulse control, no boundaries on his passions. He becomes sexually promiscuous, which often happens to adults who are caught in this phase. And he ends up dead: "till an arrow pierces his liver, like a bird darting into a snare, little knowing it will cost him his life" (Prov. 7:23).

Practicers feel that they'll never be caught. But life does catch up with them.

What practicing infants (the ones for whom omnipotence *is* appropriate!) need most from parents is a responsive delight in their delight, exhilaration at their exhilaration, and some safe limits to practice. Good parents have fun with toddlers who jump on the bed. Poor parents either quench their children's desire by not allowing any jumping, or they set no limits and allow them to jump all over Mom and Dad's orange juice and coffee. (Derek's parents were the second type.)

In the practicing phase children learn that aggressiveness and taking initiative are good. Parents who firmly and consistently set realistic boundaries with children in this period, but without spoiling their enthusiasm, help them through the transition.

Have you ever seen the posters depicting "baby's first steps"? Some of these portray a wrong notion. They present the child taking hesitant steps toward a waiting mother, arms outstretched. The truth is different. Most mothers report, "I watched my baby's first steps from behind!" The practicing toddler moves from safety and warmth to excitement and discovery. Physical and geographical boundaries help the child learn action without danger.

The practicing phase provides the child with the energy and drive to make the final step toward becoming an individual, but energetic exhilaration can't last forever. Cars can't always run at full speed. Sprinters can't keep up the pace for miles. And practicing children must give way to the next phase, *rapprochement.*

Rapprochement: "I Can't Do Everything"

Rapprochement, which occurs from around eighteen months to three years, comes from a French word meaning "a restoration of harmonious relations." In other words, the child comes back to reality. The grandiosity of the past few months slowly gives way to the realization that "I can't do everything I want." Children become anxious and aware that the world's a scary place. They realize that they still need Mother.

The rapprochement phase is a return to connection with Mother, but this time it's different. This time the child brings a more separate self into the relationship. There are two people now, with differing thoughts and feelings. And the child is ready to relate to the outside world without losing a sense of self.

Typically, this is a difficult period for both children and parents. Rapprochement toddlers are obnoxious, opposition-al, temperamental, and downright angry. They can remind you of someone with a chronic toothache.

Let's look at some of the tools toddlers use to build boundaries in this stage.

Anger. Anger is a friend. It was created by God for a purpose: to tell us that there's a problem that needs to be confronted. Anger is a way for children to know that their experience is different from someone else's. The ability to use anger to distinguish between self and others is a boundary. Children who can appropriately express anger are children who will understand, later in life, when someone is trying to control or hurt them.

Ownership. Sometimes misunderstood as simply a "selfish" stage, rapprochement introduces words to the youngster's vocabulary such as, *mine, my,* and *me.* Suzy doesn't want anyone else to hold her doll. Billy doesn't want to share his trucks with a visiting toddler. This important part of becoming a self is often quite difficult for Christian parents to understand. "Well, that old sinful nature is rearing its ugly head in my little girl," the parents will remark while their friends nod sagely. "We're trying to help her share and love others, but she's caught up in that selfishness we all have."

This is neither accurate nor biblical. The child's new-found fondness for "mine" does have roots in our innate self-centeredness—part of the sinful depravity in all of us that wants to, as did Satan, "make myself like the Most High" (Isa. 14:14). However, this simplistic understanding of our character doesn't take into consideration the full picture of what being in the image of God truly is.

Being created in God's image also means having owner-ship, or *stewardship*. As Adam and Eve were given domin-ion over the earth to subdue and rule it, we are also given stewardship over our time, energy, talents, values, feelings, behavior, money, and all the other things mentioned in chapter 2. Without a "mine," we have no sense of responsi-bility to develop, nurture, and protect these resources. Without a "mine," we have no self to give to God and his kingdom.

Children desperately need to know that *mine, my,* and *me* aren't swear words. With correct biblical parenting, they'll learn sacrifice and develop a giving, loving heart, but not until they have a personality that has been loved enough to give love away: "We love because he first loved us" (1 John 4:19).

No: The One-Word Boundary. Toddlers going through rapprochement frequently use one of the most important words in the human language: the word *no*. While it can emerge during hatching, *no* is perfected during rapproche-ment. It's the first verbal boundary children learn.

The word *no* helps children separate from what they don't like. It gives them the power to make choices. It protects them. Learning to deal with a child's no is crucial to that child's development. One couple who didn't attend to their child's refusal to eat certain foods found out later that she was allergic to one of them!

Often, children at this age become "no" addicts. They'll not only refuse vegetables and nap time, but also turn away

from Popsicles and favorite toys! It's worth it for them to
have the no. It keeps them from feeling completely helpless
and powerless.

Parents have two tasks associated with no. First, they
need to help their child feel safe enough to say no, thereby
encouraging his or her own boundaries. Though they
certainly can't make all the choices they'd like, young
children should be able to have a no that is listened to.
Informed parents won't be insulted or enraged by their
child's resistance. They will help the child feel that his no is
just as loveable as his yes. They won't withdraw emotionally
from the child who says no, but will stay connected. One
parent must often support another who is being worn down
by their baby's no. This process takes work!

One couple was faced with an aunt whose feelings were
hurt by their daughter's refusal to kiss and hug her upon
every visit. Sometimes the child wanted to be close; sometimes she wanted to stand back and watch. The couple
responded to the aunt's complaint by saying, "We don't want
Casey to feel that her affection is something she owes
people. We'd like her to be in charge of her life." These
parents wanted their daughter's yes to be yes, and her no to
be no (Matt. 5:37). They wanted her to be able to say no, so
that in the future she would have the ability to say no to evil.

The second task facing parents of children in rapprochement is that of *helping the child respect others' boundaries.*
Children need to be able to not only give a no, but also take a
no.

Parents need to be able to set and keep age-appropriate
boundaries with children. It means not giving in to temper
tantrums at the toy shop, though it would be less humiliating
to quiet the child by purchasing half of the store. It means
time-outs, appropriate confrontations, and spanking, when
necessary. "Discipline your son, for in that there is hope; do
not be a willing party to his death" (Prov. 19:18). In other
words, help the child learn to take limits before it's too late.

Boundary construction is most evident in three-year-olds.
By this time, they should have mastered the following tasks:

1. The ability to be emotionally attached to others, yet

without giving up a sense of self and one's freedom to be apart.

2. The ability to say appropriate no's to others without fear of loss of love.

3. The ability to take appropriate no's from others without withdrawing emotionally.

Noting these tasks, a friend said half-joking, "They need to learn this by age three? How about by forty-three?" Yes, these are tall orders. But boundary development is essential in the early years of life.

Two additional periods of life focus on boundaries. The first is adolescence. The adolescent years are a reenactment of the first years of life. They involve more mature issues, such as sexuality, gender identity, competition, and adult identity. But the same issues of knowing when to say yes and no and to whom are central during this confusing time.

The second period is young adulthood, the time when children leave home or college and start a career or get married. Young adults suffer a loss of structure during this period. There are no class bells, no schedules imposed by others, and a great deal of very scary freedom and responsibility, as well as the demands of intimacy and commitment. This can often become an intense time of learning more about setting good boundaries.

The earlier the child learns good boundaries, the less turmoil he or she experiences later in life. A successful first three years of life will mean a smoother (but not smooth!) adolescence and a better transition into adulthood. A problematic childhood can be helped greatly by lots of hard work in the family during adolescence. But serious boundary problems during both these periods can be devastating during the adult years.

"It helps to know the way it should have been for me," said one woman who attended a talk on child development. "But what would really help is to know what went wrong for me." Let's look next at where our boundary development goes wrong.

Boundary Injuries: What Goes Wrong?

Boundary problems are rooted in thousands of encounters with others, as well in our own nature and personality. The most important boundary conflicts, however, occur in the crucial first few years of life. They may happen in any or all of the three phases of separation-individuation: hatching, practicing, or rapprochement. Generally, the earlier and more severe the injury, the deeper the boundary problem.

Withdrawal from Boundaries

"I don't know why it happens, but it happens," mused Ingrid over coffee with her friend Alice. "Every time I disagree with my mother, even on little things, I feel this terrible sense that she's not there anymore. It's like she's hurt and withdrawn, and I can't get her back. It's really a horrible feeling to think you've lost someone you love."

Let's be honest. None of us enjoys being told no. It's difficult to accept another person's refusal to give support, to be intimate, or to forgive. Yet good relationships are built on the freedom to refuse and confront: "As iron sharpens iron, so one man sharpens another" (Prov. 27:17).

Not only good relationships but also mature characters are built on appropriate nos. Developing children need to know their boundaries will be honored. *It is crucial that their disagreements, their practicing, their experimentation not result in a withdrawal of love.*

Please don't misunderstand this. Parental limits are crucial. Children need to know behavioral lines that should not be crossed. They need to suffer biblical, age-appropriate consequences for acting out. (In fact, when parents do not set and maintain good boundaries with their children, the children suffer another type of boundary injury, which we will discuss shortly.) What we're talking about here isn't allowing the child free rein. Parents need to stay attached and connected to their children *even when they disagree with them.* That doesn't mean they shouldn't get angry. It means they shouldn't withdraw.

How often do we hear the statement that "God loves the

sinner, but hates the sin"? It's true. His love is constant and "never fails" (1 Cor. 13:8). When parents detach from a misbehaving young child instead of staying connected and dealing with the problem, God's constant love is misrepresented. When parents pull away in hurt, disappointment, or passive rage, they are sending this message to their youngster: *You're loveable when you behave. You aren't loveable when you don't behave.*

The child translates that message something like this: *When I'm good, I am loved. When I'm bad, I am cut off.*

Put yourself in the child's place. What would you do? It's not a difficult decision. God created people with a need for attachment and relationship. Parents who pull away from their child are, in essence, practicing *spiritual and emotional blackmail.* The child can either pretend to not disagree and keep the relationship, or he can continue to separate and lose his most important relationship in the world. He will most likely keep quiet.

Children whose parents withdraw when they start setting limits learn to accentuate and develop their compliant, loving, sensitive parts. At the same time, they learn to fear, distrust, and hate their aggressive, truth-telling, and separate parts. If someone they love pulls away when they become angry, cantankerous, or experimental, children learn to hide these parts of themselves.

Parents who tell their children, "It hurts us when you're angry" make the child responsible for the emotional health of the parent. In effect, *the child has just been made the parent of the parent*—sometimes at two or three years old. It's far, far better to say, "I know you're angry, but you still can't have that toy." And then to take your hurt feelings to a spouse, friend, or the Lord.

By nature, children are omnipotent. They live in a world where the sun shines because they were good, and it rains because they were naughty. Children will give up this omnipotence gradually over time, as they learn that needs and events besides theirs are important. But during the early years, this omnipotence plays right into boundary injury. When children feel parents withdrawing, they readily believe that they are responsible for Mom and Dad's feelings.

That's what *omnipotent* means: "I am powerful enough to make Mom and Dad pull away. I'd better watch it."

A parent's emotional withdrawal can be subtle: A hurt tone of voice. Long silences for no reason. Or it can be overt: Crying spells. Illness. Yelling. Children of parents like these grow up to be adults who are terrified that setting boundaries will cause severe isolation and abandonment.

Hostility Against Boundaries

"Do *I* understand why I can't say no?" Larry chuckled. "Why don't you ask me a hard one? I grew up in the military. Dad's word was law. And disagreeing was always rebellion. I contradicted him once when I was nine. All I remember is waking up on the other side of the room with a whopping headache. And lots of hurt feelings."

The second boundary injury, easier to spot than the first, is a parent's hostility against boundaries. The parent becomes angry at the child's attempts at separating from him or her. Hostility can emerge in the form of angry words, physical punishment, or inappropriate consequences.

Some parents will say to the child, "You'll do what I say." This is fair enough. God meant for parents to be in charge of children. But then they'll say, "And you'll like doing it." This makes a child crazy, because it's a denial of the separate soul of the child. To "make the child like it" is to pressure the child into becoming a "people pleaser," not a "God pleaser" (Gal. 1:10).

Some parents criticize the boundaries of their children:

"If you disagree with me, I'll . . ."
"You'll do it my way or else."
"Don't question your mother."
"You need an attitude adjustment."
"You've got no reason to feel bad."

Children need to be under the authority and control of their parents, but when parents punish their child for his growing independence, he will usually retreat into hurt and resentment.

This hostility is a poor counterfeit of God's program of learning discipline. Discipline is the art of teaching children self-control by using consequences. Irresponsible actions should cause discomfort that motivates us to become more responsible.

The "my-way-or-else" approach teaches children to pretend to be obedient, at least when the parent is in earshot. The "you-have-a-choice" approach teaches children to be responsible for their own actions. Instead of saying, "You'll make your bed or you'll be grounded for a month," the parent says, "You have a choice: Make your bed, and I'll let you play Nintendo; don't make your bed and you lose your Nintendo privileges for the rest of the day." The child decides how much pain he is willing to endure to be disobedient.

God's discipline teaches, not punishes:

> God disciplines us for our good, that we may share in his holiness. No discipline seems pleasant at the time, but painful. Later on, however, it produces a harvest of righteousness and peace for those who have been trained by it. (Heb. 12:10–11)

When parents greet their children's disagreement, disobedience, or practicing with simple hostility, the children are denied the benefit of being trained. They don't learn that delaying gratification and being responsible have benefits. They only learn how to avoid someone's wrath. Ever wonder why some Christians fear an angry God, no matter how much they read about his love?

The results of this hostility are difficult to see because these children quickly learn how to hide under a compliant smile. When these children grow up they suffer depression, anxiety, relationship conflicts, and substance-abuse problems. For the first time in their lives, many boundary-injured individuals realize they have a problem.

Hostility can create problems in both saying and hearing no. Some children become pliably enmeshed with others. But some react outwardly and become controlling people—just like the hostile parent.

The Bible addresses two distinct reactions to hostility in

parents: Fathers are told not to "embitter [their] children, or they will become discouraged" (Col. 3:21). Some children respond to harshness with compliance and depression. At the same time, fathers are told not to "exasperate [their] children" (Eph. 6:4). Other children react to hostility with rage. Many grow up to be just like the hostile parent who hurt them.

Overcontrol

Overcontrol occurs when otherwise loving parents try to protect their children from making mistakes by having too-strict rules and limits. For example, they may keep their children from playing with other kids to protect them from being hurt or learning bad habits. They may be so concerned about their children catching a cold that they make them wear galoshes on cloudy days.

The problem with overcontrol is this: while a major responsibility of good parents is certainly to control and protect, they must make room for their children to make mistakes. Remember that we learn maturity "by constant use" (Heb. 5:14). Overcontrolled children are subject to dependency, enmeshment conflicts, and difficulty setting and keeping firm boundaries. They also have problems taking risks and being creative.

Lack of Limits

Eileen sighed. Her husband Bruce was in his twice-a-week mode of throwing fits whenever she "dropped the ball." This time he was yelling about having to reschedule their night out with the Billingses. Eileen had forgotten to call a babysitter for the kids until four that afternoon.

She couldn't understand why Bruce got so wound up about such little things. Maybe he just needed some time off. *That was it!* Eileen brightened up. *We need a vacation!* She forgot that they'd had one a month ago.

Eileen had very loving, but very indulgent parents. They couldn't stand to make her do anything, to discipline her with time-outs, consequences, or spankings. Her folks thought that lots of love and lots of forgiveness would help her be the adult she needed to be.

So whenever Eileen didn't pick up after herself, her mother would cover for her. When she wrecked the family car three times, her dad got her her own car. And when she overdrew her checking account, her parents quietly put more money in it. *After all, isn't love patient?* they'd say.

Eileen's parents' lack of limits on her hurt her character development. Though she was a loving wife, mother, and worker, others were constantly frustrated at her undisciplined, careless way of living. It cost others a lot to be in relationship with her. Yet she was so loveable that most of her friends didn't want to hurt her feelings by confronting her. So the problem remained unsolved.

Lack of parental boundaries is the opposite of hostility. Again, biblical discipline would have provided the necessary structure to help Eileen develop her character.

Sometimes a lack of parental limits, coupled with a lack of connection, can produce an aggressively controlling person. We all know the experience of going into a supermarket and observing a four-year-old in total control of a mother. The mother begs, pleads, and threatens her son to stop having his tantrum. Then, at her wits' end, she gives him the candy bar he's been screaming for. "But that's the last one," she says, struggling for some control. But by then control is an illusion.

Now imagine that four-year-old as a forty-year-old man. The scenario has changed, but the script is the same. When he is crossed, or when someone sets a limit with him, the same tantrum erupts. And by then, he's had thirty-six more years of having the world cater to him. His recovery program will need to be very strong and consistent to help him. Sometimes recovery comes in the form of hospitalization, sometimes in divorce, sometimes in jail, and sometimes in disease. But no one can really escape the disciplines of life. They will always win out. We always reap what we sow. And the later in life it is, the sadder a picture it is, for the stakes are higher.

Obviously, we're describing the person who has a difficult time hearing others' boundaries and/or needs. These people have been as injured by a lack of boundaries as others are by too-rigid boundaries.

Inconsistent Limits

Sometimes, due to their confusion about rearing children or their own injuries, some parents combine strict and lax limits, sending conflicting messages to children. The children don't know what the rules of family and life are.

Alcoholic families often exhibit inconsistent limits. A parent may be loving and kind one day, unreasonably harsh the next. This is particularly true because of the behavior changes brought on by drinking.

Alcoholism causes massive boundary confusion in the child. Adult children of alcoholics never feel safe in relationships. They're always waiting for the other person to let them down or attack them unexpectedly. They keep their guard up constantly.

Setting limits is traumatic for adult children of alcoholics. Saying no might bring respect, or it might bring rage. They feel like the double-minded person described in James 1:6: "like a wave of the sea, blown and tossed by the wind." They are uncertain about what they are and aren't responsible for.

Trauma

Up until now, we've dealt with characteristics of family relating. Withdrawal, hostility, and setting inappropriate limits are ways parents act toward their children. Over time, these become ingrained in the soul of the child.

In addition, specific traumas can injure boundary development. A trauma is an intensely painful emotional experience, rather than a character pattern. Emotional, physical, and sexual abuse are traumatic. Accidents and debilitating illnesses are traumatic. Severe losses such as the death of a parent, divorce, or extreme financial hardship are also traumatic.

A good way to look at the difference between character-relating patterns, such as withdrawal and hostility, and trauma, is to look at how a tree in a forest can be hurt. It can be fed inappropriately, through bad ingredients in the soil, or it can be given too much or too little sun or water. That's an illustration of character-pattern problems. Trauma is like lightning hitting the tree.

A trauma can affect boundary development because it shakes up two necessary foundations to children's growth:

1. The world is reasonably safe.
2. They have control over their lives.

Children who undergo trauma feel these foundations shaken up. They become unsure that they are safe and protected in the world, and they become frightened that they have no say-so in any danger that approaches them.

Jerry had been physically abused by both of his parents for years. He had left home early, joined the Marines, and had several bad marriages. In therapy as an adult in his thirties, he began realizing why, under his tough exterior, he always longed for controlling women. He'd fall madly in love with the fact that they could "handle" him. Then a pattern of compliance to the woman would emerge, with Jerry always on the losing end.

One day in session, Jerry remembered his mother striking him across the face for some small infraction. He vividly remembered his vain attempts to protect himself, pleading, "Please, Mom—I'm sorry. I'll do anything you say. Please, Mom." When he promised unquestioning obedience, the hitting would stop. That memory tied in with his lack of power and self-control with his wives and girlfriends. Their anger always terrified him, and he would instantly comply. Jerry's boundary development was seriously injured by his mother's abuse.

The heart of God seems to beat especially close to the victim of trauma: "He has sent me to bind up the broken-hearted" (Isa. 61:1). God desires the wounds of the trauma-tized to be bound up by loving people.

Victims of trauma in the family are almost always recipients of poor or sinful character-relating patterns. Withdrawal from our boundaries and hostility toward our boundaries are the ground from which trauma springs.

Our Own Character Traits

Have you ever heard someone described as being that way "from the womb"? Perhaps you were always active and confrontive, always exploring new horizons. Or maybe you liked to be quiet and reflective "since forever."

We contribute to our boundary issues by our own individual character styles. For example, some people with a constitutionally greater amount of aggression deal with boundary problems more confrontationally. And some with less aggression shy more from boundaries.

Our Own Sinfulness

We also contribute to our own boundary development problems by our own depravity. Depravity is what we inherited from Adam and Eve. It is our resistance to being creatures under God, our resistance to humility. It's a refusal to accept our position, and a lust for being omnipotent and "in charge," not needing anyone and not accountable to anyone. Our depravity enslaves us to the law of sin and death, from which only Christ can save us (Rom. 8:2).

By now you should be gaining a clearer picture of what goes into boundary problems and boundary development. It's time now to look at what the Bible says about how boundaries should operate in our lives, and how they can be developed—all through our lives.

5

Ten Laws of Boundaries

I magine for a moment that you live on another planet operating under different principles. Suppose your planet has no gravity and no need for a medium of exchange such as money. You get your energy and fuel from osmosis, instead of eating and drinking. Suddenly, without warning, you find yourself transported to Earth.

When you awake from your trip, you step out of your hovering spacecraft and fall abruptly to the ground. "Ouch!" you say, not knowing exactly why you fell. After regaining your composure, you decide to travel around a bit, but are unable to fly, because of this new phenomenon called gravity. So you start walking.

After a while, you notice that, strangely, you feel hungry and thirsty. You wonder why. Where you come from, the galactic system rejuvenates your body automatically. Luckily, you run across an earthling who diagnoses your problem and tells you that you need food. Better yet, he recommends a place where you can eat, called Jack's Diner.

You follow his directions, go into the restaurant, and manage to order some of this Earth food that contains all the nutrients you need. You immediately feel better. But then, the man who gave you the food wants "seven dollars" for what he gave you. You have no idea what he's talking about. After quite an argument, some men in uniforms come and take you away and put you in a small room with bars. *What in the world is going on,* you wonder.

You didn't mean anyone harm, yet you are in "jail," whatever that is. You can no longer move about as you want, and you resent it. You only tried to be about your own business, and now you have a sore leg, fatigue from your long walk, and a stomachache from eating too much. Nice place, this Earth.

Does this sound farfetched? People raised in dysfunctional families, or families where God's ways of boundaries are not practiced, have experiences similar to that of the alien. They find themselves transported into adult life where spiritual principles that have never been explained to them govern their relationships and well-being. They hurt, are hungry, and may end up in jail, but they never know the principles that could have helped them operate in accord with reality instead of against it. So, they are prisoners of their own ignorance.

God's world is set up with laws and principles. Spiritual realities are as real as gravity, and if you do not know them, you will discover their effects. Just because we have not been taught these principles of life and relationships does not mean they will not rule. We need to know the principles God has woven into life and operate according to them. Below are ten laws of boundaries that you can learn to begin to experience life differently.

Law #1: The Law of Sowing and Reaping

The law of cause and effect is a basic law of life. The Bible calls it the Law of Sowing and Reaping. "You reap whatever you sow. If you sow to your own flesh, you will reap corruption from the flesh; but if you sow to the Spirit, you will reap eternal life from the Spirit" (Gal. 6:7–8 NRSV).

When God tells us that we will reap what we sow, he is not punishing us; he's telling us how things really are. If you smoke cigarettes, you most likely will develop a smoker's hack, and you may even get lung cancer. If you overspend, you most likely will get calls from creditors, and you may even go hungry because you have no money for food. On the other hand, if you eat right and exercise regularly, you may suffer from fewer colds and bouts with the flu. If you budget wisely, you will have money for the bill collectors and for the grocery store.

Sometimes, however, people don't reap what they sow, because someone else steps in and reaps the consequences for them. If every time you overspent, your mother sent you money to cover check overdrafts or high credit-card balances, you wouldn't reap the consequences of your spendthrift ways. Your mother would be protecting you from the natural consequences: the hounding of creditors or going hungry.

As the mother in the above example demonstrates, the Law of Sowing and Reaping can be interrupted. And it is often people who have no boundaries who do the interrupting. Just as we can interfere with the law of gravity by catching a glass tumbling off the table, people can interfere with the Law of Cause and Effect by stepping in and rescuing irresponsible people. Rescuing a person from the natural consequences of his behavior enables him to continue in irresponsible behavior. The Law of Sowing and Reaping has not been repealed. It is still operating. But the doer is not suffering the consequences; someone else is.

Today we call a person who continually rescues another person a codependent. In effect, codependent, boundaryless people "co-sign the note" of life for the irresponsible person. Then they end up paying the bills—physically, emotionally, and spiritually—and the spendthrift continues out of control with no consequences. He continues to be loved, pampered, and treated nicely.

Establishing boundaries helps codependent people stop interrupting the Law of Sowing and Reaping in their loved one's life. Boundaries force the person who is doing the sowing to also do the reaping.

It doesn't help just to confront the irresponsible person. A client will often say to me, "But I do confront Jack. I have tried many times to let him know what I think about his behavior and that he needs to change." In reality, my client is only nagging Jack. Jack will not feel the need to change because his behavior is not causing him any pain. *Confronting an irresponsible person is not painful to him; only consequences are.*

If Jack is wise, confrontation might change his behavior. But people caught in destructive patterns are usually not wise. They need to suffer consequences before they change their behavior. The Bible tells us it is worthless to confront foolish people: "Do not rebuke a mocker or he will hate you; rebuke a wise man and he will love you" (Prov. 9:8).

Codependent people bring insults and pain onto themselves when they confront irresponsible people. In reality, they just need to stop interrupting the law of sowing and reaping in someone's life.

Law #2: The Law of Responsibility

Many times when people hear a talk on boundaries and taking responsibility for their own lives, they say, "That's so self-centered. We should love one another and deny ourselves." Or, they actually become selfish and self-centered. Or, they feel "guilty" when they do someone a favor. These are unbiblical views of responsibility.

The Law of Responsibility includes loving others. The commandment to love is the entire law for Christians (Gal. 5:13–14). Jesus calls it "my" commandment, "Love each other as I have loved you" (John 15:12). Anytime you are *not* loving others, you are not taking full responsibility for yourself; you have disowned your heart.

Problems arise when boundaries of responsibility are confused. We are to *love* one another, not *be* one another. I can't feel your feelings for you. I can't think for you. I can't behave for you. I can't work through the disappointment that limits bring for you. In short, I can't grow for you; only you can. Likewise, you can't grow for me. The biblical mandate for our own personal growth is "Continue to work out your salvation with fear and trembling, for it is God who works in you to will and to act according to his good purpose" (Phil. 2:12–13). You are responsible for *yourself.* I am responsible for *myself.*

An additional theme in the Bible says that we are to treat others the way we would want to be treated. If we were down and out, helpless and without hope, we would certainly want help and provision. This is a very important side of being responsible "to."

Another aspect of being responsible "to" is not only in the giving but in the setting of limits on another's destructive and irresponsible behavior. It is not good to rescue someone from the consequences of their sin, for you will only have to do it again. You have reinforced the pattern (Prov. 19:19). It is the same principle spoken of in child rearing; it is hurtful to not have limits with others. It leads them to destruction (Prov. 23:13).

A strong strand throughout the Bible stresses that you are to *give* to needs and put *limits* on sin. Boundaries help you do just that.

Law #3: The Law of Power

As the Twelve Step movement grows within the church, Christians in therapy and recovery voice a common confusion. Am I powerless over my behavior? If I am, how can I become responsible? What *do* I have the power to do?

The Twelve Steps and the Bible teach that people must admit that they are moral failures. Alcoholics admit that they are powerless over alcohol; they don't have the fruit of self-control. They are powerless over their addiction, much like Paul was: "I do not understand what I do. For what I want to do I do not do, but what I hate I do. . . . For what I do is not the good I want to do; no, the evil I do not want to do—this I keep on doing . . . waging war against the law of my mind and making me a prisoner of the law of sin at work within my members" (Rom. 7:15, 19, 23). This is powerlessness. John says that we are all in that state, and that anyone that denies it is lying (1 John 1:8).

Though you do not have the power in and of yourself to overcome these patterns, you do have the power to do some things that will bring fruits of victory later:

1. *You have the power to agree with the truth about your problems.* In the Bible this is called "confession." To confess means to "agree with." You have the ability to at least say "that is me." You may not be able to change it yet, but you can confess.

2. You have the power to submit your inability to God.
You always have the power to ask for help and yield. You
have the power to humble yourself and turn your life over to
him. You may not be able to make yourself well, but you can
call the Doctor! The humbling of yourself commanded in the
Bible is always coupled with great promises. If you do what
you are able—confess, believe, and ask for help—God will
do what you are unable to do—bring about change (1 John
1:9; James 4:7–10; Matt. 5:3, 6).

*3. You have the power to search and ask God and others
to reveal more and more about what is within your
boundaries.*

*4. You have the power to turn from the evil that you find
within you.* This is called *repentance.* This does not mean
that you'll be perfect; it means that you can see your sinful
parts as aspects that you want to change.

*5. You have the power to humble yourself and ask God
and others to help you with your developmental injuries and
leftover childhood needs.* Many of your problematic parts
come from being empty inside, and you need to seek God
and others to have those needs met.

*6. You have the power to seek out those that you have
injured and make amends.* You need to do this in order to be
responsible for yourself and your sin, and be responsible to
those you have injured. Matthew 5:23–24 says, "Therefore,
if you are offering your gift at the altar and there remember
that your brother has something against you, leave your gift
there in front of the altar. First go and be reconciled to your
brother; then come and offer your gift."

On the other side of the coin, your boundaries help
define what you do not have power over: *everything outside
of them!* Listen to the way the serenity prayer (probably the
best boundary prayer ever written) says it:

> God grant me the serenity to accept the things I cannot
> change, the courage to change the things I can, and the
> wisdom to know the difference.

In other words, God, clarify my boundaries! You can
work on submitting yourself to the process and working with
God to change you. You cannot change anything else: not the

weather, the past, the economy—and especially not other people. *You cannot change others.* More people suffer from trying to change others than from any other sickness. And it is impossible.

What you *can* do is *influence* others. But there is a trick. Since you cannot get *them* to change, you must change *yourself* so that their destructive patterns no longer work on you. Change your way of dealing with them; they may be motivated to change if their old ways no longer work.

Another dynamic that happens when you let go of others is that you begin to get healthy, and they may notice and envy your health. They may want some of what you have.

One more thing. You need the wisdom to know what is you and what is not you. Pray for the wisdom to know the difference between what you have the power to change and what you do not.

Law #4: The Law of Respect

One word comes up again and again when people describe their problems with boundaries: *they.* "But *they* won't accept me if I say no." "But *they* will get angry if I set limits." "But *they* won't speak to me for a week if I tell them how I really feel."

We fear that others will not respect our boundaries. We focus on others and lose clarity about ourselves. Sometimes the problem is that we judge others' boundaries. We say or think things such as this:

"How could he refuse to come by and pick me up? It's right on his way! He could find some 'time alone' some other time."

"That's so selfish of her to not come to the luncheon. After all, the rest of us are sacrificing."

"What do you mean, 'no'? I just need the money for a little while."

"It seems that, after all I do for you, you could at least do me this one little favor."

We judge the boundary decisions of others, thinking that we know best how they "ought" to give, and usually that means "they ought to give to me the way I want them to!"

But the Bible says whenever we judge, we will be judged (Matt. 7:1–2). When we judge others' boundaries, ours will fall under the same judgment. If we condemn others' boundaries, we expect them to condemn ours. This sets up a fear cycle inside that makes us afraid to set the boundaries that we need to set. As a result, we comply, then we resent, and the "love" that we have "given" goes sour.

This is where the Law of Respect comes in. As Jesus said, "So in everything, do to others what you would have them do to you" (Matt. 7:12). We need to respect the boundaries of others. We need to love the boundaries of others in order to command respect for our own. We need to treat their boundaries the way we want them to treat ours.

If we love and respect people who tell us no, they will love and respect our no. Freedom begets freedom. If we are walking in the Spirit, we give people the freedom to make their own choices. "Where the Spirit of the Lord is, there is freedom" (2 Cor. 3:17). If we are going to judge at all, it needs to be by the "perfect law that gives freedom" (James 1:25).

Our real concern with others should not be "Are they doing what I would do or what I want them to do?" but "Are they really making a free choice?" When we accept others' freedom, we don't get angry, feel guilty, or withdraw our love when they set boundaries with us. When we accept others' freedom, we feel better about our own.

Law #5: The Law of Motivation

Stan was confused. He read in the Bible and was taught in church that it was more blessed to give than to receive, but he found that this often was not true. He frequently felt unappreciated for "all he was doing." He wished people would have more consideration for his time and energy. Yet, whenever someone wanted something from him, he would do it. He thought this was loving, and he wanted to be a loving person.

Finally, when the fatigue grew into depression, he came to see me.

When I asked what was wrong, Stan replied that he was "loving too much."

"How can you 'love too much?' " I asked. "I've never heard of such a thing."

"Oh, it's very simple," replied Stan. "I do far more for people than I should. And that makes me very depressed."

"I'm not quite sure what you are doing," I said, "but it certainly isn't love. The Bible says that true love leads to a blessed state and a state of cheer. Love brings happiness, not depression. If your loving is depressing you, it's probably not love."

"I don't see how you can say that. I do so much for everyone. I give and give and give. How can you say that I'm not loving?"

"I can say that because of the fruit of your actions. You should be feeling happy, not depressed. Why don't you tell me some of the things you do for people?"

As we spent more time together, Stan learned that a lot of his "doing" and sacrificing was not motivated by love but by fear. Stan had learned early in life that if he did not do what his mother wanted, she would withdraw love from him. As a result, Stan learned to give reluctantly. His motive for giving was not love, but fear of losing love.

Stan was also afraid of other people's anger. Because his father frequently yelled at him when he was a boy, he learned to fear angry confrontations. This fear kept him from saying no to others. Self-centered people often get angry when someone tells them no.

Stan said yes out of fear that he would lose love and that other people would get angry at him. These false motives and others keep us from setting boundaries:

1. *Fear of loss of love, or abandonment.* People who say yes and then resent saying yes fear losing someone's love. This is the dominant motive of martyrs. They give to get love, and when they don't get it, they feel abandoned.

2. *Fear of others' anger.* Because of old hurts and poor boundaries, some people can't stand for anyone to be mad at them.

3. *Fear of loneliness.* Some people give in to others because they feel that that will "win" love and end their loneliness.

4. *Fear of losing the "good me" inside.* We are made to love. As a result, when we are not loving, we are in pain. Many people cannot say, "I love you *and* I do not want to do that." Such a statement does not make sense to them. They think that to love means to always say yes.

5. *Guilt.* Many people's giving is motivated by guilt. They are trying to do enough good things to overcome the guilt inside and feel good about themselves. When they say no, they feel bad. So they keep trying to earn a sense of goodness.

6. *Payback.* Many people have received things with guilt messages attached. For example, their parents say things like, "I never had it as good as you." "You should be ashamed at all you get." They feel a burden to pay for all they have been given.

7. *Approval.* Many feel as if they are still children seeking parental approval. Therefore, when someone wants something from them, they need to give so that this symbolic parent will be "well pleased."

8. *Overidentification with the other's loss.* Many times people have not dealt with all their own disappointments and losses, so whenever they deprive someone else with a no, they "feel" the other person's sadness to the *n*th degree. They can't stand to hurt someone that badly, so they comply.

The point is this: we were called into freedom, and this freedom results in gratitude, an overflowing heart, and love for others. To give bountifully has great reward. It is truly more blessed to give than to receive. If your giving is not leading to cheer, then you need to examine the Law of Motivation.

The Law of Motivation says this: Freedom first, service second. If you serve to get free of your fear, you are doomed to failure. Let God work on the fears, resolve them, and create some healthy boundaries to guard the freedom you were called to.

Law #6: The Law of Evaluation

"But if I told him I wanted to do that, wouldn't he be hurt?" Jason asked. When Jason told me he wished to assume responsibility for tasks his business partner was performing poorly, I encouraged him to talk to his partner. "Sure he might be hurt," I said, in response to his question. "So, what's your problem?"

"Well, I wouldn't want to hurt him," Jason said, looking at me as though I should have known that.

"I'm sure you would not want to hurt him," I said. "But what does that have to do with the decision you have to make?"

"Well, I couldn't just make a decision without taking his feelings into account. That's cruel."

"I agree with you. That would be cruel. But, when are you going to tell him?"

"You just said that to tell him would hurt him and that would be cruel," Jason said, perplexed.

"No, I didn't," I replied. "I said to tell him *without considering his feelings* would be cruel. That is very different from not doing what you need to do."

"I don't see any difference. It would still hurt him."

"But it would not *harm* him, and that's the big difference. If anything, the hurt would help him."

"Now I'm really confused. How can it possibly help to hurt him?"

"Well, have you ever gone to the dentist?" I asked.

"Sure."

"Did the dentist hurt you when he drilled your tooth to remove the cavity?"

"Yes."

"Did he harm you?"

"No, he made me feel better."

"*Hurt* and *harm* are different," I pointed out. "When you ate the sugar that gave you the cavity, did that hurt?"

"No, it tasted good," he said, with a smile that told me he was catching on.

"Did it harm you?"

"Yes."

"That's my point. Things can hurt and not harm us. In fact they can even be good for us. And things that feel good can be very harmful to us."

You need to evaluate the effects of setting boundaries and be responsible to the other person, but that does not mean you should avoid setting boundaries because someone responds with hurt or anger. To have boundaries—in this instance, Jason's saying no to his partner—is to live a purposeful life.

Jesus refers to it as the "narrow gate." It is always easier to go through the "broad gate of destruction" and continue to not set boundaries where we need to. But, the result is always the same: destruction. Only the honest, purposeful life leads to good fruit. Deciding to set boundaries is difficult because it requires decision making and confrontation, which, in turn, may cause pain to someone you love.

We need to evaluate the pain caused by our making choices and empathize with it. Take Sandy, for example. Sandy chose to go skiing with friends instead of going home for Christmas vacation. Her mother was sad and disappointed, but she was not harmed. Sandy's decision caused sadness, but her mother's sadness should not cause Sandy to change her mind. A loving response to her mother's hurt would be, "Oh, Mom, I'm sad that we won't be together too. I'm looking forward to next summer's visit."

If Sandy's mother respected her freedom to make choices, she would say something like this: "I'm so disappointed that you're not coming home for Christmas, but I hope you all have a great time." She would be owning her disappointment and respecting Sandy's choice to spend her time with friends.

We cause pain by making choices that others do not like, but we also cause pain by confronting people when they are wrong. But if we do not share our anger with another, bitterness and hatred can set in. We need to be honest with one another about how we are hurt. "Speak truthfully to [your] neighbor, for [you] are all members of one body" (Eph. 4.25).

As iron sharpens iron, we need confrontation and truth

from others to grow. No one likes to hear negative things about him or herself. But in the long run it may be good for us. The Bible says that if we are wise, we will learn from it. Admonition from a friend, while it can hurt, can also help.

We need to evaluate the pain our confrontation causes other people. We need to see how this hurt is helpful to others and sometimes the best thing that we can do for them and the relationship. We need to evaluate the pain in a positive light.

Law #7: The Law of Proactivity

For every action, there is an equal and opposite reaction. Paul says that wrath and sinful passions are a direct reaction to the severity of the law (Rom. 4:15; 5:20; 7:5). In Ephesians and Colossians he says wrath and disillusionment can be reactions to parental injustice (Eph. 6:4; Col. 3:21).

Many of us have known people who, after years of being passive and compliant, suddenly go ballistic, and we wonder what happened. We blame it on the counselor they are seeing or the company they've been keeping.

In reality, they had been complying for years, and their pent-up rage explodes. This reactive phase of boundary creation is helpful, especially for victims. They need to get out of the powerless, victimized place in which they may have been forced by physical and sexual abuse, or by emotional blackmail and manipulation. We should herald their emancipation.

But when is enough enough? Reaction phases are *necessary but not sufficient* for the establishment of boundaries. It is crucial for the two-year-old to throw the peas at Mommy, but to continue that until forty-three is too much. It is crucial for victims of abuse to feel the rage and hatred of being powerless, but to be screaming "victim rights" for the rest of their lives is being stuck in a "victim mentality."

Emotionally, the reactive stance brings diminishing returns. You must react to find your own boundaries, but having found them, you must "not use your freedom to indulge the sinful nature.... If you keep on biting and devouring each other, watch out or you will be destroyed by each other" (Gal. 5:13, 15). Eventually, you must rejoin the human race you have reacted to, and establish connections as equals, loving your neighbor as yourself.

This is the beginning of the establishment of *proactive,* instead of reactive, boundaries. This is where you are able to use the freedom you gained through reacting to love, enjoy, and serve one another. Proactive people show you what they love, what they want, what they purpose, and what they stand for. These people are very different from those who are known by what they hate, what they don't like, what they stand against, and what they will not do.

While reactive victims are primarily known by their "against" stances, proactive people do not demand rights, they *live them.* Power is not something you demand or deserve, it is something you express. The ultimate expression of power is love; it is the ability not to express power, but to restrain it. Proactive people are able to "love others as themselves." They have mutual respect. They are able to "die to self" and not "return evil for evil." They have gotten past the reactive stance of the law and are able to love and not react.

Listen to Jesus compare the reactive person who is still controlled by the law and others with the free person: "You have heard that it was said, 'Eye for eye, and tooth for tooth.' But I tell you, Do not resist an evil person. If someone strikes you on your right cheek, turn to him the other also" (Matt. 5:38–39).

Do not try to get to freedom without owning your reactive period and feelings. You do not need to act this out, but you do need to express the feelings. You need to practice and gain assertiveness. You need to get far enough away from abusive people to be able to fence your property against further invasion. And then you need to own the treasures you find in your soul.

But, do not stay there. Spiritual adulthood has higher goals than "finding yourself." A reactive stage is a stage, not an identity. It is necessary, but not sufficient.

Law #8: The Law of Envy

The New Testament speaks strongly against the envious heart. Consider James: "You want something but don't get it. You kill and covet, but you cannot have what you want. You quarrel and fight" (James 4:2).

What does envy have to do with boundaries? Envy is probably the basest emotion we have. A direct result of the Fall, it was Satan's sin. The Bible says that he had a wish to "be like the Most High." He envied God. In turn, he tempted Adam and Eve with the same idea, telling them that they could be like God also. Satan and our parents, Adam and Eve, were not satisfied with who they were and could rightfully become. They wanted what they did not have, and it destroyed them.

Envy defines "good" as "what I do not possess," and hates the good that it has. How many times have you heard someone subtly put down the accomplishments of others, somehow robbing them of the goodness they had attained? We all have envious parts to our personalities. But what is so destructive about this particular sin is that it guarantees that we will not get what we want and keeps us perpetually insatiable and dissatisfied.

This is not to say that it is wrong to want things we do not have. God has said that he will give us the desires of our heart. The problem with envy is that it focuses outside our boundaries, onto others. If we are focusing on what others have or have accomplished, we are neglecting our responsibilities and will ultimately have an empty heart. Look at the difference in Galatians 6:4: "Each one should test his own actions. Then he can take pride in himself, without comparing himself to somebody else."

Envy is a self-perpetuating cycle. Boundaryless people feel empty and unfulfilled. They look at another's sense of fullness and feel envious. This time and energy needs to be spent on taking responsibility for their lack and doing something about it. Taking action is the only way out. "You have not because you ask not." And the Bible adds "because you work not." Possessions and accomplishments are not the only things we envy. We can envy a person's character and personality, instead of developing the gifts God has given us (Rom. 12:6).

Think of these situations:

A lonely person stays isolated and envious of the close relationships others have.

A single woman withdraws from social life, envying the marriages and families of her friends.

A middle-aged woman feels stuck in her career and wants to pursue something she would enjoy, yet always has a "yes, but . . ." reason why she can't, resenting and envying those who have "gone for it."

A person chooses the righteous life, but envies and resents those who seem to be "having all the fun."

These people are all negating their own actions (Gal. 6:4) and comparing themselves to others, staying stuck and resentful. Notice the difference between those statements and these:

A lonely person owns his lack of relationships and asks himself and God, "I wonder why I always withdraw from people. I can at least go and talk to a counselor about this. Even if I am afraid of social situations, I could seek some help. No one should live this way. I'll make the call."

The single woman asks, "I wonder why I never get asked out, or why I keep getting turned down for dates? What is wrong about what I am doing or how I'm communicating, or where I'm going to meet people? How could I become a more interesting person? Maybe I could join a therapy group to find out why or I could subscribe to a dating service to find people with interests similar to mine."

The middle-aged woman asks herself, "Why am I reluctant to pursue my interests? Why do I feel selfish when I want to quit my job to do something I enjoy? What am I afraid of? If I were really honest, I would notice that the ones who are doing what they like have had to take some risks and sometimes work and go to school to change jobs. That may just be more than I am willing to do."

The righteous person asks himself, "If I am really 'choosing' to love and serve God, why do I feel like a slave? What

is wrong with my spiritual life? What is it about me that
envies someone living in the gutter?"

These people are questioning themselves instead of
envying others. Your envy should always be a sign to you
that you are lacking something. At that moment, you should
ask God to help you understand what you resent, why you do
not have whatever you are envying, and whether you truly
desire it. Ask him to show you what you need to do to get
there, or to give up the desire.

Law #9: The Law of Activity

Human beings are responders and initiators. Many times
we have boundary problems because we lack initiative—the
God-given ability to propel ourselves into life. We respond
to invitations *and* push ourselves into life.

The best boundaries are formed when a child is pushing
against the world naturally, and the outside world sets its
limits on the child. In this way, the aggressive child has
learned limits without losing his or her spirit. Our spiritual
and emotional well-being depends on our having this spirit.

Consider the contrast in the parable of the talents. The
ones who succeeded were active and assertive. *They initi-
ated and pushed.* The one who lost out was passive and
inactive.

The sad thing is that many people who are passive are
not inherently evil or bad people. But evil is an active force,
and passivity can become an ally of evil by not pushing
against it. Passivity never pays off. God will match our effort,
but he will never do our work for us. That would be an
invasion of our boundaries. He wants us to be assertive and
active, seeking and knocking on the door of life.

We know that God is not mean to people who are afraid;
the Scripture is full of examples of his compassion. But he
will not enable passivity. The "wicked and lazy" servant was
passive. He did not try. God's grace covers failure, but it
cannot make up for passivity. We have to do our part.

The sin God rebukes is not trying and failing, but failing
to try. Trying, failing, and trying again is called learning.

Failing to try will have no good result; evil will triumph. God expresses his opinion toward passivity in Hebrews 10:38–39: "'But my righteous one will live by faith. And if he shrinks back, I will not be pleased with him.' But we are not of those who shrink back and are destroyed, but of those who believe and are saved." Passive "shrinking back" is intolerable to God, and when we understand how destructive it is to the soul, we can see why God does not tolerate it. God wants us to "preserve our souls." That is the role of boundaries; they define and preserve our property, our soul.

I have been told that when a baby bird is ready to hatch, if you break the egg for the bird, it will die. The bird must peck its own way out of the egg into the world. This aggressive "workout" strengthens the bird, allowing it to function in the outside world. Robbed of this responsibility, it will die.

This is also the way God has made us. If he "hatches" us, does our work for us, invades our boundaries, we will die. We must not shrink back passively. Our boundaries can only be created by our being active and aggressive, by our knocking, seeking, and asking (Matt. 7:7–8).

Law #10: The Law of Exposure

A boundary is a property line. It defines where you begin and end. We have been discussing why you need such a line. One reason stands above all the others: You do not exist in a vacuum. You exist in relation to God and others. Your boundaries define you in relation to others.

The whole concept of boundaries has to do with the fact that we exist in relationship. Therefore, boundaries are really about relationship, and finally about love. That's why the Law of Exposure is so important.

The Law of Exposure says that your boundaries need to be made visible to others and communicated to them in relationship. We have many boundary problems because of relational fears. We are beset by fears of guilt, not being liked, loss of love, loss of connection, loss of approval, receiving anger, being known, and so on. These are all failures in love, and God's plan is that we learn how to love.

These relational problems can only be solved in relationships, for that is the context of the problems themselves, and the context of spiritual existence. Because of these fears, we try to have secret boundaries. We withdraw passively and quietly, instead of communicating an honest no to someone we love. We secretly resent instead of telling someone that we are angry about how they have hurt us. Often, we will privately endure the pain of someone's irresponsibility instead of telling them how their behavior affects us and other loved ones, information that would be helpful to their soul.

In other situations, a partner will secretly comply with her spouse, not offering her feelings or opinions for twenty years, and then suddenly "express" her boundaries by filing for divorce. Or parents will "love" their children by giving in over and over for years, not setting limits, and resenting the love they are showing. The children grow up never feeling loved, because of the lack of honesty, and their parents are befuddled, thinking, "After all we've done."

In these instances, because of unexpressed boundaries, the relationships suffered. An important thing to remember about boundaries is that they exist, and they will affect us, whether or not we communicate them. In the same way that the alien suffered from not knowing the laws of Earth, we suffer when we do not communicate the reality of our boundaries. If our boundaries are not communicated and exposed directly, they will be communicated indirectly or through manipulation.

The Bible speaks to this issue in many places. Listen to the words of Paul: "Therefore each of you must put off falsehood and speak truthfully to his neighbor, for we are all members of one body. 'In your anger do not sin': Do not let the sun go down while you are still angry" (Eph. 4:25–26). The biblical mandate is *be honest* and *be in the light.* Listen further, "But everything exposed by the light becomes visible, for it is light that makes everything visible. This is why it is said: 'Wake up, O sleeper, rise from the dead, and Christ will shine on you'" (Eph. 5:13–14).

The Bible continually speaks of our being in the light and of the light as the only place where we have access to

God and others. But, because of our fears, we hide aspects of ourselves in the darkness, where the devil has an opportunity. When our boundaries are in the light, that is, are communicated openly, our personalities begin to integrate for the first time. They become "visible," in Paul's words, and then they become light. They are transformed and changed. Healing always takes place in the light.

David speaks of it in this way: "Surely you desire truth in the inner parts; you teach me wisdom in the inmost place" (Ps. 51:6). God wants real relationship with us and wants us to have real relationship with each other. Real relationship means that I am in the light with my boundaries and other aspects of myself that are difficult to communicate. Our boundaries are affected by sin; they "miss the mark," and need to be brought into the light for God to heal them and others to benefit from them. This is the path to real love: Communicate your boundaries openly.

Remember the story of the alien. The good news is that when God brings us out from an alien land, he does not leave us untaught. He rescued his people from the Egyptians, but, he taught them his principles and ways. These proved to be life to them. But, they had to learn them, practice them, and fight many battles to internalize these principles of faith.

God has probably led you out of captivity also. Whether it was from a dysfunctional family, the world, your own religious self-righteousness, or the scatteredness of being lost, he has been your Redeemer. But what he has secured needs to be possessed. The land to which he has brought you has certain realities and principles. Learn these as set forth in his Word, and you'll find his kingdom a wonderful place to live.

6

Common Boundary Myths

O ne of the definitions of a myth is a fiction that looks like a truth. Sometimes it sounds so true that Christians will believe it automatically. Some of these myths come from our family backgrounds. Some come from our church or theological foundations. And some come from our own misunderstandings. Whatever the source, prayerfully investigate the following "sounds-like-truths."

Myth #1: If I Set Boundaries, I'm Being Selfish

"Now, wait a minute," Teresa said, shaking her head. "How can I set limits on those who need me? Isn't that living for me and not for God?"

Teresa was voicing one of the main objections to boundary setting for Christians: a deep-seated fear of being self-centered, interested only in one's own concerns and not those of others.

It is absolutely true that we are to be a loving people. Concerned for the welfare of others. In fact, *the number-one hallmark of Christians is that we love others* (John 13:35).

So don't boundaries turn us from other-centeredness to self-centeredness? The answer is no. *Appropriate boundaries actually increase our ability to care about others.* People with highly developed limits are the most caring people on earth. How can this be true?

First, let's make a distinction between *selfishness* and *stewardship*. Selfishness has to do with a fixation on our own wishes and desires, to the exclusion of our responsibility to

103

love others. Though having wishes and desires is a God-given trait (Prov. 13:4), we are to keep them in line with healthy goals and responsibility.

For one thing, we may not *want* what we *need*. Mr. Insensitive may desperately need help with the fact that he's a terrible listener. But he may not want it. God is much more interested in meeting our needs than he is granting all our wishes. For example, he denied Paul's wish to heal his "thorn in the flesh" (2 Cor. 12:7–10). At the same time, he met Paul's needs to the point that Paul felt content and full:

> I know what it is to be in need, and I know what it is to have plenty. I have learned the secret of being content in any and every situation, whether well fed or hungry, whether living in plenty or in want. I can do everything through him who gives me strength. (Phil. 4:12–13)

It helps the Christian afraid of setting boundaries to know that God meets our needs. "God will meet all your needs according to his glorious riches in Christ Jesus" (Phil. 4:19). At the same time, God does not make our wishes and desires "all bad" either. He will meet many of them.

Our Needs Are Our Responsibility

Even with God's help, however, it is crucial to understand that meeting our own needs is basically *our* job. We can't wait passively for others to take care of us. Jesus told us to "Ask . . . seek . . . knock" (Matt. 7:7). We are to "work out [our] salvation with fear and trembling" (Phil. 2:12). Even knowing that "it is God who works in [us]" (Phil. 2:13), we are our own responsibility.

This is a very different picture than many of us are used to. Some individuals see their needs as bad, selfish, and at best, a luxury. Others see them as something that God or others should do for them. But the biblical picture is clear: our lives are our responsibility.

At the end of our lives this truth becomes crystal clear. We will all "appear before the judgment seat of Christ, that each one may receive what is due him for the things done while in the body, whether good or bad" (2 Cor. 5:10). A sobering thought.

Stewardship

A helpful way to understand setting limits is that our lives are a gift from God. Just as a store manager takes good care of a shop for the owner, we are to do the same with our souls. If a lack of boundaries causes us to mismanage the store, the owner has a right to be upset with us.

We are to develop our lives, abilities, feelings, thoughts, and behaviors. Our spiritual and emotional growth is God's "interest" on his investment in us. When we say no to people and activities that are hurtful to us, we are protecting God's investment. As you can see, there's quite a difference between selfishness and stewardship.

Myth #2: Boundaries Are a Sign of Disobedience

Many Christians fear that setting and keeping limits signals rebellion, or disobedience. In religious circles you'll often hear statements such as, "Your unwillingness to go along with our program shows an unresponsive heart." Because of this myth, countless individuals remain trapped in endless activities of no genuine spiritual and emotional value.

The truth is life-changing: a *lack* of boundaries is often a sign of disobedience. People who have shaky limits are often compliant on the outside, but rebellious and resentful on the inside. They would like to be able to say no, but are afraid. So they cover their fear with a half-hearted yes, as Barry did.

Barry had almost made it to his car after church when Ken caught up with him. *Here goes,* Barry thought. *Maybe I can still get out of this one.*

Barry!" Ken boomed. "Glad I caught you!"

The singles class officer in charge of Bible studies, Ken was a dedicated recruiter to the studies he presided over; however, he was often insensitive to the fact that not everyone wanted to attend his meetings.

"So which study can I put you down for, Barry? The one on prophecy, evangelism, or Mark?"

Barry thought desperately to himself. *I could say, "None of the above interest me. Don't call me—I'll call you." But he's a ranking officer in the singles class. He could jeopardize my relationships with others in the group. I wonder which class will be the shortest?*

"How about the one on prophecy?" Barry guessed. He was wrong.

"Great! We'll be studying end times for the next eighteen months! See you Monday." Ken walked off triumphantly.

Let's take a look at what just happened. Barry avoided saying no to Ken. At first glance, it looks like he made a choice for obedience. He committed himself to a Bible study. That's a good thing, right? Absolutely.

But take a second look. What were Barry's motives for not saying no to Ken? What were the "thoughts and attitudes of the heart" (Heb. 4:12)? Fear. Barry was afraid of Ken's political clout in the singles group. He feared that he would lose other relationships if he disappointed Ken.

Why is this important? Because it illustrates a biblical principle: *an internal no nullifies an external yes.* God is more concerned with our hearts than he is with our outward compliance. "For I desire mercy, not sacrifice, and acknowledgment of God rather than burnt offerings" (Hos. 6:6).

In other words, if we say yes to God or anyone else when we really mean no, we move into a position of *compliance.* And that is the same as lying. Our lips say yes, but our hearts (and often our half-hearted actions) say no. Do you really think Barry will finish out his year and a half with Ken's Bible study? The odds are that some priority will arise to sabotage Barry's commitment, and he'll leave—but without telling Ken the real reason why.

Here's a good way to look at this myth that boundaries are a sign of disobedience: *if we can't say no, we can't say yes.* Why is this? It has to do with our motivation to obey, to love, or to be responsible. We must always say yes out of a heart of love. When our motive is fear, we love not.

The Bible tells us how to be obedient: "Each of you must give as you have *made up your mind,* not *reluctantly* or *under compulsion,* for God loves a *cheerful* giver" (2 Cor. 9:7 NRSV, italics mine).

Look at the first two ways of giving: "reluctantly" and "under compulsion." They both involve fear—either of a real person or a guilty conscience. These motives can't exist side by side with love, because "there is no fear in love; but perfect love casts out fear" (1 John 4:18 NASB). Each of us must give as we have made up our minds. When we are afraid to say no, our yes is compromised.

God has no interest in our obeying out of fear "because fear has to do with punishment. The one who fears is not made perfect in love" (1 John 4:18). God wants a response of love.

Are boundaries a sign of disobedience? They can be. We can say no to good things for wrong reasons. But having a "no" helps us to clarify, to be honest, to tell the truth about our motives; then we can allow God to work in us. This process cannot be accomplished in a fearful heart.

Myth #3: If I Begin Setting Boundaries, I Will Be Hurt by Others

Usually the quiet one in her women's Bible study group, Debbie spoke up. The topic of the evening was "biblical conflict resolution," and she couldn't be silent another second. "I know how to present facts and arguments about my opinion in a caring way. But my husband will walk out on me if I start disagreeing! Now what do I do?"

Debbie's problem is shared by many. She genuinely believes in boundaries, but she is terrified of their consequences.

Is it possible that others will become angry at our boundaries and attack or withdraw from us? Absolutely. God never gave us the power or the right to control how others respond to our no. Some will welcome it; some will hate it.

Jesus told the rich young man a hard truth about eternal life. He understood that the man worshiped money. So he told him to give it away—to make room in his heart for God. The results were not encouraging: "When the young man

heard this, he went away sad, because he had great wealth"
(Matt. 19:22).

Jesus could have manipulated the situation so that it was
less hard to swallow. He could have said, "Well, how about
ninety percent?" After all, he's God, and he makes up the
rules! But he didn't. He knew that the young man had to
know whom to worship. So he let him walk away.

We can do no less. We can't manipulate people into
swallowing our boundaries by sugarcoating them. *Boundaries are a "litmus test" for the quality of our relationships.*
Those people in our lives who can respect our boundaries
will love our wills, our opinions, our separateness. Those
who can't respect our boundaries are telling us that they
don't love our no. They only love our yes, our compliance.

When Jesus said, "Woe to you when all men speak well
of you, for that is how their fathers treated the false
prophets" (Luke 6:26), he was saying, "Don't be an ear
tickler. Don't be a chronic peacemaker." If everything you
say is loved by everyone, the odds are good that you're
bending the truth.

Setting limits has to do with telling the truth. The Bible
clearly distinguishes between those who love truth and
those who don't. First, there is the person who welcomes
your boundaries. Who accepts them. Who listens to them.
Who says, "I'm glad you have a separate opinion. It makes
me a better person." This person is called *wise*, or *righteous*.

The second type hates limits. Resents your difference.
Tries to manipulate you into giving up your treasures. Try
our "litmus test" experiment with your significant relationships. Tell them no in some area. You'll either come out with
increased intimacy—or learn that there was very little to
begin with.

So what does Debbie, whose husband is an avowed
"boundary buster," do? Will her husband carry out his threat
to walk out on her? He might. We can't control the other
person. But if the only thing keeping Debbie's husband
home is her total compliance, is this a marriage at all? And
how will problems ever be addressed when she and he avoid
them?

Do Debbie's boundaries condemn her to a life of

isolation? Absolutely not. If telling the truth causes someone to leave you, this gives the church an opportunity to provide support and a spiritual and emotional "home" to the abandoned person.

In no way are we advocating divorce. The point is that you can't make anyone stay with or love you. Ultimately that is up to your partner. Sometimes setting boundaries clarifies that you were left a long time ago, in every way, perhaps, except physically. Often, when a crisis like this occurs, it helps the struggling couple reconcile and remake their marriage into a more biblical one. The problem was raised, and now can be addressed.

Warning: the boundaryless spouse who develops limits begins changing in the marriage. There are more disagreements. There are more conflicts over values, schedules, money, kids, and sex. Quite often, however, the limits help the out-of-control spouse begin to experience the necessary pain that can motivate him or her to take more responsibility in the marriage. Many marriages are strengthened after boundaries are set because the spouse begins to miss the relationship.

Will some people abandon or attack us for having boundaries? Yes. Better to learn about their character and take steps to fix the problem than never to know.

Bonding First, Boundaries Second

Gina listened attentively to her counselor as he presented her boundary problems. "It all seems to make sense now, " she said as she left the session. "I can see changes I'm going to have to make."

The next session was quite different. She entered the office defeated and hurt. "These boundaries aren't what they're cracked up to be," she said sadly. "This week I confronted my husband, my kids, my parents, and my friends on how they don't respect my boundaries. And now nobody will talk to me!"

What was the problem? Gina certainly jumped into her boundary work with both feet—but she neglected to find a safe place to work on boundaries. It isn't wise to immediately alienate yourself from everyone important to you. Remember that you are made for relationship. You need people. You must have places where you are connected, where you are loved unconditionally. It's only from that place of being "rooted and grounded in love" (Eph. 3:17 NASB) that you can safely begin learning to tell the truth. This is how you can prepare yourself for the resistance of others to your setting of biblical boundaries.

Myth #4: If I Set Boundaries, I Will Hurt Others

"The biggest problem with telling my mother no is the 'hurt silence,'" Barbara said. "It lasts about forty-five seconds, and it always happens after I tell her I can't visit her. It's only broken by my apologizing for my selfishness and setting up a time to visit. Then she's fine. I'll do *anything* to avoid that silence."

If you set boundaries, you fear that your limits will injure someone else—someone you would genuinely like to see happy and fulfilled:

- The friend who wants to borrow your car when you need it
- The relative in chronic financial straits who desperately asks for a loan
- The person who calls for support when you are in bad shape yourself

The problem is that sometimes *you see boundaries as an offensive weapon.* Nothing could be further from the truth. *Boundaries are a defensive tool.* Appropriate boundaries don't control, attack, or hurt anyone. They simply prevent your treasures from being taken at the wrong time. Saying no to adults, who are responsible for getting their own needs met, may cause some discomfort. They may have to look elsewhere. But it doesn't cause injury.

This principle doesn't speak only to those who would like to control or manipulate us. It also applies to the legitimate needs of others. Even when someone has a valid problem, there are times when we can't sacrifice for some reason or another. Jesus left the multitudes, for example, to be alone with his Father (Matt. 14:22–23). In these instances, we have to allow others to take responsibility for their "knapsacks" (Gal. 6:5) and to look elsewhere to get their needs met.

This is a crucial point. We all need more than God and a best friend. We need a group of supportive relationships. The reason is simple: having more than one person in our lives allows our friends to be human. To be busy. To be unavailable at times. To hurt and have problems of their own. To have time alone.

Then, when one person can't be there for us, there's another phone number to call. Another person who may have something to offer. And we aren't enslaved to the schedule conflicts of one person.

This is the beauty behind the Bible's teachings on the church, the body of Christ. We're all a group of lumpy, bumpy, unfinished sinners, who ask for help and give help, who ask again and give again. And when our supportive network is strong enough, we all help each other mature into what God intended us to be: "showing forbearance to one another in love, being diligent to preserve the unity of the Spirit in the bond of peace" (Eph. 4:2–3).

When we've taken the responsibility to develop several supportive relationships in this biblical fashion, we can take a no from someone. Why? Because we have somewhere else to go.

Remember that God had no problem telling Paul that he would not take away his thorn. He tells all of us no quite often! God doesn't worry that his boundaries will injure us. He knows we are to take responsibility for our lives—and sometimes no helps us do just that.

Myth #5: Boundaries Mean That I Am Angry

Brenda had finally mustered up the courage to tell her boss she was no longer going to work weekends for no pay. She had asked for a meeting, which had gone well. Her boss had been understanding, and the situation was being ironed out. Everything had gone well, except inside Brenda.

It had begun innocently enough. Brenda had itemized her issues with the work situation and had presented her view and suggestions. But midway through her presentation, she'd been surprised by a sense of rage welling up inside. Her feeling of anger and injustice had been difficult to keep hidden. It had even slipped out in a couple of sarcastic comments about the boss's "golfing Fridays," comments that Brenda had had no intention of making.

Sitting at her desk, Brenda felt confused. Where had the anger come from? Was she "that kind of person"? Maybe the culprit was these boundaries she'd been setting.

It's no secret that quite often, when people begin telling the truth, setting limits, and taking responsibility, an "angry cloud" follows them around for a while. They become touchy and easily offended, and they discover a hair-trigger temper that frightens them. Friends will make comments like, "You're not the nice, loving person I used to know." The guilt and shame caused by these remarks can further confuse new boundary setters.

So do boundaries cause anger in us? Absolutely not. This myth is a misunderstanding of emotions in general, and anger specifically. Emotions, or feelings, have a function. They tell us something. They are a signal.

Here are some of the things our "negative" emotions tell us. Fear tells us to move away from danger, to be careful. Sadness tells us that we've lost something—a relationship, an opportunity, or an idea. Anger is also a signal. Like fear, anger signals danger. However, rather than urging us to withdraw, anger is a sign that we need to move forward to confront the threat. Jesus' rage at the defilement of the temple is an example of how this feeling functions (John 2:13–17).

Anger tells us that our boundaries have been violated. Much like a nation's radar defense system, angry feelings serve as an "early warning system," telling us we're in danger of being injured or controlled.

"So that's why I find myself hostile to pushy salesmen!" Carl exclaimed. He couldn't understand why he had a hard time loving sales personnel who couldn't hear his no. They were attempting to get inside his financial boundaries, and Carl's anger was simply doing its job.

Anger also provides us with a sense of power to solve a problem. It energizes us to protect ourselves, those we love, and our principles. In fact, a common Old Testament illustration of an angry person is someone with a "hard-breathing nose."[1] Imagine a bull in a ring, snorting and pawing, getting the steam up to attack, and you'll get the picture.

However, as with all emotions, anger doesn't understand time. Anger doesn't dissipate automatically if the danger occurred two minutes ago—or twenty years ago! It has to be worked through appropriately. Otherwise, anger simply lives inside the heart.

This is why individuals with injured boundaries often are shocked by the rage they feel inside when they begin setting limits. This is generally not "new anger"—it's "old anger." It's often years of nos that were never voiced, never respected, and never listened to. The protests against all the evil and violation of our souls sit inside us, waiting to tell their truths.

The Scriptures say that the earth quakes "under a slave when he becomes king" (Prov. 30:22). The only difference between a slave and a king is that one has *no choices* and the other has *all choices* available to him. When you suddenly give those who have been imprisoned all their lives a great deal of power, the result is often an angry tyrant. Years of constant boundary violations generate great anger.

It's very common for boundary-injured people to do some "catching up" with anger. They may have a season of looking at boundary violations of the past that they never realized existed.

Nathan's family was known in his small town as the ideal family. Other kids envied him growing up, saying, "You're lucky your parents are so close to you—mine couldn't care less about me." Feeling a great deal of gratitude for his close family, Nathan never noticed that his family carefully controlled differences and separateness. No one ever really disagreed or fought over values or feelings. "I always thought conflict meant a loss of love," he would say.

It wasn't until Nathan's marriage began suffering that he began questioning his past. He naively married a woman who manipulated and controlled him. Several years into the marriage, he knew it was in serious trouble. But to Nathan's surprise, he was not only angry at himself for getting into this mess, but also at his parents for not equipping him with tools for handling life better.

Because he genuinely loved the warm family in which he was raised, Nathan felt guilty and disloyal when he remembered occasions in which his attempts to separate from his parents and set his own limits were constantly and lovingly frustrated. Mom would cry about his argumentativeness. Dad would tell Nathan not to upset his mom. And Nathan's boundaries remained immature and nonfunctional. The more clearly he saw what this had cost him, the angrier he felt. "I made my own choices in life," he said. "But life would have been a lot better had they helped me learn to say no to people."

Did Nathan remain angry at his parents forever? No, and neither do you have to. As hostile feelings surface, bring them to relationship. Confess them. The Bible tells us to tell the truth to each other about our lacks, so that we may be healed (James 5:16). Experience the grace of God through others who love you in your anger. This is a first step toward resolving past anger.

A second step is to rebuild the injured parts of your soul. Take responsibility for healing the "treasures" that may have been violated. In Nathan's case, his sense of personal autonomy and safety had been deeply wounded. He had to practice for a long time to regain this in his primary relationships. But the more he healed, the less anger he felt.

Finally, as you develop a sense of biblical boundaries, you develop more safety in the present. You develop more confidence. You are less enslaved to the fear of other people. In Nathan's case, he set better limits with his wife and improved his marriage. As you develop better boundaries, you have less need for anger. This is because in many cases, anger was the only boundary you had. Once you have your no intact, you no longer need the "rage signal." You can see evil coming your way and prevent it from harming you by your boundaries.

Don't fear the rage you discover when you first begin your boundary development. It is the protest of earlier parts of your soul. Those parts need to be unveiled, understood, and loved by God and people. And then you need to take responsibility for healing them and developing better boundaries.

Boundaries Decrease Anger

This brings us to an important point about anger: The more biblical our boundaries are, the less anger we experience! Individuals with mature boundaries are the least angry people in the world. While those who are just beginning boundary work see their anger increase, this passes as boundaries grow and develop.

Why is this? Remember the "early warning system" function of anger. We feel it when we are violated. If you can prevent boundary violation in the first place, you don't need the anger. You are more in control of your life and values.

Tina resented her husband's coming home forty-five minutes late to dinner every night. She had a hard time keeping the food hot; the kids were hungry and crabby, and their evening study schedule was thrown off. Things changed, however, when she began serving dinner on time, with or without her husband. He came home to refrigerated leftovers that he had to reheat and eat alone. Three or four "sessions" like this prompted Tina's husband to tear himself away from work earlier!

Tina's boundary (eating with the kids on time) kept her from feeling violated and victimized. She got her needs met, the kids' needs met, and she didn't feel angry anymore. The old saying, "Don't get mad. Just get even" isn't accurate. It's far better to say, "Don't get mad. Set a limit!"

Myth #6: When Others Set Boundaries, It Injures Me

"Randy, I'm sorry, but I can't lend you the money," Pete said. "This is just a bad time for me."

My best friend, Randy thought to himself. *I come to him in need, and he refuses me. What a blow! I guess that shows me what kind of friendship we really have.*

Randy is preparing to embark on a life of boundary-lessness with others. Why? Because being on the "receiving end" was hurtful to him. He even made an emotional vow never to put anyone else through his experience.

Many of us are like Randy. Having someone say no to our request for support leaves a bad taste in our mouths. It feels hurtful, rejecting, or cold. It becomes difficult to conceive of setting limits as being helpful or good.

Having to accept the boundaries of others is certainly not pleasant. None of us enjoys hearing the word no. Let's look at why accepting others' boundaries is such a problem.

First, *having inappropriate boundaries set on us can injure us, especially in childhood.* A parent can hurt a child by not providing the correct amount of emotional connection at the appropriate time. Children's emotional and psycholog-ical needs are primarily the responsibility of the parents. The younger the child, the fewer places he or she can go to get those needs met. A self-centered, immature, or depen-dent parent can hurt a child by saying no at the wrong times.

Robert's earliest memories were of being in his crib, alone in the room, for hours at a time. His parents would simply leave him there, thinking he was fine if he wasn't crying. Actually, he had moved past crying to infant depres-sion. Their no created a deep sense of being unwanted, which followed him into adulthood.

Second, *we project our own injuries onto others.* When we feel pain, one response is to "disown" the bad feeling and to throw it onto others. This is called *projection.* Quite often, people who have been hurt by inappropriate child-hood boundaries will throw their fragility onto others. Sensing their own pain in others, they will avoid setting limits on others, as they imagine how devastating it would be to them.

Robert had extreme difficulty setting nighttime limits with his three-year-old daughter, Abby. Whenever she would cry about having to go to bed, he would panic inside, thinking, *I'm abandoning my daughter—she needs me and*

I'm not there for her. Actually, he was a wonderful father, who read stories at night, prayed, and sang songs with his little girl. But he read his own pain in her tears. Robert's injuries kept him from setting the correct limits on Abby's wish to keep him singing songs and playing—until sunrise.

Third, *an inability to receive someone's boundary may mean there is an idolatrous relationship.* Kathy felt wounded and isolated when her husband wouldn't want to talk at night. His silence resulted in severe feelings of alienation. She began wondering if she were being injured by her husband's boundaries.

The real problem, however, lay in Kathy's dependence on her husband. Her emotional well-being rested on his being there for her at all times. He was to have provided everything that her own alcoholic parents hadn't. When he had a bad day and withdrew, her own day was a disaster.

Though we certainly need each other, no one but God is indispensable. When a conflict with one significant person can bring us to despair, it is possible that we are putting that person on a throne that should only be occupied by God. We should never see one other person as the only source of good in the world. It hurts our spiritual and emotional freedom, and our development.

Ask yourself: "If the person I can't hear no from were to die tonight, to whom would I go?" It's crucial to develop several deep, significant relationships. This allows those in our lives to feel free to say no to us without guilt because we have somewhere else to go.

When we have a person we can't take no from, we have, in effect, handed over the control of our lives to them. All they have to do is threaten withdrawal, and we will comply. This occurs quite often in marriages, where one spouse is kept in emotional blackmail by the other's threat to leave. Not only is this no way to live—it doesn't work, either. The controller continues withdrawing whenever he or she is displeased. And the boundaryless person continues frantically scrambling to keep him or her happy. Dr. James Dobson's *Love Must Be Tough* is a classic work on this kind of boundary problem.[2]

Fourth, *an inability to accept others' boundaries can*

indicate a problem in taking responsibility. Randy, who
needed a loan from his best friend, is an example of this
problem. He was making Pete responsible for his own
financial woes. Some people become so accustomed to
others rescuing them that they begin to believe that their
well-being is someone else's problem. They feel let down
and unloved when they aren't bailed out. They fail to accept
responsibility for their own lives.

Paul strongly confronted the Corinthians in a letter that
has since been lost. He set limits on their rebelliousness.
Thankfully, they responded well:

> Even if I caused you sorrow by my letter, I do not regret it.
> Though I did regret it—I see that my letter hurt you, but
> only for a little while—yet now I am happy, not because
> you were made sorry, but because your sorrow led you to
> repentance. (2 Cor. 7:8–9)

The Corinthians took, accepted, and responded well to
Paul's boundaries, whatever they were. That's a sign of
taking responsibility.

It's helpful to remember Jesus' Golden Rule here: "In
everything, do to others what you would have them do to
you" (Matt. 7:12). Apply it to setting limits. Do you want
others to respect your boundaries? Then you must be willing
to respect the boundaries of others.

Myth #7: Boundaries Cause Feelings of Guilt

Edward shook his head. "There's something not right
about all this for me," he said. My folks were always so
caring and concerned about me. It's been such a great
relationship. And then . . ." He paused, groping for words.

"And then I met Judy and we got married. And that was
wonderful. We saw my folks every week, sometimes more.
Then the kids came along. Everything was fine. Until I got
the job offer from across the country. It was the position of
my dreams—Judy was excited about it, too.

"But as soon as I told my parents about the offer, things
changed. I started hearing them talk about Dad's health—I
hadn't realized it was that bad. About Mom's loneliness—

about how we were the only bright spots in their lives. And about all the sacrifices they'd made for me.

"What do I do? They're right . . . they've given their lives to me. How can I leave them after all that?"

Edward isn't alone in his dilemma. One of the major obstacles to setting boundaries with others in our lives is our feelings of obligation. What do we owe not only our parents, but anyone who's been loving toward us? What's appropriate and biblical, and what isn't?

Many individuals solve this dilemma by avoiding boundary setting with those to whom they feel an obligation. In this sense, they can avoid the guilty feelings that occur when they say no to someone who has been kind to them. They never leave home, never change schools or churches, and never switch jobs or friends. Even when it would be an otherwise mature move.

The idea is that *because we have received something, we owe something*. The problem is the nonexistent debt. The love we receive, or money, or time—or anything which causes us to feel obligated—should be accepted as a gift.

"Gift" implies no strings attached. All that's really needed is gratitude. The giver has no second thought that the present will provide a return. It was simply provided because someone loved someone and wanted to do something for him or her. Period.

That is how God views his gift of salvation to us. It cost him his Son. It was motivated out of love for us. And our response is to receive it, and to be grateful. Why is gratitude so important? Because God knows that our gratitude for what he has done for us will move us to love others: "as you were taught, and overflowing with thankfulness" (Col. 2:7).

What do we owe those who are kind to us, who have genuinely cared for us? We owe them thanks. And from our grateful heart, we should go out and help others.

We need to distinguish here between those who "give to get" and those who truly give selflessly. It's generally easy to tell the difference. If the giver is hurt or angered by a sincere thanks, the gift was probably a loan. If the gratitude is enough, you probably received a legitimate gift with no feelings of guilt attached.

God does an instructive job of keeping the issue of gratitude and boundaries separate. In Revelation's letters to the seven churches, he singles out three churches (Ephesus, Pergamum, and Thyatira):

1. He praises their accomplishments (gratitude).
2. He then tells them that even so, he has "something against" them (2:4, 14, 20).
3. He finally confronts their irresponsibilities (boundaries).

He doesn't allow the two issues to be confused. Neither should we.

Myth #8: Boundaries Are Permanent, and I'm Afraid of Burning My Bridges

"But what if I change my mind?" Carla asked. "I'm scared that I'll set a boundary with my best friend, and then she'll leave and forget about me."

It's important to understand that your no is always subject to you. You own your boundaries. They don't own you. If you set limits with someone, and she responds maturely and lovingly, you can renegotiate the boundary. In addition, you can change the boundary if you are in a safer place.

Changing and renegotiating boundaries has many biblical precedents: God chose not to destroy Nineveh, for example, when the city repented (Jonah 3:10). In addition, Paul rejected John Mark for a mission trip because the younger man had deserted Paul (Acts 15:37–39). Yet, years later, Paul requested John Mark's companionship (2 Tim. 4:11). The timing was ripe to change his boundary.

As you've probably noticed, some of these myths are genuine misconceptions you may have learned from distorted teachings. Yet others simply result from the fear of standing up and saying no to unbiblical responsibility. Prayerfully review which myths have entangled and ensnared you. Search the Scripture mentioned in this chapter. And ask God to give you a sense of confidence that he believes in good boundaries more than you do.

PART TWO

———

BOUNDARY CONFLICTS

7

Boundaries and Your Family

S usie had a problem that I had seen countless times before. This thirty-year-old woman would return from a visit to her parents' home and suffer a deep depression.

When she described her problem to me, I asked her if she noticed that every time she went home to visit, she came back extremely depressed.

"Why that's ridiculous," she said. "I don't live there anymore. How could the trip affect me this way?"

When I asked her to describe the trip, Susie told of social gatherings with old friends and family times around the dinner table. These were fun, she said, especially when it was only family.

"What do you mean 'only family'?" I asked.

"Well, other times my parents would invite some of my friends over, and I didn't like those dinners as well."

"Why was that?"

Susie thought for a minute and then replied, "I guess I start to feel guilty." She began to recount the subtle remarks her parents would make comparing her friends' lives to hers. They would talk of how wonderful it is for grandparents to have a "hands on" role in raising the children. They would talk of the community activities her friends were doing and how wonderful she would be at those activities if she only lived there. The list went on and on.

Susie soon discovered that, when she returned home, she felt as if she were bad for living where she lived. She had a nagging sense that she really should do what her parents wanted her to do.

Susie had a common problem. She had made choices *on the outside*. She had moved away from the family she grew up in to pursue a career on her own. She had been paying her own bills. She had even gotten married and had a child. But *on the inside*, things were different. She did not have emotional permission to be a separate person, make free choices about her life, and not feel guilty when she did not do what her parents wanted. She could still yield to pressure.

The real problem is on the inside. Remember, boundaries define someone's property. Susie, and others like her, do not really "own" themselves. People who own their lives do not feel guilty when they make choices about where they are going. They take other people into consideration, but when they make choices for the wishes of others, they are choosing out of love, not guilt; to advance a good, not to avoid being bad.

Signs of a Lack of Boundaries

Let's look at some common signs of a lack of boundaries with the family we grew up in.

Catching the Virus

A common scenario is this: one spouse doesn't have good emotional boundaries with the family he grew up in—his family of origin. Then when he has contact with them by phone or in person, he becomes depressed, argumentative, self-critical, perfectionistic, angry, combative, or withdrawn. It is as though he "catches" something from his family of origin and passes it on to his immediate family.

His family of origin has the power to affect his new family in a trickle-down effect. One sure sign of boundary problems is when your relationship with one person has the power to affect your relationships with others. You are giving one person way too much power in your life.

I remember one young woman who made steady gains in therapy until she talked to her mother, when she would withdraw for three weeks. She would say things like, "I'm not changing at all. I'm not getting any better." Fusing with many of her mother's ideas about her, she wasn't able to stay separate. This fusion with her mother affected her other relationships. She virtually shut everyone out of her life after an interaction with her mother. Her mother owned her life; she was not her own.

Second Fiddle

"You wouldn't believe how she is with him," Dan said. "She totally focuses on his every wish. When he criticizes her, she tries harder. And she practically ignores me. I'm tired of being the 'second man' in her life."

Dan wasn't talking about Jane's lover. He was talking about her father. Dan was tired of feeling like Jane cared more about her father's wishes than his.

This is a common sign of a lack of boundaries with the family of origin: the spouse feels like he gets leftovers. He feels as if his mate's real allegiance is to her parents. This spouse hasn't completed the "leaving before cleaving" process; she has a boundary problem. God has designed the process whereby a "man shall leave his father and his mother and shall cleave to his wife; and they shall become one flesh" (Gen. 2:24 NASB). The Hebrew word for "leave" comes from a root word that means to "loosen," or to relinquish or forsake. For marriage to work, the spouse needs to loosen her ties with her family of origin and forge new ones with the new family she is creating through marriage.

This does not mean that husbands and wives shouldn't have a relationship with their extended families. But they do need to set clear boundaries with their families of origin. Many marriages fail because one partner fails to set clear boundaries with the family of origin, and the spouse and children get leftovers.

May I Have My Allowance, Please?

Terry and Sherry were an attractive couple. They owned a big house and went on lavish vacations; their children took piano lessons and ballet, and they had their own skis, roller blades, ice skates, and wind surfers. Terry and Sherry had all the trappings of success. But, there was one problem. This lifestyle was not supported by Terry's paycheck. Terry and Sherry received much financial help from his family.

Terry's family had always wanted the best for him, and they had always helped him get it. They had contributed to the house, the vacations, and the children's hobbies. While this allowed Terry and Sherry to have things they could not otherwise have, it cost them dearly as well.

The periodic bailouts from his parents cut into Terry's self-respect. And Sherry felt as if she couldn't spend any money without consulting her in-laws, since they contributed the funds.

Terry illustrates a common boundary problem for young adults today, both married and single: he was not yet an adult financially. He could not set boundaries on his parents' desire for him and Sherry to "have everything we have." He also found that he had so fused with their ideas of success that he had trouble saying no to these wishes in himself. He wasn't sure he wanted to forsake the gifts and handouts for a greater sense of independence.

Terry's story is the "up" side of the financial boundary problem. There is also the "I'm in trouble" side. Many adult children perpetually get into financial messes because of irresponsibility, drug or alcohol use, out-of-control spending, or the modern "I haven't found my niche" syndrome. Their parents continue to finance this road of failure and irresponsibility, thinking that "this time they'll do better." In reality, they are crippling their children for life, preventing them from achieving independence.

An adult who does not stand on his own financially is still a child. To be an adult, you must live within your means and pay for your own failures.

Mom, Where Are My Socks?

In the *perpetual child syndrome*, a person may be financially on his own, but allows his family of origin to perform certain life management functions.

This adult child often hangs out at Mom and Dad's

house, vacations with them, drops off laundry, and eats many meals there. He is Mom or Dad's closest confidant, sharing "everything" with them. At thirtysomething, he hasn't found his career niche, and he has no savings, no retirement plan, and no health insurance. On the surface these things do not appear to be serious problems. But often, Mom and Dad are symbolically keeping their adult child from emotionally leaving home.

This often happens in friendly, loving families, where things are so nice it's hard to leave. (Psychologists often refer to this as the "enmeshed family," one in which the children do not separate with clear boundaries.) It does not look like a problem, because everyone gets along so well. The family is very happy with one another.

However, the adult children's *other* adult relationships may be dysfunctional. They may choose "black sheep" friends and lovers. They may be unable to commit to a member of the opposite sex or to a career.

Often their finances are a problem. They have large and multiple credit-card balances and usually are behind on their taxes. Although they may be earning their own way daily, they never think about the future. This is essentially an adolescent financial life. Adolescents make enough money to buy a surfboard, stereo, or dress, but do not think past the immediate present to the future. Did I make enough money for the pleasures of this weekend? Adolescents—and adult children who have not separated from their parents—are still under parental protection, and it's a parent's job to think about the future.

Three's a Crowd

Dysfunctional families are known for a certain type of boundary problem called *triangulation*. It goes something like this: Person A is angry at Person B. Person A does not tell Person B. Person A calls Person C and gripes about Person B. Person C enjoys Person A's confidence and listens whenever A wants to play the triangle game.

By this time, Person B, feeling lonely, calls C, and, in passing, mentions the conflict with A. Person C becomes the confidant of B as well as A. Persons A and B have not resolved their conflict, and C has two "friends."

Triangulation is the failure to resolve a conflict between two persons and the pulling in of a third to take sides. This is a boundary problem because the third person has no business in the conflict, but *is used for comfort and validation by the ones who are afraid to confront each other.* This is how conflicts persist, people don't change, and enemies are made unnecessarily.

What happens in the triangle is that people speak falsely, covering up their hatred with nice words and flattery. Person A is usually very cordial, nice, and even complimentary to B in person, but when A talks to C, the anger comes out.

This is a clear lack of boundaries because Person A is not "owning" his anger. The person with whom A is angry deserves to hear it straight from him. How many times have you been hurt by a "Do you know what John said about you?" And the last time you talked to John things were fine.

In addition, Person C is being drawn into the conflict and his knowledge of the conflict gets in the way of his relationship with Person B. Gossip gets between people. It affects our opinions of the people being gossiped about without their having a chance to defend themselves. Many times what we hear from a third person is inaccurate. This is why the Bible commands us to listen to at least two or three witnesses, not just one.

Triangulation is a common boundary problem with families of origin. Old patterns of conflict between a parent and a child, or between two parents, result in one family member calling another family member and talking about the third family member. These extremely destructive patterns keep people dysfunctional.

The Scripture is very serious about dealing with conflict *directly* with the one you are angry with:

> He who rebukes a man will in the end gain more favor than he who has a flattering tongue. (Prov. 28:23)

> Do not hate your brother in your heart. Rebuke your neighbor frankly so you will not share in his guilt. (Lev. 19:17)

Therefore, if you are offering your gift at the altar and there remember that your brother has something against you, leave your gift there in front of the altar. First go and be reconciled to your brother; then come and offer your gift. (Matt. 5:23–24)

If your brother sins against you, go and show him his fault, just between the two of you. (Matt. 18:15)

These Scriptures show that a simple way to avoid triangulation is to always talk to the person with whom you have a conflict first. Work it out with her, and only if she denies the problem, talk to someone else to get insight about how to resolve it, not to gossip and to bleed off anger. Then you *both* go to talk to her together to try to solve the problem.

Never say to a third party something about someone that you do not plan to say to the person himself.

Who's the Child Here, Anyhow?

"Children should not have to save up for their parents, but parents for their children" (2 Cor. 12:14).

Some people were born to take care of their parents. They did not sign up for this duty; they inherited it. Today we call these people "codependent." Early in life they learned they were responsible for their parents, who were stuck in childish patterns of irresponsibility. When they became adults, they had a difficult time setting boundaries between themselves and their irresponsible parents. Every time they tried to have separate lives, they felt selfish.

Indeed, the Bible teaches that adult children should take care of their elderly parents. "Give proper recognition to those widows who are really in need. But if a widow has children or grandchildren, these should learn first of all to put their religion into practice by caring for their own family and so repaying their parents and grandparents, for this is pleasing to God" (1 Tim. 5:3–4). It is good to feel grateful to our parents and to repay them for what they have done for us.

But two problems generally crop up. First, your parents may not be "really in need." They may be irresponsible, demanding, or acting like martyrs. They may need to take responsibility for their own knapsacks.

Second, when they are "really in need," you may not have clear boundaries to determine what you can give and what you can't give. You may not be able to limit your giving, and your parents' inability to adjust to old age, for example, will dominate your family. Such domination can ruin marriages and hurt children. A family needs to decide what they want to give and what they do not want to give, so they will continue to love and appreciate the parent, and not grow resentful.

Good boundaries prevent resentment. *It is good to give.* Make sure, however, that it is the proper amount for your situation and resources.

But I'm Your Brother

Another frequent dynamic is the grown sibling relationship. An irresponsible adult child depends on a responsible adult sibling to avoid growing up and leaving the family. (We are not talking about a true needy sibling who has a mental or physical impairment.) The irresponsible child continues to play old family games well into adulthood.

The tough issue here is the guilt and pressure you feel because it is your brother or sister. I have seen people do totally crazy and unhelpful things for a brother or sister that they would never do for their closest friend. Our families can tear down our best-built fences because they are "family."

But Why Do We Do That?

Why in the world do we choose to continue these sorts of patterns? What is wrong?

One reason is that we did not learn the laws of boundaries in our family of origin, and our adult boundary problems are actually old boundary problems that have been there since childhood.

Another reason is that we may not have gone through the biblical transition into adulthood and the spiritual adoption into the family of God. Let's look at both.

Continuation of Old Boundary Problems

Remember the story about the alien? He had grown up on another planet and was unfamiliar with the laws of Earth, such as gravity and money as a medium of exchange.

The patterns you learn at home growing up are continued into adulthood with the same players: lack of consequences for irresponsible behavior, lack of confrontation, lack of limits, taking responsibility for others instead of yourself, giving out of compulsion and resentment, envy, passivity, and secrecy. These patterns are not new, they have just never been confronted and repented of.

These patterns run deep. Your family members are the ones you learned to organize your life around, so they are able to send you back to old patterns by their very presence. You begin to act automatically out of *memory* instead of growth.

To change, you must identify these "sins of the family" and turn from them. You must confess them as sins, repent of them, and change the way you handle them. The first step in establishing boundaries is becoming aware of old family patterns that you are still continuing in the present.

Look at the struggles you are having with boundaries in your family of origin, identify which laws are being broken, and then pinpoint the resulting negative fruit in your life.

Adoption

This is not a book about spiritual development, but boundaries are an essential aspect of growing up. One step in growing up is coming out from under parental authority and putting yourself under God's authority.

The Bible says that children are *under* the authority of their parents until they become adults (Gal. 4:1–7). In a real sense their parents are responsible for them. But when adulthood and the "age of accountability" comes, that person comes out from under guardians and managers and becomes responsible for him or herself. Christians move into another parental relationship with God as Father. God does not leave us as orphans, but takes us into his family.

Numerous New Testament passages teach that we need to forsake our allegiance to our original family and become adopted by God (Matt. 23:9). God commands us to look to him as our father and to have no parental intermediaries. Adults who are still holding an allegiance to earthly parents have not realized their new adoptive status.

Many times we are not obeying the Word of God because we have not spiritually left home. We feel we still need to please our parents and their traditional ways of doing things rather than obey our new Father (Matt. 15:1–6).

When we become part of God's family, obeying his ways will sometimes cause conflict in our families and sometimes separate us (Matt. 10:35–37). Jesus says that our spiritual ties are the closest and most important (Matt. 12:46–50). Our true family is the family of God.

In this family, which is to be our strongest tie, things are done a certain way. We are to tell the truth, set limits, take and require responsibility, confront each other, forgive each other, and so on. Strong standards and values make this family run. And God will not allow it any other way in his family.

This in no way means that we are to cut other ties. We are to have friends outside of God's family and strong ties with our family of origin. However, we need to ask two questions: Do these ties keep us from doing the right thing in any situation? and Have we really become an adult in relation to our family of origin?

If our ties are truly loving, we will be separate and free and give out of love and a "purposeful" heart. We will stay away from resentment, we will love with limits, and we will not enable evil behavior.

If we are not "under guardians and managers" as adults, we can make truly *adult* decisions, having control over our own will (1 Cor. 7:37), subject to our true Father.

Resolution of Boundary Problems with Family

Establishing boundaries with families of origin is a tough task, but one with great reward. It is a process, with certain distinguishable steps.

Identify the Symptom

Look at your own life situation and see where boundary problems exist with your parents and siblings. The basic question is this: *Where have you lost control of your property?* Identify those areas and see their connection with the family you grew up in, and you are on your way.

Identify the Conflict

Discover what dynamic is being played out. For example, what "law of boundaries" are you violating? Do you triangulate? Do you take responsibility *for* a sibling or parent instead of being responsible *to* them? Do you fail to enforce consequences and end up paying for their behavior? Are you passive and reactive toward them and the conflict?

You cannot stop acting out a dynamic until you understand what you are doing. "Take the log out" of your own eye. Then, you will be able to see clearly to deal with your family members. See yourself as the problem and find your boundary violations.

Identify the Need That Drives the Conflict

You do not act in inappropriate ways for no reason. You are often trying to meet some underlying need that your family of origin did not meet. Maybe we are still entangled because of a need to be loved, or approved of, or accepted. You must face this deficit and accept that it can only be met in your new family of God, those who are now your true "mother, father, brothers, and sisters," those who do God's will and can love you the way he designed.

Take in and Receive the Good

It is not enough to understand your need. *You must get it met.* God is willing to meet your needs through his people, but you must humble yourself, reach out to a good support system, and take in the good. Do not continue to hide your talent in the ground and expect to get better. Learn to respond to and receive love, even if you're clumsy at first.

Practice Boundary Skills

Your boundary skills are fragile and new. You can't take them immediately into a difficult situation. Practice them in situations where they will be honored and respected. Begin saying no to people in your supportive group who will love and respect your boundaries.

When you are recovering from a physical injury, you do not pick up the heaviest weight first. You build up to the heavy stuff. Look at it as you would physical therapy.

Say No to the Bad

In addition to practicing new skills in safe situations, avoid hurtful situations. When you are in the beginning stages of recovery, you need to avoid people who have abused and controlled you in the past.

When you think you are ready to reestablish a relationship with someone who has been abusive and controlling in the past, bring a friend or supporter along. Be aware of your pull toward hurtful situations and relationships. The injury you are recovering from is serious, and you can't reestablish a relationship until you have the proper tools. Be careful to not get sucked into a controlling situation again because your wish for reconciliation is so strong.

Forgive the Aggressor

Nothing clarifies boundaries more than forgiveness. To forgive someone means to let him off the hook, or to cancel a debt he owes you. When you refuse to forgive someone, you still want something from that person, and even if it is revenge that you want, it *keeps you tied to him forever.*

Refusing to forgive a family member is one of the main reasons people are stuck for years, unable to separate from their dysfunctional families. They still want something from them. It is much better to receive grace from God, who has something to give, and to forgive those who have no money to pay their debt with. This ends your suffering, because it ends the wish for repayment that is never forthcoming and that makes your heart sick because your hope is deferred (Prov. 13:12).

If you do not forgive, you are demanding something your offender does not choose to give, even if it is only confession of what he did. This "ties" him to you and ruins boundaries. Let the dysfunctional family you came from go. Cut it loose, and you will be free.

Respond, Don't React

When you *react* to something that someone says or does, you may have a problem with boundaries. If someone is able to cause havoc by doing or saying something, she is in control of you at that point, and your boundaries are lost. When you *respond,* you remain in control, with options and choices.

If you feel yourself reacting, step away and regain control of yourself so family members can't force you to do or say something you do not want to do or say and something that violates your separateness. When you have kept your boundaries, choose the best option. The difference between responding and reacting is choice. When you are reacting, *they* are in control. When you respond, *you* are.

Learn to Love in Freedom and Responsibility, Not in Guilt

The best boundaries are loving ones. The person who has to remain forever in a protective mode is losing out on love and freedom. Boundaries in no way mean to stop loving. They mean the opposite: you are gaining freedom to love. It is good to sacrifice and deny yourself for the sake of others. But you need boundaries to make that choice.

Practice purposeful giving to increase your freedom. Sometimes people who are building boundaries feel that to do someone a favor is codependent. Nothing is farther from the truth. Doing good for someone, when you freely choose to do it, is boundary enhancing. Codependents are not doing good; they are allowing evil because they are afraid.

8

Boundaries and Your Friends

Marsha switched on the television, not even noticing which show was on. She was thinking about her phone call with her best friend, Tammy. She had asked Tammy to go to a movie with her. Tammy had had other plans for the evening. Once again, Marsha had taken the initiative. Once again, she was disappointed. Tammy never called her. Was this what friendship was supposed to be about?

Friendship. The word conjures up images of intimacy, fondness, and a mutual drawing together of two people. Friends are symbols of how meaningful our lives have been. The saddest people on earth are those who end their days with no relationships in which they are truly known and truly loved.

Friendship can be a broad category; most of the relationships mentioned in this book have friendship components. But for our purposes, let's define friendship as *a nonromantic relationship that is attachment-based rather than function-based.* In other words, let's exclude relationships based on a common task, like work or ministry. Let's look at friendship as comprising people we want to be around just for their own sake.

Boundary conflicts with friends come in all sizes and shapes. To understand the various issues, let's look at a few conflicts and how they can be resolved with boundaries.

Conflict #1: Compliant/Compliant

In some ways it was a great friendship; in other ways, it was awful. Sean and Tim enjoyed the same sports, activities, and recreation. They went to the same church and liked the same restaurants. But they were just too nice to each other. They both had difficulty saying no to each other.

Their realization of the problem came up one weekend when a white-water rafting trip and a sixties concert were scheduled on the same day. Sean and Tim enjoyed both activities, but they couldn't do both. Sean called Tim, suggesting they go rafting. "Absolutely," answered his friend. However, unbeknownst to each other, neither Sean nor Tim really wanted to go rafting. In their heart of hearts, both men had been looking forward to going to the concert.

Halfway down the river, Sean and Tim got honest with each other. Tired and wet, Tim blurted out, "It was your big idea to come on this trip."

"Tim," Sean said with surprise. "I thought *you* wanted to go rafting."

"Oh, no! Since you called me, I figured that's what *you* wanted! Old buddy," he continued ruefully, "maybe it's time we stopped treating each other like china dolls."

The result of two compliants' interacting is that neither does what he really wants. Each is so afraid of telling the other the truth that neither ever does.

Let's apply a boundary checklist to this conflict. This checklist of questions will not only help you locate where you are in setting boundaries, but also show you how to get where you want to go.

1. *What are the symptoms?* One symptom of a compliant/compliant conflict is dissatisfaction—a sense that you allowed something you shouldn't have.

2. *What are the roots?* Compliants come from backgrounds where they had to avoid saying no to keep others happy. Since their roots are similar, it's often hard for two compliant people to help each other.

3. *What is the boundary conflict?* Compliant people politely deny their own boundaries to keep the peace.

4. *Who needs to take ownership?* Each compliant needs to take responsibility for his or her attempts to appease or please the other. Sean and Tim both need to admit that they each control the other by being nice.

5. *What do they need?* Compliant people need to have

supportive relationships to plug into, be they support groups, home Bible studies, or counselors. Their fear of hurting the other person makes it difficult for them to set boundaries on their own.

6. *How do they begin?* Both compliants practice setting limits on trivial things. They may begin with being honest about things like tastes in restaurants, church liturgies, music, and the like.

7. *How do they set boundaries with each other?* Sean and Tim talk with each other face-to-face, finally telling the truth and revealing limits they'd like to start setting. They commit themselves to better boundaries with each other.

8. *What happens next?* Sean and Tim may have to admit that their interests are not as similar as they'd thought. They may need to separate more from each other. Having different friends for different activities is no blot on the relationship; it might help their friendship in the long run.

Conflict #2: Compliant/Aggressive Controller

The compliant/aggressive controller conflict, the most identifiable of friendship conflicts, has classic symptoms. The compliant feels intimidated and inferior in the relationship; the aggressive controller feels irritated at being nagged by the compliant.

"Well, all right, if you insist" is a catchphrase of the compliant. Usually, the aggressive controller is insisting on using some of the compliant's time, talents, or treasures. The aggressive controller has no problem demanding what she wants. Sometimes she just takes what she wants without asking. "I needed it" is enough reason for the aggressive controller to help herself to whatever the compliant has, be it car keys, a cup of sugar, or three hours of time.

Since the compliant is usually unhappy in this relationship, he is the one who needs to take action. Let's put this relationship through the boundary checklist:

1. *What are the symptoms?* The compliant feels controlled and resentful; the aggressive controller feels good, except she doesn't like to be nagged.

2. *What are the roots?* The compliant probably grew up

in a family who taught him to avoid conflict, rather than embrace it. The aggressive controller never received training in delaying gratification and in taking responsibility for herself.

3. *What is the boundary conflict?* Two specific boundary conflicts are the inability of the compliant to set clear limits with his friend, and the inability of the aggressive controller to respect the compliant's limits.

4. *Who needs to take ownership?* The compliant needs to see that he isn't a victim of the aggressive controller; he is volunteering his power to his friend on a silver platter. Giving up his power is his way of controlling his friend. The compliant controls the aggressive controller by pleasing her, hoping it will appease her and cause her to change her behavior. The aggressive controller needs to own that she has difficulty listening to no and accepting the limits of others. She needs to take responsibility for her need to control her friend.

5. *What is needed?* The unhappier one in the friendship, the compliant, needs to plug into a supportive group of people to help him with this boundary conflict.

6. *How do they begin?* In preparation for confronting his friend, the compliant needs to practice setting limits in his support group. The aggressive controller could really benefit from honest feedback from loving friends on how she runs over people and how she can learn to respect the limits of others.

7. *How do they set boundaries?* The compliant applies biblical principles to his friendship (see Matthew 18). He confronts his friend on her control and intimidation. He tells her that the next time she tries to control him, he will leave.

He does not attempt to control her. Confrontation isn't an ultimatum meant to rob her of her choices. He sets limits to let her know that her control hurts him and wounds their friendship. Such limits protect the compliant from further hurt. The aggressive controller can become as angry or intimidating as she wants, but the compliant won't be around to get hurt. He will be out of the room, the house, or the friendship—until it's safe to come back.

The aggressive controller experiences the consequences

of her actions. Not having her friend around may force her to miss the attachment, and she can begin to take responsibility for the control that ran her friend off.

8. *Now what?* At this point, if both friends are open, the two can renegotiate the relationship. They can set new ground rules, such as, "I'll stop nagging if you'll stop being critical," and can build a new friendship.

Conflict #3: Compliant/Manipulative Controller

"Cathy, I'm in a real jam, and you're the only one I can depend on to help me out. I can't get a baby-sitter for the kids, and I have this church meeting...."

Cathy listened to the plight of her friend, Sharon. It was the usual story. Sharon neglected to plan for events, to call ahead for sitters. She often called Cathy to help out in these self-induced emergencies.

Cathy hated being stuck in this position. Sharon didn't do it on purpose, and she needed her for a good cause, but Cathy still felt used and exploited. What was she to do?

Many friendships get stuck in this interaction between compliants and manipulative controllers. Why do we call Sharon controlling? She's not consciously trying to manipulate her friend; however, no matter what her good intentions are, when she's in a jam, Sharon uses her friends. She takes them for granted, thinking that they shouldn't mind doing a friend a favor. Her friends go along, saying, "Well, that's just Sharon." They stifle their resentment.

Let's run this conflict through our boundary checklist:

1. *What are the symptoms?* The compliant (Cathy) feels resentment at the manipulative controller's (Sharon's) last-minute requests. Cathy feels as though her friendship is being taken for granted. She begins to avoid her friend.

2. *What are the roots?* Sharon's parents rescued her from every jam, from finishing term papers at 3:00 A.M. to lending her money when she was well into her thirties. She lived in a very forgiving universe, where nice people would always help her out. She never had to face her own irresponsibility and lack of discipline and planning.

As a child, Cathy didn't like her mother's hurt look when

she said no. She grew up afraid of hurting others by setting boundaries. Cathy would do anything to avoid conflict with friends—especially with Sharon.

3. *What is the boundary conflict?* Sharon doesn't plan ahead and take responsibility for her schedule. When responsibilities "get away from her," she calls out to the nearest compliant for help. And Cathy comes running.

4. *Who needs to take ownership?* Cathy, the motivated party in this conflict, sees how her never-ending yes contributes to Sharon's illusion that she doesn't ever have to plan ahead. Cathy needs to stop feeling like a victim and take responsibility for saying no.

5. *What does she need?* Cathy needs to connect with others who will support her as she looks at the boundary issues between her and her friend.

6. *How does she begin?* Cathy practices saying no with supportive friends. In a supportive atmosphere she learns to disagree, to state her opinion, and to confront. They all pray for strength and guidance in this relationship.

7. *How does she set boundaries?* At their next lunch, Cathy tells Sharon about her feelings of being used and taken advantage of. She explains how she'd like a more mutual relationship. Then she lets her friend know that she won't be taking any more "emergency" baby-sitting jobs.

Sharon, unaware of how she was hurting her friend, is genuinely sorry about the problem. She begins to take more responsibility for her schedule. After a few futile attempts to get Cathy to baby-sit at the last minute and having to miss a few important meetings, she starts planning for events a week or two ahead of time.

8. *What happens next?* The friendship grows and deepens. Over time, Cathy and Sharon laugh over the conflict that actually brought them closer.

Conflict #4: Compliant/Nonresponsive

Remember the Marsha-Tammy friendship at the beginning of this chapter? One friend doing all the work and the other coasting illustrates the compliant/nonresponsive conflict. One party feels frustrated and resentful; the other wonders what the problem is. Marsha sensed that the friendship wasn't as important to Tammy as it was to her.

Let's analyze the situation:

1. *What are the symptoms?* Marsha feels depressed, resentful, and unimportant. Tammy, however, may feel guilty or overwhelmed by her friend's needs and demands.

2. *What are the roots?* Marsha always feared that if she didn't control her important attachments by doing all the work, she'd be abandoned. So she became a Martha to everyone else's Mary, a worker instead of a lover (Luke 10:38–42).

Tammy has never had to work hard for friendships. Always popular and in demand, she's passively taken from important friendships. She's never lost anyone by not being responsive. In fact, they work harder to keep her around.

3. *What is the boundary conflict?* There could be two boundary conflicts here. First, Marsha takes on too much responsibility for the friendship. She's not letting her friend bear her own load (Gal. 6:5). Second, Tammy doesn't take enough responsibility for the friendship. She knows that Marsha will come up with activities from which she can pick and choose. Why work when someone else will?

4. *Who needs to take ownership?* Marsha needs to take responsibility for making it too easy for Tammy to do nothing. She sees that her attempts to plan, call, and do all the work are disguised attempts to control love.

5. *What do they need?* Both women need support from other friends. They can't look objectively at this problem without a relationship or two of unconditional love around them.

6. *How do they begin?* Marsha practices setting limits with supportive friends. She realizes that she will still have friendships in which each friend carries her own weight if she and Tammy break off their friendship.

7. *How do they set boundaries?* Marsha tells Tammy about her feelings and informs her that she will need to take equal responsibility for their friendship in the future. In other words, after Marsha calls, she won't call again unless Tammy does. Marsha hopes that Tammy will miss her and begin calling.

If worst comes to worst and the friendship atrophies due to Tammy's unresponsiveness, Marsha has gained something. She's learned it wasn't a mutual connection in the first place. Now she can grieve, get over it, and move on to find real friends.

8. *What happens next?* The mini-crisis changes the character of the friendship permanently. It either exposes it for a nonrelationship—or it provides soil for the rebuilding of a better one.

Questions about Friendship Boundary Conflicts

Boundary conflicts in friendships are difficult to deal with because the only cord tying the relationship together is the attachment itself. There's no wedding ring. There's no job connection. There's just the friendship—and it often seems all too fragile and in danger of being severed.

People who are in the above conflicts often raise the following questions when they consider setting boundaries on their friendships.

Question #1: Aren't Friendships Easily Broken?

Most friendships have no external commitment, such as marriage, work, or church, to keep the friends together. The phone could just stop ringing and the relationship die with no real ripples in the lives of the participants. So aren't friendships at greater risk of breaking up when boundary conflicts arise?

This type of thinking has two problems. First, it assumes that external institutions such as marriage, work, and church are the glue that holds relationships together. It assumes that our commitments are what hold us together, not our attachments. Biblically and practically, nothing could be further from the truth.

We hear this thinking in many Christian circles: "If you don't like someone, act like you do." Or, "make yourself love them." Or, "commit to loving someone." Or, "choose to love someone, and the feelings will come."

Choice and commitment *are* elements of a good friendship. We do need more than fair-weather friends. However, Scripture teaches us that we can't depend on commitment or sheer willpower, for they will always let us down. Paul cried out that he did what he didn't want to do, and he didn't do what he wanted to do (Rom. 7:19). He was stuck. We all experience the same conflict. Even when we commit to a loving friendship, bad things happen. We let them down. Feelings go sour. Simply white-knuckling it won't reestablish the relationship.

We can solve our dilemma the same way Paul solved his: "Therefore, there is now no condemnation for those who are in Christ Jesus" (Rom. 8:1). The answer is being "in Christ Jesus"—in other words, in relationship with Christ, both vertically and horizontally. As we stay connected to God, to our friends, and to our support groups, we are filled up with the grace to hang in there and fight out the boundary conflicts that arise. Without this external source of connection, we're doomed to an empty willpower that ultimately fails or makes us think we're omnipotent.

Again, the Bible teaches that all commitment is based on a loving relationship. Being loved leads to commitment and willful decision-making—not the reverse.

How does this apply to friendships? Look at it this way. How would you feel if your best buddy approached you and said: "I just wanted to tell you that the only reason we're friends is because I'm committed to our friendship. There's nothing that draws me to you. I don't particularly enjoy your company. But I will keep choosing to be your friend."

You probably wouldn't feel very safe or cherished in this relationship. You'd suspect you were being befriended out of obligation, not out of love. Don't let anyone fool you. All friendships need to be based on attachment, or they have a shaky foundation.

The second problem with thinking that friendships are weaker than institutionalized relationships such as marriage, church, and work is in assuming that those three aren't attachment-based. It simply isn't true. If it were, wedding vows would ensure a zero percent divorce rate. Professions of faith would ensure faithful church attendance. A hiring would ensure one hundred percent attendance at work.

These three important institutions, so crucial to our lives, are, to a large degree, attachment-based.

It's scary to realize that the only thing holding our friends to us isn't our performance, or our lovability, or their guilt, or their obligation. The only thing that will keep them calling, spending time with us, and putting up with us is love. And that's the one thing we can't control.

At any moment, any person can walk away from a friendship. However, as we enter more and more into an attachment-based life, we learn to trust love. We learn that the bonds of a true friendship are not easily broken. And we learn that, in a good relationship, we can set limits that will strengthen, not injure, the connection.

Question #2: How Can I Set Boundaries in Romantic Friendships?

Single Christians have tremendous struggles with learning to be truth-tellers and limit-setters in romantic, dating friendships. Most of the conflicts revolve around the fear of losing the relationship. A client may say: "There's someone in my life whom I like a lot—but I'm afraid if I say no to him, I'll never see him again."

A couple of unique principles operate in the romantic sphere:

1. *Romantic relationships are, by nature, risky.* Many singles who have not developed good attachments with other people and who have not had their boundaries respected try to learn the rules of biblical friendships by dating. They hope that the safety of these relationships will help them learn to love, be loved, and set limits.

Quite often, these individuals come out of a few months of dating more injured than when they went in. They may feel let down, put down, or used. This is not a dating problem. It's a problem in understanding the purpose of dating.

The purpose of dating is to practice and experiment. The end goal of dating is generally to decide, sooner or later, whether or not to marry. Dating is a means to find out what kind of person we complement and with whom we are spiritually and emotionally compatible. It's a training ground for marriage.

This fact causes a built-in conflict. When we date, we have the freedom to say, at any time, "This isn't working out," and to end the relationship. The other person has the same freedom.

What does this mean for the person whose boundaries have been injured? Often, she brings immature, undeveloped aspects of her character to an adult romantic situation. In an arena of low commitment and high risk, she seeks the safety, bonding, and consistency that her wounds need. She entrusts herself too quickly to someone whom she is dating because her needs are so intense. And she will be devastated when things "don't work out."

This is a little like sending a three-year-old to the front lines of battle. Dating is a way for adults to find out about each other's suitability for marriage; it's not a place for young, injured souls to find healing. This healing can best be found in nonromantic arenas, such as support groups, church groups, therapy, and same-sex friendships. We need to keep separate the purposes of romantic and nonromantic friendships.

It's best to learn the skill of setting boundaries in these nonromantic arenas, where the attachments and commitments are greater. Once we've learned to recognize, set, and keep our biblical boundaries, we can use them on the adult playground called dating.

2. *Setting limits in romance is necessary.* Individuals with mature boundaries sometimes suspend them in the initial stages of a dating relationship in order to please the other person. However, truth-telling in romance helps define the relationship. It helps each person to know where he starts and the other person stops.

Ignorance of one another's boundaries is one of the most blatant red flags of the poor health of a dating relationship. We'll ask a couple in premarital counseling, "Where do you disagree? Where do you lock horns?" When the answer is, "It's just amazing, we're so compatible, we have very few differences," we'll give the couple homework: Find out what you've been lying about to each other. If the relationship has any hope, that assignment will generally help.

Question #3: What If My Closest Friends Are My Family?

Boundary-developing individuals sometimes say, "But my mother (or father, or sister, or brother) is my best friend." They often feel fortunate that, in these times of family stress, their best friends are the family in which they were raised. They don't think they need an intimate circle of friends besides their own parents and siblings.

They misunderstand the biblical function of the family. God intended the family to be an incubator in which we grow the maturity, tools, and abilities we need. Once the incubator has done its job, then, it's supposed to encourage the young adult to leave the nest and connect to the outside world (Gen. 2:24), to establish a spiritual and emotional family system on one's own. The adult is free to do whatever God has designed for him or her.

Over time, we are to accomplish God's purposes of spreading his love to the world, to make disciples of all the nations (Matt. 28:19–20). Staying emotionally locked in to the family of origin frustrates this purpose. It's hard to see how we'll change the world when we have to live on the same street.

No one can become a truly biblical adult without setting some limits, leaving home, and cleaving somewhere else. Otherwise, we never know if we have forged our own values, beliefs, and convictions—our very identity—or if we are mimicking the ideas of our family.

Can family be friends? Absolutely. But if you have never questioned, set boundaries, or experienced conflict with your family members, you may not have an adult-to-adult connection with your family. If you have no other "best friends" than your family, you need to take a close look at those relationships. You may be afraid of separating and individuating, of becoming an autonomous adult.

Question #4: How Can I Set Limits with Needy Friends?

I was talking to a woman one day in session who felt extremely isolated and out of control. Setting limits with her friends seemed impossible for her; they were in perpetual crisis.

I asked her to describe the quality of her relationships. "Oh, I've got lots of friends. I volunteer at the church two nights a week. I teach a Bible study once a week. I'm on a couple of church committees, and I sing in the choir."

"I'm getting exhausted just listening to you describe your week," I said. "But what about the quality of these relationships?"

"They're great. People are being helped. They're growing in their faith, and troubled marriages are getting healed."

"You know," I said, "I'm asking you about friendships, and you're answering about ministries. They're not the same thing."

She had never considered the difference. Her concept of friendship was to find people with needs and throw herself into a relationship with them. She didn't know how to ask for things for herself.

And that was the source of her boundary conflicts. Without these "ministry relationships," this woman would have had nothing. So she couldn't say no. Saying no would have plummeted her into isolation, which would have been intolerable.

But it had happened anyway: she had come for help because of burnout.

When the Bible tells us to comfort with the comfort with which we are comforted (2 Cor. 1:4), it's telling us something. We need to be comforted before we can comfort. That may mean setting boundaries on our ministries so that we can be nurtured by our friends. We must distinguish between the two.

A prayerful look at your friendships will determine whether you need to begin building boundaries with some of your friends. By setting boundaries, you may save some important ones from declining. And when romantic, dating relationships lead to marriage, you will still need to remember how to build and maintain boundaries even in this most intimate of human relationships.

9

Boundaries and Your Spouse

I f there were ever a relationship where boundaries could get confused, it is marriage, where by design husband and wife "become one flesh" (Eph. 5:31). Boundaries foster separateness. Marriage has as one of its goals the giving up of separateness and becoming, instead of two, one. What a potential state of confusion, especially for someone who does not have clear boundaries to begin with!

More marriages fail because of poor boundaries than for any other reason. This chapter will apply the laws of boundaries, as well as its myths, to the marital relationship.

Is This Yours, Mine, or Ours?

A marriage mirrors the relationship that Christ has with his bride, the church. Christ has some things that only he can do, the church has some things that only it can do, and they have some things they do together. Only Christ could die. Only the church can represent him on earth in his absence and obey his commands. And together, they work on many things, such as saving the lost. Similarly, in marriage, some duties one spouse does, some the other does, and some they do together. When the two become one on their wedding day, spouses do not lose their individual identities. Each participates in the relationship, and each has his or her own life.

No one would have a problem deciding who wears the dress and who wears the tie. It's a little trickier to decide who balances the checkbook and who mows the lawn. But these duties can be worked out according to the spouses' individual abilities and interests. Where boundaries can get confusing is in the elements of personhood—the elements of the soul that each person possesses and can choose to share with someone else.

The problem arises when one trespasses on the other's personhood, when one crosses a line and tries to control the feelings, attitudes, behaviors, choices, and values of the other. These things only each individual can control. To try to control these things is to violate someone's boundaries, and ultimately, it will fail. Our relationship with Christ— and any other successful relationship—is based on freedom.

Let's look at some common examples:

Feelings

One of the most important elements that promotes intimacy between two people is the ability of each to take responsibility for his or her own feelings.

I was counseling a couple who were having marital problems because of the husband's drinking. I asked the wife to tell her husband how she felt when he drank.

"I feel like he doesn't think about what he's doing. I feel like he . . ."

"No, you are evaluating his drinking. How do you feel about it?"

"I feel like he doesn't care. . . ."

"No," I said, "That is what you *think* about him. How do you *feel* when he drinks?"

She started to cry. "I feel very alone and afraid." She had finally said what she felt.

At that point her husband reached out and put his hand on her arm. "I never knew you were afraid," he said. "I would never want to make you afraid."

This conversation was a real turning point in their relationship. For years the wife had been nagging her husband about the way he was and about the way he should be. He responded by blaming her and justifying his actions. In spite of hours and hours of talking, they had continued to talk past each other. Neither was taking responsibility for his or her own feelings and communicating them.

We do not communicate our feelings by saying, "I feel that you ..." We communicate our feelings by saying, "I feel sad, or hurt, or lonely, or scared, or ..." Such vulnerability is the beginning of intimacy and caring.

Feelings are also a warning signal telling us that we need to do something. For example, if you are angry at someone for something she did, it is your responsibility to go to her and tell her you are angry and why. If you think that your anger is her problem and that she needs to fix it, you may wait years. And your anger may turn to bitterness. If you are angry, even if someone else has sinned against you, it is your responsibility to do something about it.

This was a lesson Susan needed to learn. When her husband, Jim, did not come home from work early enough for them to have time together, Susan became angry. Instead of confronting her husband, she would become very quiet for the rest of the evening. Jim became annoyed with having to pull out of her what was wrong. Eventually, hating her pouting, he left her alone.

Not dealing with hurt or anger can kill a relationship. Susan needed to talk with Jim about how she was feeling, instead of waiting for him to draw her out. Even though she felt he had been the one who had hurt her, she needed to take responsibility for her own hurt and anger.

Jim and Susan did not solve their problem by her simply expressing her anger to him. She needed to go one more step. She needed to clarify her desires in the conflict.

Desires

Desires are another element of personhood that each spouse needs to take responsibility for. Susan was angry because she wanted Jim to be home. She blamed him for being late. When they came in for counseling, our conversation went like this:

"Susan, tell me why you get angry at Jim," I said.

"Because he's late," she replied.

"That can't be the reason," I said. "People don't make

other people angry. Your anger has to come from something inside of you."

"What do you mean? He's the one who comes home late."

"Well, what if you had plans to go out with your friends that night? Would you still be angry at him for being late?"

"Well, no. That's different."

"What's different? You said you were angry because he was late, and he would still be late, yet you wouldn't be angry."

"Well, in that situation, he wouldn't be doing anything to hurt me."

"Not exactly," I pointed out. "The difference is that you wouldn't be wanting something that he didn't want to give. Your disappointed desire is what hurts you, not his being late. The problem lies in who is responsible for the want. It is your want, not his. You are responsible for getting it fulfilled. That is a rule of life. We do not get everything we want, and we all must grieve over our disappointments instead of punish others for them."

"What about common respect? Staying at the office is selfish," she said.

"Well, he wants to work some nights and you want him home. Both of you want something for yourselves. We could say that you are as selfish as he is. The truth is that neither one of you is selfish. You just have conflicting wants. This is what marriage is about—getting conflicting wants worked out."

There was no "bad guy" in this situation. Both Jim and Susan had needs. Jim needed to work late, and Susan needed him home. Problems arise when we make someone else responsible for our needs and wants, and when we blame them for our disappointments.

Limits on What I Can Give

We are finite creatures and must give as we "decide in [our] heart to give" (2 Cor. 9:7), being aware of when we are giving past the love point to the resentment point. Problems arise when we blame someone else for our own lack of limits. Often spouses will do more than they really want to and then resent the other for not stopping them from overgiving.

Bob had this problem. His wife, Nancy, wanted the perfect home, including handmade patios, landscaping, and remodeling. She was always coming up with something for him to do around the house. He was beginning to resent her projects.

When he came to see me, I asked him why he was angry.

"Well, because she wants so much. I can't find any time for myself," he said.

"What do you mean 'can't'? Don't you mean 'won't'?"

"No, I *can't*. She would be angry if I didn't do the work."

"Well, that's her problem; it's her anger."

"Yes, but I have to listen to it."

"No, you don't," I said. "You are choosing to do all of these things for her, and you are choosing to take the tongue lashings that happen if you don't. Any time you spend doing things for her is a gift from you; if you do not want to give it, you don't have to. Stop blaming her for all of this."

Bob didn't like that. He wanted her to stop wanting instead of his learning to say no.

"How much time do you want to give her each week for home improvement?" I asked.

He thought for a minute. "About four hours. I could work on things for her and still have a little time left for a hobby."

"Then tell her that you have been thinking about your time and that with all the other things you are doing for the family, you would like to give her four hours a week to work around the house. She is free to use that time any way she chooses."

"But what if she says that four hours is not enough?"

"Explain to her that you understand that this may not be enough time to complete all the jobs she wants done, but those are her wants, not yours. Therefore, she is responsible for her own wants, and she is free to be creative in how she gets them done. She could earn some extra money and hire someone. She could learn to do them herself. She could ask a friend to help. Or, she could cut down on her wants. It is important that she learns that you are not going to take responsibility for her wants. You're going to give as you choose, and she is responsible for the rest."

Bob saw the logic in my suggestion and decided to talk with Nancy. It was not pretty at first. No one had ever said no to Nancy before, and she did not take well to it. But, over time, Bob took responsibility for his limits instead of wishing that Nancy would not want so much, and his limits took effect. She learned something that she had never learned before: the world does not exist for her. Other people are not extensions of her wants and desires. Other people have wants and needs of their own, and we must negotiate a fair and loving relationship and respect each other's limits.

The key here is that the other person is not responsible for our limits; we are. Only we know what we can and want to give, and only we can be responsible for drawing that line. If we do not draw it, we can quickly become resentful.

Applying the Laws of Boundaries to Marriage

In Chapter 5 we talked about the ten laws of boundaries. Let's apply a few of those laws to troubled marital situations.

The Law of Sowing and Reaping

Many times one spouse may be out of control and may not suffer the consequences of this behavior. The husband yells at his wife, and she tries to be more loving. In effect, the evil (yelling) produces good things (more loving) for him. Or, a wife overspends, and her husband pays the consequences. He gets a second job to cover the mound of bills.

Natural consequences are needed to resolve these problems. A wife needs to tell her overly critical husband that if he continues to berate her, she will go into another room until he can discuss the problem rationally. Or, she could say something like, "I will not talk about this issue with you anymore alone. I will only talk in the presence of a counselor." Or, "If you start yelling at me again, I will go to Jane's house to spend the night." The husband with the spendthrift wife needs to cancel the credit cards or tell her *she* needs to get a second job to pay the bills. These spouses

all need to let the out-of-control spouses suffer the consequences of their actions.

A friend of mine decided to let his wife suffer the
consequences of her chronic lateness. He had nagged and
nagged his wife about her tardiness, to no avail. Finally, he
realized he could not change her; he could only change his
response to her. Tired of suffering the consequences of her
behavior, he decided to give them back to her.

One night they had plans to go to a banquet, and he did
not want to be late. In advance, he told her that he wanted to
be on time and that if she were not ready by 6:00 P.M., he
would leave without her. She was late, and he left. When he
came home that night, she screamed, "How could you leave
without me!" He let her know that her lateness was what
caused her to miss the banquet and that he was sad to have to
go alone, but he did not want to miss the dinner. After a few
more incidents like this, she knew that her lateness would
affect her and not him, and she changed.

These moves are not manipulative, as the other spouse
will accuse. They are examples of someone limiting how
they will allow themselves to be treated and exhibiting self-
control. The natural consequences are falling on the should-
ers of the responsible party.

The Law of Responsibility

We talked earlier about taking responsibility *for* ourselves and having responsibility *to* others. The above
examples show that. People who set limits exhibit self-
control and show responsibility for themselves. They act
responsible to their partner by confronting him or her.
Setting limits is an act of love in the marriage; by binding
and limiting the evil, they protect the good.

Taking responsibility for someone's anger, pouting, and
disappointments by giving in to that person's demands or
controlling behavior destroys love in a marriage. Instead of
taking responsibility for people we love, or rescuing them,
we need to show responsibility to them by confronting evil
when we see it. This is truly loving our partner and the

marriage. The most responsible behavior possible is usually the most difficult.

The Law of Power

We have looked at our basic inability to change another person. A nagging spouse, in effect, keeps the problem going. Accepting someone as she is, respecting her choice to be that way, and then giving her appropriate consequences is the better path. When we do this, we execute the power we do have, and we stop trying to wield the power no one has. Contrast these ways of reacting:

BEFORE BOUNDARIES	AFTER BOUNDARIES
1. "Stop yelling at me. You must be nicer."	1. "You can continue to yell if you choose to. But I will choose not to be in your presence when you act that way."
2. "You've just got to stop drinking. It's ruining our family. Please listen. You're wrecking our lives."	2. "You may choose to not deal with your drinking if you want. But I will not continue to expose myself and the children to this chaos. The next time you are drunk, we will go to the Wilsons' for the night, and we will tell them why we are there. Your drinking is your choice. What I will put up with is mine."
3. "You are a pervert to look at pornography. That's so degrading. What kind of a sick person are you anyway?"	3. "I will not choose to share you sexually with naked women in magazines. It's up to you. I will only sleep with someone who is interested in me. Make up your mind and choose."

These are all examples of taking power over what you do have power over—yourself—and giving up trying to control and have power over someone else.

The Law of Evaluation

When you confront your husband or wife and begin to set boundaries, your partner may be hurt. In evaluating the pain that your boundary setting causes your spouse, remember that love and limits go together. When you set boundaries, be lovingly responsible to the person in pain.

Spouses who are wise and loving will accept boundaries and act responsibly toward them. Spouses who are controlling and self-centered will react angrily.

Remember that a boundary always deals with yourself, not the other person. You are not demanding that your spouse do something—even respect your boundaries. You are setting boundaries to say what you will do or will not do. Only these kinds of boundaries are enforceable, for you *do* have control over yourself. Do not confuse boundaries with a new way to control a spouse. It is the opposite. It is giving up control and beginning to love. You are giving up trying to control your spouse and allowing him to take responsibility for his own behavior.

The Law of Exposure

In a marriage, as in no other relationship, the need for revealing your boundaries is important. Passive boundaries, such as withdrawal, triangulation, pouting, affairs, and passive-aggressive behavior, are extremely destructive to a relationship. Passive ways of showing people that they do not have control over you never lead to intimacy. They never educate the other on who you really are; they only estrange.

Boundaries need to be communicated first verbally and then with actions. They need to be clear and unapologetic. Remember the types of boundaries we listed earlier: skin, words, truth, physical space, time, emotional distance, other people, consequences. All of these boundaries need to be respected and revealed at different times in marriage.

Skin. Each spouse needs to respect the other's physical body boundaries. Physical boundary violations can range from hurtful displays of affection to physical abuse. The Bible says that the husband and wife have "authority" over each other's body (1 Cor. 7:4–6 NASB); this is mutual authority, given freely. One should always remember Jesus' principle: "Treat others as you would want to be treated."

Words. Your words need to be clear and spoken in love. Confront your spouse directly. Say no. Don't use passive resistance. Don't pout or withdraw. Say things like, "I do not feel comfortable with that. I do not want to. I won't."

Truth. Paul says that "each of you must put off falsehood and speak truthfully" (Eph. 4:25). Honest communication is always best. This includes telling the other person when he is not aware that he is violating one of God's standards. You also need to own the truth about your feelings and hurts and communicate those feelings directly to your spouse with love.

Physical Space. When you need time away, tell your spouse. Sometimes you need space for nourishment; other times you need space for limit setting. In either instance, your spouse should not have to guess why you do not want him around for a while. Communicate clearly so your spouse does not feel as though he is being punished, but knows he is experiencing the consequences of his out-of-control behavior (Matt. 18:17; 1 Cor. 5:9–13).

Emotional Distance. If you are in a troubled marriage, where your partner has had an affair, for example, you may need emotional space. Waiting to trust again is wise. You need to see if your spouse is truly repentant, and your spouse needs to see that her behavior has a cost. Your spouse may interpret this as punishment, but the Bible teaches that we are to judge a person by her actions, not by her words (James 2:14–26).

In addition, a hurt heart takes time to heal. You cannot rush back into a position of trust with too much unresolved hurt. That hurt needs to be exposed and communicated. If you are hurting, you need to own that hurt.

Time. Each spouse needs time apart from the relationship. Not just for limit setting, as we pointed out above, but for self-nourishment. The Proverbs 31 wife has a life of her own; she is out doing many things. The same is true of her husband. They have their own time for doing what they like and for seeing their own friends.

Many couples have trouble with this aspect of marriage. They feel abandoned when their spouse wants time apart. In reality, spouses need time apart, which makes them realize the need to be back together. Spouses in healthy relationships cherish each other's space and are champions of each other's causes.

Other People. Some spouses need the support of others to set boundaries. If they haven't ever stood up for themselves, they need help from friends and the church in learning how. If you are too weak to set and enforce boundaries, get help from supporters outside your marriage. Do not, however, seek support from someone of the opposite sex that could lead to an affair. Get help from other people within relationships that have built-in boundaries, such as counselors or support groups.

Consequences. Communicate consequences clearly and enforce them firmly as you have said you would. Spelling out consequences in advance and enforcing them gives your spouse a choice about whether or not he or she wants the consequences to happen. Because people have control over their own behavior, they have control over the consequences of that behavior.

But That Doesn't Sound Submissive

Whenever we talk about a wife setting boundaries, someone asks about the biblical idea of submission. What follows is not a full treatise on submission, but some general issues you should keep in mind.

First, both husbands and wives are supposed to practice submission, not just wives. "Submit to one another out of reverence for Christ" (Eph. 5:21). Submission is always the free choice of one party to another. Wives choose to submit to their husbands, and husbands choose to submit to their wives.

Christ's relationship with the church is a picture of how a

husband and wife should relate: "Now as the church submits to Christ, so also wives should submit to their husbands in everything. Husbands, love your wives, just as Christ loved the church and gave himself up for her to make her holy, cleansing her by the washing with water through the word, and to present her to himself as a radiant church, without stain or wrinkle or any other blemish, but holy and blameless" (Eph. 5:24–27).

Whenever submission issues are raised, the first question that needs to be asked is, What is the nature of the marital relationship? Is the husband's relationship with his wife similar to Christ's relationship with the church? Does she have free choice, or is she a slave "under the law"? Many marital problems arise when a husband tries to keep his wife "under the law," and she feels all the emotions the Bible promises the law will bring: wrath, guilt, insecurity, and alienation (Rom. 4:15; James 2:10; Gal. 5:4).

Freedom is one issue that needs to be examined; grace is another. Is the husband's relationship with his wife full of grace and unconditional love? Is she in a position of "no condemnation" as the church is (Rom. 8:1), or does her husband fail to "wash her" of all guilt? Usually husbands who quote Ephesians 5 turn their wives into slaves and condemn them for not submitting. If she incurs wrath or condemnation for not submitting, she and her husband do not have a grace-filled Christian marriage; they have a marriage "under the law."

Often, in these situations, the husband is trying to get his wife to do something that either is hurtful or takes away her will. Both of these actions are sins against himself. "Husbands ought to love their wives as their own bodies. He who loves his wife loves himself. After all, no one ever hated his own body, but he feeds and cares for it, just as Christ does the church" (Eph. 5:28–29). Given this, the idea of slavelike submission is impossible to hold. Christ never takes away our will or asks us to do something hurtful. He never pushes us past our limits. He never uses us as objects. Christ "gave himself up" for us. He takes care of us as he would his own body.

We have never seen a "submission problem" that did not

have a controlling husband at its root. When the wife begins to set clear boundaries, the lack of Christlikeness in a controlling husband becomes evident because the wife is no longer enabling his immature behavior. She is confronting the truth and setting biblical limits on hurtful behavior. Often, when the wife sets boundaries, the husband begins to grow up.

A Question of Balance

"I can't get him to spend any time with me. All he wants to do is go with his friends to sporting events. He never wants to see me," Meredith complained.

"What do you say to that?" I asked her husband.

"That's not true at all," Paul replied. "It feels like all we have is togetherness. She calls me at work two or three times a day. She is waiting at the door when I get home and wants to talk. She has our evenings and weekends all planned out. It drives me crazy. So, I try to get away and go to a game or to play golf. I feel smothered."

"How often do you try to get out?"

"Any time I can. Probably about two nights a week and one afternoon on the weekend."

"What do you do at those times?" I asked Meredith.

"Well, I wait for him to come home. I miss him very much."

"Don't you have something you want to do for yourself?"

"No. My family is my life. I live for them. I hate it when they are gone and we can't have time together."

"Well, it's not like you never have time together," I said. "But it is true that you don't have all the time together. And when that happens, Paul seems to be relieved and you are distressed. Can you explain that imbalance?"

"What do you mean, 'imbalance'?" she asked.

"Every marriage is made up of two ingredients, togetherness and separateness. In good marriages, the partners carry equal loads of both of those. Let's say there are 100 points of togetherness and 100 points of separateness. In a good relationship, one partner expresses 50 points of togetherness and 50 points of separateness, and the other does the same. They both do things on their own, and that creates some mutual longing for the other, and the togetherness creates some need for separateness. But in your relationship, you have divided the 200 points differently. You are expressing all of the 100 together points, and he is expressing the 100 points of separateness.

"If you want him to move toward you," I continued, "you need to move away from him and create some space for longing. I don't think Paul ever gets a chance to miss you. You're always pursuing him, and he is turning away to create space. If you would create some space, he would have some space to long for you in, and then he would pursue you."

"That's exactly right," Paul broke in. "Honey, it's like when you were getting your graduate degree and were gone so much. Remember? I used to long to see you. I don't get a chance to miss you now. You're always around."

Meredith was reluctant to concede my point, but eager to explore with Paul ways to bring balance to their marital relationship.

Balance. It's something that God has wired into every system. Every system tries to find balance in any way it can. And many dimensions need to be balanced in a marriage: power, strength, togetherness, sex, and so on. Problems come when, instead of trading places in these areas, one spouse is always powerful and the other powerless; one spouse is always strong and the other weak; one spouse always wants togetherness and the other wants separateness; one spouse always wants sex and the other doesn't. In each case, the couple has struck a balance, but it is not a *mutual* balance.

Boundaries help create mutual balance, instead of split balance. They help couples keep each other accountable. If someone does not have boundaries and begins to do another's work for him, such as creating all the togetherness in the relationship, that person is on the road to codependency or worse. The other partner will live out the opposite side of the split. Boundaries keep partners accountable through consequences and force the balance to become mutual.

The Preacher in Ecclesiastes says, "There is a time for everything, and a season for every activity under heaven"

(3:1). There are balanced polarities in life and relationship. When you find yourself in an unequal relationship, you may lack boundaries. Setting boundaries may correct the imbalance. For example, when Paul sets boundaries on Meredith's demands, he forces her to become more independent.

Resolution

It is often easy to see problems, but difficult to make the hard choices and risks that result in change. Let's look at the steps toward personal change in a marital relationship.

1. *Inventory the symptom.* First, you need to recognize the problem and agree to take action to solve it. You will not resolve the problem by wishing. You need to own the problem, whether it be sex, discipline of the children, lack of togetherness, or unfair spending of money.

2. *Identify the specific boundary problem.* One step beyond identifying the symptom is putting your finger on the specific boundary issue. For instance, the symptom may be that one person does not want sex; the boundary problem may be that this person does not say no often enough in other areas of the relationship so that this is the one place that she has some power. Or, she may feel as if she does not have enough control in the sexual arena. She may feel powerless; she may feel that her choices are not honored.

3. *Find the origins of the conflict.* This is probably not the first relationship in which this boundary issue has arisen. You probably learned to relate this way in a significant relationship in the family in which you grew up. Certain fears that were developed in that relationship are still operative. You need to name these original issues; you may need to stop confusing your parent with your spouse. No other relationship repeats parental conflicts more often than the marriage relationship.

4. *Take in the good.* This step involves establishing a support system. Remember, "Boundaries are not built in a vacuum." We need bonding and support before we build boundaries; the fear of abandonment keeps many people from setting boundaries in the first place.

For this reason, establish a support system that will

encourage boundary setting in your marriage. This may be a co-dependency group, Al-Anon, a therapist, a marriage counselor, or a pastor. Do not set boundaries alone. You have not set boundaries because you are afraid; the only way out is through support. "And if one can overpower him who is alone, two can resist him. A cord of three strands is not quickly torn apart" (Ecc. 4:12). Boundaries are like muscles. They need to be built up in a safe support system and allowed to grow. If you try to shoulder too much weight too quickly, your muscles may tear or be pulled. Get help.

5. *Practice.* Practice new boundaries in safe relationships, relationships in which people love you unconditionally. Tell a good friend no when you can't do lunch, or let her know when your opinion differs from hers, or give something to her without expecting anything in return. As you practice setting limits with safe people, you will begin to grow in your ability to set limits in your marriage.

6. *Say no to the bad.* Put limits on the bad in your marriage. Stand up to abuse; say no to unreasonable demands. Remember the parable of the talents. There was no growth without risk and a facing up to fear. Being successful is not as important as stepping out and trying.

7. *Forgive.* To not forgive is to lack boundaries. Unforgiving people allow other people to control them. Setting people who have hurt you free from an old debt is to stop wanting something from them; it sets you free as well. Forgiving can lead to proactive behavior in the present, instead of passive wishes from the past.

8. *Become proactive.* Instead of allowing someone else to be in control, figure out what you want to do, set your course, and stick to it. Decide what your limits are, what you will allow yourself to be a party to, what you will no longer tolerate, and what consequences you will set. Define yourself proactively, and you will be ready to maintain your boundaries when the time comes.

9. *Learn to love in freedom and responsibility.* Remember the goal of boundaries: love coming out of freedom. This is the true self-denial of the New Testament. When you are in control of yourself, you can give and sacrifice for loved ones in a helpful way instead of giving in to destructive

behavior and self-centeredness. This kind of freedom allows one to give in a way that leads to fruit. Remember, "no greater love has anyone than to lay down his life for his friends." This is to live up to the law of Christ, to serve one another. But this must be done out of freedom, not boundaryless compliance.

Setting and receiving firm boundaries with your spouse can lead to a much greater intimacy. But you not only need to address boundaries with your spouse; you need to address boundaries with your children. And it's never too late to start.

10

Boundaries and Your Children

S hannon couldn't stop crying. A young mother of two preschool children, she couldn't imagine herself being angry, out of control, and certainly not abusive. Yet a week ago, she had picked up three-year-old Robby and shaken him. Hard. She had screamed at him. Loudly. And it wasn't the first time. She had done it numerous times in the past year. The only difference was that this time, Shannon almost physically injured her son. She was frightened.

The experience had so shaken Shannon and her husband, Gerald, that they called and made an appointment with me to discuss what had happened. Her shame and guilt were intense. She avoided eye contact with me as she told her story.

The several hours before Shannon had lost control with Robby had been horrible. Gerald and she had had an argument over breakfast. He had left for work without saying good-bye. Then one-year-old Tanya spilled cereal all over the floor. And Robby chose that morning to do everything he'd been told not to for the past three years. He pulled the cat's tail. He figured out how to open the front door, and he ran outside into the yard and into the street. He smeared Shannon's lipstick all over the white dining room wall, and he pushed Tanya to the floor.

This last incident was the straw that broke Shannon's back. Seeing Tanya lying on the floor, crying, with Robby standing over her with a defiantly pleased look, was too much. Shannon saw red and impulsively ran to her son. You know the rest of the story.

167

After she had calmed down a little, I asked Shannon how she and Gerald normally disciplined Robby.

"Well, we don't want to alienate Robby, or quench his spirit," Gerald began. "Being negative is so ... so ... negative. So we try to reason with him. Sometimes we'll warn him that 'you won't get ice cream tonight.' Sometimes we try to praise good things he does. And sometimes we try to ignore the bad behavior. Then maybe he'll stop it."

"Doesn't he push the limits?"

Both parents nodded. "You wouldn't believe it," Shannon said. "It's like he doesn't hear us. He keeps on doing what he jolly well pleases. And generally, he'll keep it up until one of us explodes and yells at him. I guess we just have a problem child."

"Well, there's certainly a problem," I replied. "But perhaps Robby has been trained to not respond to anything but out-of-control rage. Let's talk about boundaries and kids. . . ."

Of all the areas in which boundaries are crucially important, none is more relevant than that of raising children. How we approach boundaries and child rearing will have enormous impact on the characters of our kids. On how they develop values. On how well they do in school. On the friends they pick. On whom they marry. And on how well they do in a career.

The Importance of Family

God, at his deepest level, is a lover (1 John 4:8). He is relationally oriented and relationally driven. He desires connection with us from womb to tomb: "I have loved you with an everlasting love" (Jer. 31:3). God's loving nature isn't passive. It's active. Love multiplies itself. God the relational Lover is also God the aggressive Creator. He wants to fill up his universe with beings who care for him— and for each other.

The family is the social unit God invented to fill up the world with representatives of his loving character. It's a place for nurturing and developing babies until they're mature enough to go out of the family as adults and to multiply his image in other surroundings.

God first picked the nation Israel to be his children. After centuries of resistance by Israel, however, God chose the church: "Because of [Israel's] transgression, salvation has come to the Gentiles to make Israel envious" (Rom. 11:11). The body of Christ has the same role as Israel had—to multiply God's love and character.

The church is often described as a family. We are to do good "especially to those who belong to the family of believers" (Gal. 6:10). Believers "are members of God's household" (Eph. 2:19). We are to "know how people ought to conduct themselves in God's household" (1 Tim. 3:15).

These and many other powerful passages show us how God "thinks family." He explains his heart as a parent would. He's a daddy. He likes his job. This biblical portrayal of God helps show us how parenting is such a vital part of bringing God's own character to this planet in our own little ones.

Boundaries and Responsibility

God, the good parent, wants to help us, his children, grow up. He wants to see us "become mature, attaining to the whole measure of the fullness of Christ" (Eph. 4:13). Part of this maturing process is helping us know how to take responsibility for our lives.

It's the same with our own flesh-and-blood kids. Second only to learning how to bond, to form strong attachments, the most important thing parents can give children is a sense of responsibility—knowing what they are responsible for and knowing what they aren't responsible for, knowing how to say no and knowing how to accept no. Responsibility is a gift of enormous value.

We've all been around middle-aged people who have the boundaries of an eighteen-month-old. They have tantrums or sulk when others set limits on them, or they simply fold and comply with others just to keep the peace. Remember that these adult people started off as little people. They learned long, long ago to either fear or hate boundaries. The relearning process for adults is laborious.

Instilling vs. Repairing Boundaries

A wise mother of adult children once watched her younger friend struggle with her youngster. The child was refusing to behave, and the young mother was quickly losing her mind. Affirming the mother's decision to make the child sit on a chair by himself, the older woman said, "Do it now, Dear. Discipline the child now—and you just might survive adolescence."

Developing boundaries in young children is that proverbial ounce of prevention. If we teach responsibility, limit setting, and delay of gratification early on, the smoother our children's later years of life will be. The later we start, the harder we and they have to work.

If you're a parent of older children, don't lose heart. It just means boundary development will be met with more resistance. In their minds, they do not have a lot to gain by learning boundaries. You'll need to spend more time working on it, getting more support from friends—and praying harder! We'll review age-appropriate boundary tasks for the different stages of childhood later in this chapter.

Boundary Development in Children

The work of boundary development in children is the work of learning responsibility. As we teach them the merits and limits of responsibility, we teach them autonomy—we prepare them to take on the tasks of adulthood.

The Scriptures have much to say about the role of boundary setting in child rearing. Usually, we call it discipline. The Hebrew and Greek words that scholars translate as "discipline" mean "teaching." This teaching has both a positive and a negative slant.

The positive facets of discipline are *proactivity, prevention,* and *instruction.* Positive discipline is sitting someone down to educate and train him in a task: fathers are to raise children "in the training and instruction of the Lord" (Eph.

6:4). The negative facets of discipline are *correction, chastisement,* and *consequences.* Negative discipline is letting children suffer the results of their actions to learn a lesson in responsibility: "Stern discipline awaits him who leaves the path" (Prov. 15:10).

Good child rearing involves both preventive training and practice, and correctional consequences. For example, you set a ten o'clock bedtime for your fourteen-year-old. "It's there so that you'll get enough sleep to be alert in school," you tell her. You've just disciplined positively. Then your teen dawdles until 11:30 P.M. The next day you say, "Because you did not get to bed on time last night, you may not use the phone today." You've just disciplined negatively.

Why are both the carrot and the whip necessary in good boundary development? Because God uses practice—trial and error—to help us grow up. We learn maturity by getting information, applying it poorly, making mistakes, learning from our mistakes, and doing better the next time.

Practice is necessary in all areas of life: in learning to ski, write an essay, or operate a computer. We need practice in developing a deep love relationship and in learning to study the Bible. And it's just as true in our spiritual and emotional growth: "But solid food is for the mature, who by constant use have trained themselves to distinguish good from evil" (Heb. 5:14). Practice is important in learning boundaries and responsibility. Our mistakes are our teachers.

Discipline is an external boundary, designed to develop internal boundaries in our children. It provides a structure of safety until the child has enough structure in his character to not need it. Good discipline always moves the child toward more internal structure and more responsibility.

We need to distinguish between discipline and punishment. Punishment is payment for wrongdoing. Legally, it's paying a penalty for breaking the law. Punishment doesn't leave a lot of room for practice, however. It's not a great teacher. The price is too high: "The wages of sin is death" (Rom. 6:23), and "whoever keeps the whole law and yet stumbles at just one point is guilty of breaking all of it" (James 2:10). Punishment does not leave much room for mistakes.

Discipline, however, is different. Discipline is not payment for a wrong. It's the natural law of God: our actions reap consequences.

Discipline is different from punishment because God is finished punishing us. Punishment ended on the cross for all those who accept Christ as Savior: "He himself bore our sins in his body on the tree" (1 Peter 2:24). Christ's suffering paid for our wrongdoing.

In addition, discipline and punishment have a different relationship to time. Punishment looks back. It focuses on making payment for wrongs done in the past. Christ's suffering was payment, for example, for our sin. Discipline, however, looks forward. The lessons we learn from discipline help us to not make the same mistakes again: "God disciplines us for our good, that we may share in his holiness" (Heb. 12:10).

How does that help us? It frees us to make mistakes without fear of judgment, without fear of loss of relationship: "Therefore, there is now no condemnation for those who are in Christ Jesus" (Rom. 8:1). The freedom of the cross allows us to practice without having to pay a terrible price. The only danger is consequences—not isolation and judgment.

Take, for example, the mother who tells her ten-year-old, "You smart off again, and I won't love you anymore." The youngster is immediately in a no-win situation. She can either rebel and lose her most important relationship in life, or she can comply and become externally obedient, losing any chance of practicing confrontational skills. Now, compare that response with this, "I'll never stop loving you. That's a constant in my heart. However, if you smart off again you've lost your boom box for three days." The relationship is still intact. There's no condemnation. And the child gets an opportunity to choose responsibility or suffer consequences—with no risk of losing love and safety. This is the way to maturity, to learning to eat solid food: the safe practice of discipline.

The Boundary Needs of Children

What specific needs do boundaries meet in our kids? Limit-setting abilities have several important jobs that will pay enormous dividends throughout life.

Self-Protection

Have you ever seen anything more helpless than the human infant? Human babies are less able to take care of themselves than animal babies. God designed the newborn months as a means for the mother and father (or another caregiver) to connect deeply with their infant, knowing that without their minute-by-minute care, the baby would not survive. All this time and energy translates into an enduring attachment, in which the child learns to feel safe in the world.

God's program of maturation, however, doesn't stop there. Mom and Dad can't always be there to care and provide. The task of protection needs to ultimately pass on to the children. When they grow up, they need to protect themselves.

Boundaries are our way of protecting and safeguarding our souls. Boundaries are designed to keep the good in and the bad out. And skills such as saying no, telling the truth, and maintaining physical distance need to be developed in the family structure to allow the child to take on the responsibility of self-protection.

Consider the following two twelve-year-old boys:

Jimmy is talking with his parents at the dinner table. "Guess what—some kids wanted me to smoke pot with them. When I told them I didn't want to, they said I was a sissy. I told them they were dumb. I like some of them, but if they can't like me because I don't smoke pot, I guess they aren't really my friends."

Paul comes home after school with red eyes, slurred speech, and coordination difficulties. When asked by his concerned parents what is wrong, he denies everything until, finally, he blurts out, "Everybody's doing it. Why do you hate my friends?"

Both Jimmy and Paul come from Christian homes with lots of love and an adherence to biblical values. Why did they turn out so differently? Jimmy's family allowed disagreements between parent and child and gave him practice in the skill of boundary setting, even with them. Jimmy's mom would be holding and hugging her two-year-old when he would get fidgety. He'd say, "Down," meaning, "Let me get a little breathing space, Ma." Fighting her own impulses to hold on to her child, she would set him down on the floor and say, "Wanna play with your trucks?"

Jimmy's dad used the same philosophy. When wrestling with his son on the floor, he tried to pay attention to Jimmy's limits. When the going got too rough, or when Jimmy was tired, he could say, "Stop, Daddy," and Dad would get up. They'd go to another game.

Jimmy was receiving boundary training. He was learning that when he was scared, in discomfort, or wanted to change things, he could say no. This little word gave him a sense of power in his life. It took him out of a helpless or compliant position. And Jimmy could say it without receiving an angry and hurt response, or a manipulative countermove, such as, "But Jimmy, Mommy needs to hold you now, okay?"

Jimmy learned from infancy on that his boundaries were good and that he could use them to protect himself. He learned to resist things that weren't good for him.

A hallmark of Jimmy's family was permission to disagree. When, for example, Jimmy would fight his parents about his bedtime, they never withdrew or punished him for disagreeing. Instead, they would listen to his reasoning, and, if it seemed appropriate, they would change their minds. If not, they would maintain their boundaries.

Jimmy was also given a vote in some family matters. When family night out would come up, his parents listened to his opinion on whether they should go to a movie, play board games, or play basketball. Was this a family with no limits? On the contrary! It was a family who took boundary setting seriously—as a skill to develop in its children.

This was good practice for resisting in the evil day (Eph. 5:16), when some of Jimmy's friends turned on him and pressured him to take drugs. How was Jimmy able to refuse?

Because by then, he'd had ten or eleven years of practice disagreeing with people who were important to him without losing their love. He didn't fear abandonment in standing up against his friends. He'd done it many times successfully with his family with no loss of love.

Paul, on the other hand, came from a different family setting. In his home, no had two different responses. His mom would be hurt and withdraw and pout. She would send guilt messages, such as "How can you say no to your mom who loves you?" His dad would get angry, threaten him, and say things like, "Don't talk back to me, Mister."

It didn't take long for Paul to learn that to have his way, he had to be externally compliant. He developed a strong yes on the outside, seeming to agree with his family's values and control. Whatever he thought about a subject—the dinner menu, TV restrictions, church choices, clothes, or curfews—he stuffed inside.

Once, when he had tried to resist his mother's hug, she had immediately withdrawn from him, pushing him away with the words, "Someday you'll feel sorry for hurting your mother's feelings like that." Day by day, Paul was being trained to not set limits.

As a result of his learned boundarylessness, Paul seemed to be a content, respectful son. The teens, however, are a crucible for kids. We find out what kind of character has actually been built into our children during this difficult passage.

Paul folded. He gave in to his friends' pressure. Is it any wonder that the first people he said no to were his parents—at twelve years old? Resentment and the years of not having boundaries were beginning to erode the compliant, easy-to-live-with false self he'd developed to survive.

Taking Responsibility for One's Needs

The group therapy session I was leading was quiet. I'd just asked Janice an unanswerable question. The question was, "What do you need?" She looked confused, became thoughtful, and sat back in her chair.

Janice had just described a week of painful loss: her

husband had made moves to separate, her kids were out of control, and her job was in jeopardy. The concern on the faces of the group members, who were all working on issues of attachment and safety, was evident. Yet no one knew quite how to help. So when I asked the question, I was asking it for all of us. But Janice couldn't answer.

This was typical of Janice's background. She'd spent most of her childhood taking responsibility for her parents' feelings. The peacemaker of the house, she was always smoothing over the ruffled feathers of either parent, with soothing words like, "Mom, I'm sure Dad didn't mean to blow up at you—he's had a rough day."

The result of such unbiblical responsibility toward her family was clear in Janice's life: a sense of overresponsibility for others and a lack of attunement toward her own needs. Janice had radar out for the hurts of others; but the radar pointed her way was broken. It was no wonder she couldn't answer my question. Janice didn't understand her own God-given, legitimate needs. She had no vocabulary for this thinking.

The story does, however, have a happy ending. One of the group members said, "If I were in your shoes, I know what I'd need. I'd really need to know that you people in this room cared for me, that you didn't see me as a colossal, shameful failure, and that you'd pray for me and let me call you on the phone this week for support."

Janice's eyes began watering. Something about her friend's empathic statement touched her in a place she couldn't herself touch. And she allowed the comfort that comes from others who have been comforted to take its place inside her (2 Cor. 1:4).

Janice's story illustrates the second fruit of boundary development in our children: the ability to take ownership of, or responsibility for, our own needs. God intends for us to know when we're hungry, lonely, in trouble, overwhelmed, or in need of a break—and then to take initiative to get what we need. The Scriptures present Jesus as understanding this point when he left a crowd of people in a boat in a time of great ministry and need: "because so many people were coming and going that [he and his disciples] did not even have a chance to eat" (Mark 6:31).

Boundaries play a primary role in this process. Our limits create a spiritual and emotional space, a separateness, between ourselves and others. This allows our needs to be heard and understood. Without a solid sense of boundaries, it becomes difficult to filter out our needs from those of others. There is too much static in the relationship.

When children can be taught to experience their own needs, as opposed to those of others, they have been given a genuine advantage in life. They are able to better avoid the burnout that comes from not taking care of one's self.

How can we help our children experience their own individual needs? The best thing a parent can do is to encourage verbal expression of those needs, even when they don't "go with the family flow." When children have permission to ask for something that goes against the grain— even though they might not receive it—they develop a sense of what they need.

Below are some ways you can help your children:

- Allow them to talk about their anger.
- Allow them to express grief, loss, or sadness without trying to cheer them up and talk them out of their feelings.
- Encourage them to ask questions and not assume your words are the equivalent of Scripture (this takes a pretty secure parent!).
- Ask them what they are feeling when they seem isolated or distressed; help them put words to their negative feelings. Do not try to keep things light for a false sense of cooperation and family closeness.

The first aspect of taking ownership over one's needs, then, is to identify them. That's where our spiritual radar comes in. Janice's radar was broken and undeveloped, and she wasn't able to identify her needs.

The second aspect of taking ownership is to initiate responsible caretaking for ourselves—as opposed to placing the burden on someone else. We must allow our children to

experience the painful consequences of their own irresponsibility and mistakes. This is the "training" of Hebrews 5:14
and the "discipline" of Hebrews 12. By the time they are
ready to leave home, our children should have internalized a
deep sense of personal responsibility for their lives. They
should hold these convictions:

- My success or failure in life largely depends on me.
- Though I am to look to God and others for comfort and
  instruction, I alone am responsible for my choices.
- Though I am deeply affected by my significant relationships throughout my life, I can't blame my problems on
  anyone but myself.
- Though I will always fail and need support, I can't
  depend on some overresponsible individual to constantly bail me out of spiritual, emotional, financial, or
  relational crises.

This sense of "my life is up to me" is founded in God's
concern that we take responsibility for our lives. He wants us
to use our talents in productive ways, as Jesus discussed in
the parable of the talents (Matt. 25:14–30). And this sense of
responsibility will follow us all through our adult lives—and
even beyond the grave, at the judgment seat of Christ.

You can imagine how well not taking ownership over our
lives will come across to the Lord then: "But I had a
dysfunctional family." "But I was lonely." "But I didn't have
much energy." The rationalizing "buts" will have as much
impact as the excuses of the servant in the parable of the
talents did. This isn't to say that we aren't deeply influenced
for better or worse by our backgrounds and our various
stressors. We certainly are. But we are ultimately responsible
for what we do with our injured, immature souls.

Wise parents allow their children to undergo "safe
suffering." "Safe suffering" means allowing a child to
experience age-appropriate consequences. Allowing a six-
year-old to go outside after dark isn't training her for
adulthood. She is making decisions that she doesn't have the
maturity to make. She shouldn't be placed in a position of
making these choices in the first place.

Pat's parents allowed their daughter to experience safe suffering. At the start of senior high, they gave Pat an entire semester's allowance. Pat was responsible for paying for her school meals, clothing, social outings, and extracurricular activities. The amount was enough for this and a little more. On the surface it looked like a teenager's dream—all this money and no restrictions on how she spent it!

The first semester Pat bought some beautiful outfits. She went out to lots of functions with her friends. And she even treated them several times. That lasted for about one month out of the three and a half. The next two and a half months were lean ones. Pat stayed home a lot, saving her remaining money for school lunches, and she wore her new outfits over and over again.

The next semester was better—and by the beginning of her sophomore year, she had established a bank account and a workable budget. Pat was developing boundaries. Normally a budding shopping addict, she began saying no to clothes, CD's, food, and magazines that normally would have been a minimum requirement for her. She began learning to take responsibility for her own life. And she didn't end up like many college graduates who, after years of having someone else bail them out, can't cook, clean, or keep a checkbook balanced.

It's important to tie consequences as closely to the actions of the child as possible. This best replicates real life.

Homework projects are another area in which parents can either help the child take on responsibility—or create the illusion of the eternal, omnipresent parent who will always take up the slack. It's difficult when your child comes to you tearfully, saying, "I have a ten-page report due tomorrow— and I just started." Our impulse, as loving parents, is to bail them out by doing the research, or the organization, or the typing. Or all three.

Why do we do this? Because we love our kids. We long for the best for them just as God longs for the best for us. And yet, just as God allows us to experience our failures, we may need to let our kids mar a good report card with a bad grade. This is often the consequence of not planning ahead.

Having a Sense of Control and Choice

"I won't go to the dentist—and you can't make me go!" Pamela stamped her eleven-year-old feet and scowled at her father, Sal, who was waiting at the front door.

There had been a time when Sal would have reacted in a knee-jerk fashion to Pamela's power move. He would have said something like, "Well, we'll see about that!" and physically dragged the screaming child into the car.

However, lots of family counseling and reading up on these issues had prepared Sal for the inevitable. Calmly he said to her, "You're absolutely right, Honey. I can't make you go to the dentist. If you don't want to go, you don't have to. But remember our rule: if you choose not to go, you're also choosing not to go to the party tomorrow night. I'll certainly respect either decision. Shall I cancel your appointment?"

Pamela looked perplexed and thought a minute. Then, slowly, she replied, "I'll go. But I'm not going because I have to." Pamela was right. She was choosing to go to her appointment because she wanted to attend the party.

Children need to have a sense of control and choice in their lives. They need to see themselves not as the dependent, helpless pawns of parents, but as choosing, willing, initiative-taking agents of their own lives.

Children begin life in a helpless, dependent fashion. Godly parenting, however, seeks to help children learn to think, make decisions, and master their environment in all aspects of life. This runs the gamut of deciding what to wear in the morning to what courses to take in school. Learning to make age-appropriate decisions helps children have a sense of security and control in their lives.

Anxious and well-meaning parents attempt to prevent their children from making painful decisions. They shield them from fouling up and skinning their knees. Their motto is, "Here, let me decide that for you." The result is that kids become atrophied in a very important part of the image of God that should be developing in their character: their assertion, or change-making abilities. Children need a sense that their lives, their destinies are largely theirs to determine, within the province of God's sovereignty. This helps them weigh choices, rather than avoid them. They learn to appreciate the consequences of choices made, rather than resenting the choices made for them.

Delaying Gratification of Goals

The word *now* was made for young children. It's where they live. Try telling a two-year-old she can have dessert tomorrow. She doesn't buy it. That means "never" to her. Newborns, in fact, don't have the capacity to understand "later." That's why a six-month-old panics when Mom leaves the room. He is convinced that she is irrevocably gone forever.

Yet, sometime in our development we learn the value of "later," of delaying one good for a greater good. We call this skill *delay of gratification*. It's the ability to say no to our impulses, wishes, and desires for some gain down the road.

The Scriptures place great value on this ability. God uses this skill to help us see the benefits of planning and preparing. Jesus is our prime example, "Who for the joy set before him endured the cross, scorning its shame, and sat down at the right hand of the throne of God" (Heb. 12:2).

Generally, this skill isn't relevant until after the first year of life, as bonding needs take precedence during that time. However, teaching delay of gratification can begin quickly by the beginning of the second year. Dessert comes after carrots, not before.

Older children also need to learn this skill. The family can't buy certain clothes or recreational items until later in the year. Again, the boundaries developed during this process are invaluable later in life. They can prevent a child from becoming an adult who is a broken, chaotic, impulse-driven slave to Madison Avenue. Our children can become like ants, who are self-sufficient, instead of sluggards, who are always in crisis (Prov. 6:6–11).

Learning how to delay gratification helps children have a goal orientation. They learn to save time and money for things that are important to them, and they value what they have chosen to buy. One family I know had the son save up his money for his first car. He began with a plan, with Dad's help, when he was thirteen. When all his weekend and summer jobs finally paid off in a car when he was sixteen, he treated that car like it was fine china—you could eat lunch off the hood. He had counted the cost, and valued the result (Luke 14:28).

Respecting the Limits of Others

From an early age, children need to be able to accept the limits of parents, siblings, and friends. They need to know that others don't always want to play with them, that others may not want to watch the same TV shows they want, and that others may want to eat dinner at a different restaurant than they do. They need to know that the world doesn't revolve around them.

This is important for a couple of reasons. First, the ability to learn to accept limits teaches us to take responsibility for ourselves. Knowing that others are not always available for us, at our beck and call, helps us to become inwardly directed instead of externally driven. It helps us carry our own knapsack.

Have you ever been around a child who can't hear no, who keeps whining, cajoling, throwing a tantrum, or pouting till he gets his way? The problem is, the longer we hate and resist the limits of others, the more dependent we will be on others. We expect others to take care of us, rather than simply taking care of ourselves.

At any rate, God has constructed life itself to teach us this law. It's the only way we can live on this planet together. Sooner or later, someone will say a no to us that we can't ignore. It's built into the fabric of life. Observe the progression of nos in the life of the person who resists others' limits:

1. the no of parents
2. the no of siblings
3. the no of schoolteachers
4. the no of school friends
5. the no of bosses and supervisors
6. the no of spouses

7. the no of health problems from overeating, alcoholism, or an irresponsible lifestyle
8. the no of police, the courts, and even prison

Some people learn to accept boundaries early in life, even as early as stage number one. But some people have to go all the way to number eight before they get the picture that we have to accept life's limits: "Stop listening to instruction, my son, and you will stray from the words of knowledge" (Prov. 19:27). Many out-of-control adolescents don't mature until their thirties, when they become tired of not having a steady job and a place to stay. They have to hit bottom financially, and sometimes they may even have to live on the streets for a while. In time, they begin sticking with a career, saving money, and starting to grow up. They gradually begin to accept life's limits.

No matter how tough we think we are, there's always someone tougher. If we don't teach our children to take a no, someone who loves them far less may take on the job. Someone tougher. Someone stronger. And most parents would much rather spare having their children go through this suffering. The earlier we teach limits, the better.

A second, even more important, reason why accepting the limits of others is important for kids is this: *Heeding others' boundaries helps children to love.* At its heart, the idea of respecting others' boundaries is the basis for empathy, or loving others as we'd like to be loved. Children need to be given the grace of having their no respected, and they need to learn to give that same grace to others. As they feel empathy for the needs of others, they mature and deepen in their love for God and others: "We love because he first loved us" (1 John 4:19).

Say, for example, that your six-year-old accidentally but carelessly bonks you on the head hard with a softball. To ignore it, or act like it didn't hurt, is to give the child the feeling that his actions have no impact. He can then avoid any sense of responsibility or awareness of others' needs or hurts. However, telling him, "I know you didn't do it on purpose, but that ball really hurt me—try to be a little more careful" helps him see, without condemnation, that he can hurt people he loves and that his actions do matter.

If this principle isn't taught, it's difficult for children to grow up as loving people. Frequently, they become self-centered or controlling. At that point, God's program of maturity is more difficult. A client of mine had been trained by his family to ignore others' limits. His subsequent manipulation had landed him in jail for stealing. Yet this process, painful though it was, taught him empathy.

"I really never knew that other people had needs and hurts," he once explained to me. "I was raised to concentrate on Number One. And when I began getting confronted on my lack of respect for others' needs, something happened inside. A space opened up inside my heart for others. I didn't ignore my own needs—but for the first time, I saw progress. I actually started feeling guilty about how my actions have hurt my wife and family."

Did he have a long way to go? Absolutely. But he was on the right road. Learning boundaries later in life was a start to becoming an authentically, biblically loving person.

Seasonal Boundaries: Age-Appropriate Limits Training

If this was the first chapter you turned to when you glanced over the table of contents, chances are you're a parent. Chances are also that you may be experiencing boundary difficulties with your children. Perhaps you're reading this simply in an effort to prevent problems. But more likely you're in some pain from which you need relief: Your newborn won't stop shrieking. Your toddler runs the household. Your elementary school student has behavioral problems at school. Your junior high kid smarts off. Your high schooler is drinking.

All of these issues indicate possible boundary problems. And this section provides an outline on the age-appropriate boundary tasks your children should be learning. As parents, we need to take into consideration our children's developmental needs and abilities to avoid asking them to do something they can't do, or to avoid asking too little of them.

Below are the basic tasks for the different stages of

childhood. For more detailed information on birth to age three, refer to Chapter 4 on how boundaries are developed in childhood.

Birth to Five Months

At this stage, the newborn needs to establish an attachment with Mother, Dad, or the primary caregiver. A sense of belonging, of being safe and welcome are the tasks the child needs to accomplish. Setting limits is not as much an issue here as providing security for the infant.

The only real boundary here is the soothing presence of the mother. She protects the infant. Mom's job is to help her newborn contain intense, frightening, and conflicting feelings. Left by themselves, infants are terrorized by their aloneness and lack of internal structure.

For centuries mothers—including Mary, Jesus' mother— have swaddled their babies, or wrapped cloths tightly around them. While swaddling keeps the baby's body heat regulated, the tight wrappings also help the infant feel safe— a sort of external boundary. The baby knows where he or she begins and ends. When newborns are undressed, they often panic about the loss of structure around them.

Some well-meaning Christian teachers call for infant training theories that schedule the feeding and holding of infants. These techniques try to teach an infant not to cry or demand comfort because "the child is in control instead of the parent," or because "that demand is evidence of the child's selfish, sinful nature." These theories can be horribly destructive when not understood biblically or developmentally.

The screaming four-month-old child is trying to find out whether the world is a reasonably safe place or not. She is in a state of deep terror and isolation. She hasn't learned to feel comfort when no one is around. To put her on the parents' schedule instead of her own for holding and feeding is to "condemn the innocent," as Jesus said (Matt. 12:7).

These teachers say their programs are biblical because they work. "When I stopped picking her up from her crib at night, my four-month-old stopped crying," they'll say. That may be true. But another explanation for the cessation of crying is infant depression, a condition in which the child gives up hope and withdraws. "Hope deferred makes the heart sick" (Prov. 13:12).

Teaching delay of gratification shouldn't begin until after the first year of life, when a foundation of safety has been established between baby and mother. Just as grace always precedes truth (John 1:17), attachment must come before separation.

Five to Ten Months

As we learned in Chapter 4, children in the last half of the first year of life are in the "hatching" phase. They are learning that "Mother and I aren't the same." There's a scary, fascinating world out there that babies literally crawl toward. Though they have tremendous dependency needs, infants are beginning to move out of their oneness with their mom.

To help their children develop good boundaries during this stage, parents need to encourage attempts at separateness, while still being the anchors the child clings to. Allow your child to be fascinated with people and objects other than you. Make your home a safe place for your baby to explore.

Helping your children hatch, however, doesn't mean neglecting the deep attachment necessary for their internal foundation, their rootedness and groundedness. This is still an infant's primary work. You need to carefully tend to your child's needs for bonding and emotional safety, while at the same time allowing the child to look outward, beyond you.

Many mothers find this transition from their child's love affair with them to the big wide world difficult. The loss of such a deep intimacy is great, especially after the time spent in pregnancy and childbirth. The responsible mother, however, will strive to get her own closeness needs met by other adults in her life. She will encourage the "hatching" of her baby, knowing she is preparing him or her to be equipped to "leave and cleave."

At this point, most infants don't yet have the ability to

understand and respond appropriately to the word *no.* Keeping them out of danger by picking them up and removing them from unsafe places is the best route.

Ten to Eighteen Months

At this "practicing" stage, your baby begins not only talking, but also walking—and the possibilities stretch out before her. The world is this child's oyster—and she spends a lot of time finding ways to open it up and play with it. Now she has the emotional and cognitive ability to understand and respond to the word *no.*

Boundaries become increasingly important during this stage, both having and hearing limits. Allowing the no muscle to begin developing is crucial at this age. No is your child's way of finding out whether taking responsibility for her life has good results—or whether no causes someone to withdraw. As parents, learn to rejoice in your baby's no.

At the same time, you have the delicate task of helping your child see that she is not the center of the universe. There are limits in life. There are consequences for scribbling on doors and screaming in church. Yet you need to do this without quenching the sense of excitement and interest in the world that she has been developing.

Eighteen to Thirty-six Months

The child is now learning the important task of taking responsibility for a separate yet connected soul. The practicing child gives way to the more sober child who is realizing that life has limits, but that being separate does not mean that we can't be attached. In this phase, the following abilities are goals:

1. The ability to be emotionally attached to others, without giving up a sense of self and one's freedom to be apart.
2. The ability to say appropriate nos to others without fear of loss of love.

3. The ability to take appropriate nos from others without withdrawing emotionally.

At eighteen to thirty-six months the child needs to learn to be autonomous. She wants to be free of parental rule, but this desire is conflicted by her deep dependence on her parents. The wise parent will help her gain a sense of individualism and accept her loss of omnipotence, but without losing attachment.

To teach a child boundaries at this stage, you need to respect her no whenever appropriate, yet maintain your own firm no. It's easy for you to try to win all the skirmishes. But there are simply too many. You will end up losing the war because you've lost the big picture—the attachment. Don't waste your energy trying to control a random whirlwind. Pick your battles carefully and choose the important ones to win.

Wise parents will rejoice in children's fun times, but will consistently and uniformly keep solid limits with the practicing child. At this age, children can learn the rules of the house as well as the consequences for breaking them. One workable process of discipline is listed below:

1. *First infraction.* Tell the child not to color on the bedsheet. Try to help the child meet her need in another way—using a coloring book or a pad of plain paper to crayon on instead of a bedsheet, for example.

2. *Second infraction.* Again, tell the child no, and state the consequence. She will need to take a time out for one minute or lose the crayons for the rest of the day.

3. *Third infraction.* Administer the consequences, explaining why, then give the child a few minutes to be angry and separate from parents.

4. *Comfort and reconnection.* Hold and comfort the child, helping her reattach with you. This helps her differentiate between consequences and a loss of love. Painful consequences should never include a loss of connection.

Three to Five Years

During this phase, children move into a period of sexrole development. Each child identifies with the same-sex parent. Little boys want to be like Dad, and little girls like Mom. They also develop competitive feelings toward that same parent, wishing to marry the opposite-sex parent, defeating the same-sex parent in the process. They are preparing for adult sex roles later in life.

Boundary work by parents is important here. Gently but firmly, mothers need to allow their daughters to identify and to compete. They must also deal with the possessiveness of their sons, letting them know that "I know you'd like to marry Mom, but Mom's married to Dad." Fathers have to do the same job with their sons and daughters. This helps children learn to identify with the opposite-sex parent and take on appropriate characteristics.

Parents who fear the budding sexuality of their children will often become critical of these intense longings. Their own fear may cause them to attack or to shame their child, causing her to repress her sexuality. At the other extreme, the needy parent will sometimes emotionally, or even physically, seduce the child of the opposite sex. The mother who tells her son that "Daddy doesn't understand me— you're the only one who can" is ensuring years of confusion about sex roles for her son. Mature parents need to keep a boundary between allowing sex role typing to emerge—and keeping the lines between parent and child clear.

Six to Eleven Years

During what is called latency, or the years of industry, the child is preparing for the upcoming thrust into adolescence. These years are the last true years of childhood. They are important for learning task orientation through schoolwork and play, and for learning to connect with same-sex peers.

An extremely busy time for work and friends, this period carries its own boundary tasks for parents. Here, you need to help your kids establish the fundamentals of tasks: doing homework, house chores, and projects. They need to learn planning and the discipline of keeping at a job until it's finished. They need to learn such boundary work as delay of gratification, goal orientation, and budgeting time.

Eleven to Eighteen Years

Adolescence, the final step before adulthood, involves important tasks such as sexual maturation, a sense of solidifying identity in any surrounding, career leanings, and love choices. It can be a frightening yet exciting time for both child and parents.

By this point, the "de-parenting" process should have begun. Things are beginning to shift between you and your youngster. Instead of controlling your child, you influence her. You increase her freedom, as well as responsibility. You renegotiate restrictions, limits, and consequences with more flexibility.

All of these changes are like the countdown of a NASA space shuttle. You are preparing for the launching of a young adult into the world. Wise parents keep the imminent catapulting of their teens into society in the back of their minds at all times. The question they must always struggle with is no longer, "How can I make them behave?" but rather, "How can I help them survive on their own?"

Teens need to be setting their own relational, scheduling, values, and money boundaries as much as possible. And they should suffer real-life consequences when they cross their boundaries. The seventeen-year-old who is still disciplined with TV and phone restrictions may have real problems at college in one year. Professors, deans, and residence hall assistants don't impose these kinds of restrictions; they resort to tactics such as failing grades, suspension, and expulsion.

If you are the parent of a teen who hasn't had boundary training, you may feel at a loss about what to do. You need to begin at whatever point your teens are. When their ability to say and hear no is deficient, clarifying house rules and consequences can often help in the last few years before the youth leaves home.

Symptoms such as the following, however, may indicate a more serious problem:

• Isolation of the teen from family members
• Depressed mood

- Rebellious behavior
- Continual conflict in family
- Wrong type of friends
- School problems
- Eating disorders
- Alcohol use
- Drug use
- Suicidal ideas or behavior

Many parents, observing these problems, react with either too many boundaries, or too few. The too-strict parent runs the risk of alienating the almost-adult from the home connection. The too-lenient parent wants to be the child's best friend at a time the teen needs someone to respect. At this point, parents should consider consulting a therapist who understands teen issues. The stakes are simply too high to ignore professional help.

Types of Discipline

Many parents are confused by how to teach children to respect boundaries. They read countless books and articles on spanking, time-outs, restrictions, and allowances. While this question is beyond the scope of this book, a few thoughts may help organize the searching parent.

1. *Consequences are intended to increase the child's sense of responsibility and control over his life.* Discipline that increases the child's sense of helplessness isn't helpful. Dragging a sixteen-year-old girl to class doesn't build the internal motivation she'll need in two years when she's in college. A system of rewards and consequences that help her choose school for her own benefit has much better possibilities for success.

2. *Consequences must be age-appropriate.* You need to think through the meaning of your discipline. Spanking, for example, humiliates and angers a teenager; however, administered correctly, it can help build structure for a four-year-old.

3. *Consequences must be related to the seriousness of the infraction.* Just as the penal system has different prison stays

for different crimes, you must be able to distinguish between minor and severe infractions. Otherwise, severe penalties become meaningless.

A client once told me, "I got whippings for little things and for big things. So I started getting more involved in big things. It just seemed more efficient." Once you've been sentenced to death, you don't have much to gain by being good!

4. *The goal of boundaries is an internal sense of motivation, with self-induced consequences.* Successful parenting means that our kids want to get out of bed and go to school, be responsible, be empathic, and be caring because that's important to them, not because it's important to us. It's only when love and limits are a genuine part of the child's character that true maturity can occur. Otherwise, we are raising compliant parrots who will, in time, self-destruct.

Parents have a sober responsibility: teaching their children to have an internal sense of boundaries and to respect the boundaries of others. It's sober because the Bible says it's sober: "Not many of you should presume to be teachers, my brothers, because you know that we who teach will be judged more strictly" (James 3:1).

There are certainly no guarantees that our training will be heeded. Children have the responsibility to listen and learn. The older they are, the more responsibility they have. Yet as we learn about our own boundary issues, take responsibility for them, and grow up ourselves, we increase our kids' chances to learn boundaries in an adult world in which these abilities will be sorely needed—every day of their lives.

11

Boundaries and Work

I n Sunday school we were studying Adam and Eve and the Fall. I learned that the Fall was the beginning of everything "bad." That day I went home and said to my mother, "I don't like Adam and Eve. If it weren't for them, I wouldn't have to clean up my room!"

Work at age eight wasn't fun, and because it wasn't fun, it was bad. Because it was bad, it was Adam's fault. A simple theological theory for a youngster, but it was youthful heresy. Work existed before the Fall; it was always part of God's plan for humanity. He planned for people to do two things. They would subdue and they would rule (Gen. 1:28). They would bring the earth under their domain, and they would manage it. That sounds a lot like work!

But because Eden was paradise, our difficulties with work came later, after the Fall. God said to Adam: "Cursed is the ground because of you; through painful toil you will eat of it all the days of your life. It will produce thorns and thistles for you, and you will eat the plants of the field. By the sweat of your brow you will eat your food until you return to the ground, since from it you were taken; for dust you are and to dust you will return" (Gen. 3:17–19).

Other aspects of the Fall also affected our work. The first is the tendency toward disownership. We talked in earlier chapters about the boundary problem of not taking responsibility for what is ours. This started in the garden when Adam and Eve tried to pass the blame on to another for their original act of sinning. Adam blamed Eve; Eve blamed the serpent (Gen. 3:11–13). They were disowning their responsibility and blaming another. Their theme was "Get the attention off of me." This tendency to blame another is a key work problem.

The Fall also divided love from work. Before the Fall, Adam was connected to the love of God and from that loved state, he worked. After the Fall, he was not motivated out of perfect love, but he had to work as a part of the fallen world's curse and the law. The love-motivated "want to" became a law-motivated "should."

Paul tells us the law's "should" increases our wish to rebel (Rom. 5:20); it makes us angry at what we "should" do (Rom. 4:15); and it arouses our motivations to do the wrong thing (Rom. 7:5). All of this adds up to the human race being unable to take responsibility and work effectively by owning its behaviors, talents, and choices. No wonder we have work problems.

In this chapter, we want to look at how boundaries can help resolve many work-related problems, as well as how they can help you to be happier and more fulfilled at the work you do.

Work and Character Development

Christians often have a warped way of looking at work. Unless someone is working "in the ministry," they see his work as secular. However, this view of work distorts the biblical picture. All of us—not only full-time ministers— have gifts and talents that we contribute to humanity. We all have a vocation, a "calling" into service. Wherever we work, whatever we do, we are to do "unto the Lord" (Col. 3:23).

Jesus used parables about work to teach us how to grow spiritually. These parables deal with money, with completing tasks, with faithful stewardship of a job, and with honest emotional dealings in work. They all teach character development in the context of relating to God and others. They teach a work ethic based on love under God.

Work is a spiritual activity. In our work, we are made in the image of God, who is himself a worker, a manager, a creator, a developer, a steward, and a healer. To be a

Christian is to be a co-laborer with God in the community of humanity. By giving to others we find true fulfillment.

The New Testament teaches that jobs offer more than temporal fulfillment and rewards on earth. Work is the place to develop our character in preparation for the work that we will do forever. With that in mind, let's look at how setting boundaries in the workplace can help us to grow spiritually.

Problems in the Workplace

A lack of boundaries creates problems in the workplace. In consulting for corporations, I have seen lack of boundaries as the major problem in many management squabbles. If people took responsibility for their own work and set clear limits, most of the problems for which I get consulted would not exist.

Let's see how applying boundaries can solve some common problems in the workplace.

Problem #1: Getting Saddled with Another Person's Responsibilities

Susie is an administrative assistant in a small company that plans training sessions for industry. She's responsible for booking the training sessions and managing the speakers' schedules. A co-worker, Jack, is responsible for the training facilities. He takes the materials to the site, sets up the equipment, and orders the food. Together, Susie and Jack make the events happen.

After a few months of really liking her work, Susie began to lose energy. Eventually, her friend and co-worker, Lynda, asked her what was wrong. Susie couldn't put her finger on the problem at first. Then she realized: The problem was Jack!

Jack had been asking Susie to "pick this up for me while you're out," or "please bring this box of materials to the workshop." Slowly, Jack was shifting his responsibilities onto Susie.

"You have to stop doing Jack's work," Lynda told Susie. "Just do your own work and don't worry about him."

"But what if things go wrong?" Susie asked.

Lynda shrugged. "Then they'll blame Jack. It's not your responsibility."

"Jack will be angry with me for not helping," Susie said.

"Let him," said Lynda. "His anger can't hurt you as much as his poor work habits can."

So Susie began to set limits on Jack. She told him, "I will not have time to bring the materials for you this week." And when Jack ran out of time to do things himself, Susie said, "I'm sorry that you have not done that before now, and I understand that you are in a bind. Maybe next time you will plan better. That's not my job."

Some trainers were angry that their equipment was not set up, and customers were angry that no food was provided for the break. But the boss tracked down the problem to the person who was responsible—Jack—and told him to shape up, or find another job. In the end, Susie began to like work again, and Jack began to get more responsible. All because Susie set boundaries and stuck to them.

If you are being saddled with another person's responsibilities and feel resentful, you need to take responsibility for your feelings, and realize that your unhappiness is not your co-worker's fault, but your own. In this as in any other boundary conflict, you first must take responsibility *for* yourself.

Then you must act responsibly *to* your co-worker. Go to your co-worker and explain your situation. When he asks you to do something that is not your responsibility, say no and refuse to do whatever it is that he wants you to do. If he gets angry at you for saying no, be firm about your boundaries and empathize with his anger. Don't get angry back. To fight anger with anger is to get hooked into his game. Keep your emotional distance and say, "I am sorry if this upsets you. But that job is not my responsibility. I hope you get it worked out."

If he continues to argue, tell him that you are finished discussing it; he can come and find you when he is ready to talk about something else. Do not fall into the trap of justifying why you can't do his work for him. You will be slipping into his thinking that you should do his work if you are able to, and he will try to find a way that you can. You owe no one an explanation about why you will not do something that is not your responsibility.

Many overresponsible people who work next to under-responsible people bear the consequences for their co-workers. Always covering for them, or bailing them out, they are not enjoying their work or their relationships with these people. Their lack of boundaries is hurting them, as well as keeping the other person from growing. If you are one of these people, you need to learn to set boundaries.

Sometimes, however, a co-worker will genuinely need some extra help. It is perfectly legitimate to bail out a responsible co-worker, or to make special concessions to a colleague who uses those concessions responsibly to get well. This is love, and good companies operate lovingly.

In our work as psychologists at the same hospital, we often cover hospital duty for each other or take each other's "on call" time. But if one of us started taking advantage of the other, we would need to stop that. Covering for the other at that point would not be helpful, but would enable a bad pattern.

Favors and sacrifices are part of the Christian life. Enabling is not. Learn to tell the difference by seeing if your giving is helping the other to become better or worse. The Bible requires responsible action out of the one who is given to. If you do not see it after a season, set limits (Luke 13:9).

Problem #2: Working Too Much Overtime

When I first went into practice, I hired a woman for twenty hours a week to run my office. On her second day in the office, I gave her a pile of things to do. About ten minutes later, she knocked at my door, stack of papers in hand.

"What can I do for you, Laurie?" I asked.

"You have a problem," she told me.

"I do? What is it?" I asked, not having the vaguest idea what she was talking about.

"You hired me for twenty hours a week, and you have just given me about forty hours of work. Which twenty would you like done?"

She was right. I did have a problem. I had not managed my workload very well. I was either going to have to spend more on help, cut back on projects, or hire someone else. But she was right: it was *my* problem, not hers. I had to take responsibility for it and fix it. Laurie was telling me what that everpresent sign says: "Poor planning on your part does not constitute an emergency on my part."

Many bosses aren't so lucky. Their employees take responsibility for their lack of planning and never set limits on them. They are never forced to look at their lack of boundaries until it's too late, until they have lost a good employee to exhaustion or burnout. Such bosses need clear limits, but many employees are afraid to set them, as Laurie did, because they need the job or they fear disapproval.

If you are in a situation in which you're doing lots of extra work because you "need the job" and because you are afraid of being let go, you have a problem. If you are working more overtime than you want to, you are in bondage to your job. You are a slave, not an employee under contract. Clear and responsible contracts tell all parties involved what is expected of them, and they can be enforced. Jobs should have clear descriptions of duties and qualifications.

As hard as it sounds, you need to take responsibility for yourself and take steps to change your situation. Here are some suggested steps you may wish to take:

1. *Set boundaries on your work.* Decide how much overtime you are willing to do. Some overtime during seasonal crunches may be expected of you.

2. *Review your job description,* if one exists.

3. *Make a list of the tasks you need to complete in the next month.* Make a copy of the list and assign your own priority to each item. Indicate on this copy any tasks that are not part of your job description.

4. *Make an appointment to see your boss to discuss your job overload.* Together you should review the list of tasks you need to complete in the next month. Have your boss prioritize the tasks. If your boss wants all the tasks done, and you cannot complete these tasks in the time you are willing to give, your boss may need to hire temporary help to complete those tasks. You may also wish to review your job

description with your boss at this time if you think you are doing things that fall outside your domain.

If your boss still has unreasonable expectations of you, you may wish to take a co-worker or two along with you to a second meeting (according to the biblical model in Matthew 18), or you may wish to discuss your problem with the appropriate person in your personnel department. If even then he remains unreasonable about what he thinks you can accomplish, you may need to begin looking for other job opportunities within your company or outside.

You may need to go to night school and get some further training to open up other opportunities. You may need to chase down hundreds of employment ads and send out stacks of resumes. (Consult the book *How to Get a Job* by James Bramlett for information on job searches.[1]) You may wish to start your own business. You may wish to start an emergency fund to survive between quitting your present job and starting a new one.

Whatever you do, remember that your job overload is your responsibility and your problem. If your job is driving you crazy, you need to do something about it. Own the problem. Stop being a victim of an abusive situation and start setting some limits.

Problem #3: Misplaced Priorities

We have talked about setting limits on someone else. You also need to set limits on yourself. You need to realize how much time and energy you have, and manage your work accordingly. Know what you can do and when you can do it, and say no to everything else. Learn to know your limits and enforce them, as Laurie did. Say to your team or your boss, "If I am going to do A today, I will not be able to do B until Wednesday. Is that okay or do we need to rethink which one I need to be working on?"

Effective workers do two things: they strive to do excellent work, and they spend their time on the most important things. Many people do excellent work but allow themselves to get sidetracked by unimportant things; they may do unimportant things very well! They feel like they are doing a great job, but their boss is upset because essential goals are not being met. Then they feel unappreciated and resentful because they have put out so much effort. They were working hard, but they weren't placing boundaries on what they allowed to take up their time, and the really important things did not get their attention.

Say no to the unimportant, and say no to the inclination to do less than your best. If you are doing your best work on the most important things, you will reach your goals.

In addition to saying no to the unimportant, you need to make a plan to accomplish the important things, and erect some fences around your tasks. Realize your limits, and make sure you do not allow work to control your life. Having limits will force you to prioritize. If you make a commitment to spend only so many hours a week on work, you will spend those hours more wisely. If you think your time is limitless, you may say yes to everything. Say yes to the best, and sometimes you may need to say no to the good.

One man's ministry required a lot of travel, so he and his wife put their heads together and decided that he would spend no more than one hundred nights a year on the road. When he gets an offer he has to check his time budget and see if this is something he wants to spend some of his nights on. This plan forces him to be more selective in his travel, thereby saving time for the rest of his life.

A company president who was allowing work to keep him away from home too much made a commitment to spend only forty hours a week in the office. At first, he really struggled because he wasn't used to budgeting his time and commitments so closely. Slowly though, when he realized that he only had so much time, he began to spend it more wisely. He even got more accomplished because he was forced to work smarter.

Work will grow to fill the time you have set aside for it. If a meeting does not have an agenda with time limits, discussion could be endless. Allot time for certain things, and then keep your limits. You will work smarter and like your work more.

Take a lesson from Jethro, Moses' father-in-law, who,

seeing Moses' lack of boundaries, asked him why he was working so hard (Exod. 18:14–27).

"Because the people need me," Moses said.

"What you are doing is not good," Jethro replied. "You and these people who come to you will only wear yourselves out. The work is too heavy for you; you cannot handle it alone" (vv. 17–18). Even though Moses was doing good work, Jethro saw that he was going to burn himself out. Moses had allowed good work to go too far. Limits on good things keep them good.

Problem #4: Difficult Co-workers

A personnel counselor will often send someone to our hospital program because of stress at work. When these situations are unraveled, the "stress at work" often turns out to be somebody at the office who is driving the stressed-out person crazy. This person in the office or workplace has a strong influence over the emotional life of the person in pain, and he or she does not know how to deal with it.

In this case you need to remember the Law of Power: *You only have the power to change yourself. You can't change another person.* You must see yourself as the problem, not the other person. To see another person as the problem to be fixed is to give that person power over you and your well-being. Because you cannot change another person, you are out of control. The real problem lies in how you are relating to the problem person. *You* are the one in pain, and only *you* have the power to fix it.

Many people have found immense relief in the thought that they have no control over another person and that they must focus on changing their reactions to that person. They must refuse to allow that person to affect them. This idea is life changing, the beginning of true self-control.

Problem #5: Critical Attitudes

Stress is often caused by working with or for someone who is supercritical. People will get hooked into either trying to win over the critical person, which can almost never be done, or by allowing the person to provoke them to anger. Some people internalize the criticism and get down on themselves. All of these reactions indicate an inability to stand apart from the critical person and keep one's boundaries.

Allow these critical people to be who they are, but keep yourself separate from them and do not internalize their opinion of you. Make sure you have a more accurate appraisal of yourself, and then disagree internally.

You may also want to confront the overly critical person according to the biblical model (Matt. 18). At first tell her how you feel about her attitude and the way it affects you. If she is wise, she will listen to you. If not, and her attitude is disruptive to others as well, two or more of you might want to talk to her. If she will not agree to change, you may want to tell her that you do not wish to talk with her until she gets her attitude under control.

Or you can follow the company's grievance policy. The important thing to remember is that you can't control her, but you can choose to limit your exposure to her, either physically or emotionally distancing yourself from her. This is self-control.

Avoid trying to gain the approval of this sort of person. It will never work, and you will only feel controlled. And avoid getting in arguments and discussions. You will never win. Remember the proverb, "Whoever corrects a mocker invites insult; whoever rebukes a wicked man incurs abuse. Do not rebuke a mocker or he will hate you; rebuke a wise man and he will love you" (Prov. 9:7–8). If you allow them to draw you in, thinking that you will change them, you are asking them for trouble. Stay separate. Keep your boundaries. Don't get sucked into their game.

Problem #6: Conflicts with Authority

If you are having trouble getting along with your boss, you may be having "transference feelings." Transference is when you experience feelings in the present that really belong to some unfinished business in the past.

Transference happens frequently with bosses because

they are authority figures. The boss-employee relationship can trigger authority conflicts you might have. You can begin to have strong reactions that are not appropriate to the current relationship.

Suppose your supervisor tells you that he wants something done differently. Immediately you feel "put down." You think, *He never thinks I do anything right. I'll show him.* Your supervisor may have made the comment in passing, but the feelings it triggered were very strong indeed. The reality is that the interaction may be tapping into unresolved hurt from past authority relationships, such as parents or teachers.

When a transference relationship starts, you may begin to act out all the old patterns you did with parents. This never works. You become a child on the job.

To have boundaries is to take responsibility for your transference. If you find yourself having strong reactions to someone, take some time and look inside to see if the feelings are familiar. Do they remind you of someone from the past? Did Mom or Dad treat you like that? Do they have the same personality as this person?

You are responsible for working out these feelings. Until you face your own feelings, you can't even see who others really are. You are looking at them through your own distortions, through your own unfinished business. When you see others clearly without transference, you will know how to deal with them.

Another example would be strong feelings of competition with a co-worker. This may represent some competitive relationship from the past, such as sibling rivalry, that has not been worked through. Whenever you experience strong feelings, see them as part of your responsibility. This will lead you to any unfinished business and healing, as well as keep you from acting irrationally toward co-workers and bosses. Leave the past in the past, deal with it, and do not allow it to interfere with present relationships.

Problem #7: Expecting Too Much of Work

People increasingly come to the workplace wanting the company to be a "family." In a society where the family, church, and community are not the support structures they once were, people look to their colleagues for the emotional support a family once provided. This lack of boundaries between the personal and work life is fraught with all sorts of difficulties.

The workplace ideally should be supportive, safe, and nurturing. But this atmosphere should primarily support the employee in work-related ways—to help her learn, improve, and get a job done. The problem arises when someone wants the job to provide what her parents did not provide for her: primary nurturing, relationship, self-esteem, and approval. Work is not set up this way, nor is it what the typical job asks of someone. The inherent conflict in this set-up is this: The job expects adult functioning, and the person wants childhood needs met. These differing expectations will inevitably collide.

Health comes from owning unmet childhood needs and working them out. The problem is that the workplace is not the place to do that. There are expectations at work. They will ask from you without giving because they are going to pay you for your work. They are not obligated to provide all the emotional support you need.

You need to make sure you are meeting your needs for support and emotional repair outside of work. Plug into supportive and healing networks that will help you to grow out of your emotional hurts and unmet needs, and build you up so you can function well at the job, in the adult world that has adult expectations. Get your relationship needs met outside of work, and then you will be able to work the best without getting your needs mixed up with what the company needs from you. Keep your boundaries firm; protect those hurt places from the workplace, which is not only not set up to heal, but also may wound unintentionally.

Problem #8: Taking Work-Related Stress Home

Just as we should keep good boundaries on our personal issues and keep them out of the workplace, we need to keep some boundaries on work and keep it out of the home. This generally has two components.

The first is emotional. Conflicts at work need to be dealt with and worked through so they do not begin to affect the rest of your life. If denied, they can cause major depressions and other illnesses that begin to spill over into other areas of life.

Make sure you understand work issues and face them directly so that work does not emotionally control your life. Find out why a certain co-worker is able to get to you, or why your boss is able to control the rest of your life. Find out why your successes or failures on the job are able to bring you up or down. These important character issues need to be worked through. Otherwise, the job will own you.

The second component is finite things such as time, energy, and other resources. Make sure that the job, which is literally never done, does not continue to spill over into personal life and cost you relationships and other things that matter. Put limits on special projects that are going to take more time than usual, and make sure overtime does not become a pattern. One company we know has such a high value for family that they dock people for working overtime! They want them to put limits on their work and be home with the family. Find out your own limits and live by them. These are good boundaries.

Problem #9: Disliking Your Job

Boundaries are where our identity comes from. Boundaries define what is me and what is not me. Our work is part of our identity in that it taps into our particular giftedness and the exercise of those gifts in the community.

However, many people are unable to ever find a true work identity. They stumble from job to job, never really finding anything that is "them." More often than not, this is a boundary problem. They have not been able to own their own gifts, talents, wants, desires, and dreams because they are unable to set boundaries on others' definitions and expectations of them.

This happens with people who have not separated from the family they grew up in. A pastor was having great difficulty with his church and the board of elders. Finally, right in the middle of a consistory meeting, he said, "I never wanted to be a pastor anyway. It was my mother's wish, not mine." He did not have good enough boundaries with his mother to define his own career path. As a result, he had fused with her wishes and was miserable. His heart had not been in it from the start.

This can happen also with friends and culture. Others' expectations can be very strong influences. You must make sure that your boundaries are strong enough that you do not let others define you. Instead, work with God to find out who you really are and what kind of work you are made for. Romans 12:2 speaks of having boundaries against these kinds of pressures from others: "Do not conform any longer to the pattern of this world, but be transformed by the renewing of your mind. Then you will be able to test and approve what God's will is—his good, pleasing and perfect will." You should have a realistic expectation of yourself based on who you really are, your own true self with your own particular giftedness. You can only do this with boundaries that stand up and say, "This is me, and that is not me." Stand up against others' expectations of you.

Finding Your Life's Work

Finding your life's work involves taking risks. First you need to firmly establish your identity, separating yourself from those you are attached to and following your desires. You must take ownership of how you feel, how you think, and what you want. You must assess your talents and limitations. And then you must begin to step out as God leads you.

For God wants you to discover and use your gifts to his glory. He asks only that you include him in the process: "Delight yourself in the LORD and he will give you the desires of your heart. Commit your way to the LORD; trust in him and he will do this" (Ps. 37:4–5).

God also, however, calls you to be accountable for what you do: "Follow the ways of your heart and whatever your eyes see, but know that for all these things God will bring you to judgment" (Eccl. 11:9).

As you develop your talents, look at your work as a partnership between you and God. He has given you gifts, and he wants you to develop them. Commit your way to the Lord, and you will find your work identity. Ask him to help.

12

Boundaries and Your Self

S arah heaved a long sigh. She'd been working on major boundary issues in her therapy for a while now. She was seeing progress in resolving responsibility conflicts with her parents, her husband, and her kids. Yet today she introduced a new issue.

"I haven't told you about this relationship before, though I guess I should have. I have tremendous boundary problems with this woman. She eats too much, and has an attacking tongue. She's undependable—lets me down all the time. And she's spent money of mine and hasn't paid me back in years."

"Why haven't you mentioned her before?" I asked.

"Because she's me," Sarah replied.

Sarah was echoing the conflict most of us have. We learn that boundaries are biblical. We begin setting limits on others. We begin moving from taking too much responsibility to taking just enough. But how do we begin to set limits on ourselves? As Pogo Possum, cartoonist Walt Kelly's popular swamp character, says, "We have met the enemy, and he is us."

In this chapter, instead of looking at the control and manipulation of others, we'll be looking at our responsibility to control our own bodies (1 Thess. 4:4). Instead of examining outer boundary conflicts with other people, we will be looking at our own *internal boundary conflicts*. This can get a little touchy. As the disgruntled country church member told his pastor as he left after the Sunday sermon, "You done stopped preachin', and you done started meddlin'!"

Instead of this defensive posture, we are much better off to look humbly at ourselves. To ask for feedback from others. To listen to people we trust. And to confess, "I was wrong."

Our Out-of-Control Soul

Eating

Teresa's secret shame was becoming more difficult to keep a secret. Her five-foot-four frame could hide a little extra weight, but over the past few months she'd gradually moved into the mid-hundred mark. She hated it. Her dating life, her stamina, and her attitude toward herself were all affected.

She was out of control. In her successful but stressful career as an attorney, cookies and candy were the only place she could go when everything was falling down around her. Twelve-hour days meant lots of isolation, and absolutely nothing filled the void like fatty foods. *No wonder they call it comfort food,* Teresa would think.

What makes overeating especially painful is that overweight is visible to others. The overweight person feels enormous self-hate and shame about her condition. And, like others who suffer from out-of-control behaviors, the overweight person feels overwhelming shame for her behavior, which drives her away from relationship and back to food.

Both chronic and bingeing overeaters suffer from an internal self-boundary problem. For overeaters, food serves as a false boundary. They might use food to avoid intimacy by gaining weight and becoming less attractive. Or they might binge as a way to get false closeness. For bingers, the "comfort" from food is less scary than the prospect of real relationships, where boundaries would be necessary.

Money

A now-famous bumper sticker reads, "I can't be overdrawn—I still have checks left!" People have tremendous problems in many different areas dealing with money, including the following:

- impulse spending
- careless budgeting
- living beyond one's means
- credit problems
- chronically borrowing from friends
- ineffectual savings plans
- working more to pay all the bills
- enabling others

God intended for money to be a blessing to us and others: "Give, and it will be given to you" (Luke 6:38). In fact, the Bible says that the problem isn't money, it's the love of money that is "a root of all kinds of evil" (1 Tim. 6:10).

Most of us would certainly agree that we need to be in control of our finances. Saving money, keeping costs down, and shopping for discounts are all good things. It's tempting to see money problems as simply a need for more income; however, the problem often isn't the high cost of living—it's the cost of high living.

The problem of our financial outgo exceeding our input is a self-boundary issue. When we have difficulty saying no to spending more than we should, we run the risk of becoming someone else's servant: "The rich rule over the poor, and the borrower is servant to the lender" (Prov. 22:7).

Time

Many people feel that their time is out of control. They are "eleventh-hour people," constantly on the edge of deadlines. Try as they might, they find the day—every day—getting away from them. There just aren't enough hours to accomplish their tasks. The word *early* doesn't seem to be part of their personal experience. Some of the time binds these strugglers deal with are these:

- business meetings
- luncheon appointments
- project deadlines
- church and school activities
- holiday mailings

These people breeze into meetings fifteen minutes late and breathlessly apologize, talking about traffic, overwhelming job responsibilities, or kid emergencies.

People whose time is out of control inconvenience others whether they mean to or not. The problem often stems from one or more of the following causes:

1. *Omnipotence.* These people have unrealistic, somewhat grandiose expectations of what they can accomplish in a given amount of time. "No problem—I'll do it" is their motto.

2. *Overresponsibility for the feelings of others.* They think that leaving a party too early will cause the host to feel abandoned.

3. *Lack of realistic anxiety.* They live so much in the present that they neglect to plan ahead for traffic, parking the car, or dressing for an outing.

4. *Rationalization.* They minimize the distress and inconvenience that others must put up with because of their lateness. They think, "They're my friends—they'll understand."

The person with undeveloped time self-boundaries ends up frustrating not only others, but himself. He ends the day without the sense that a "desire realized is sweet to the soul" (Prov. 13:19 NASB). Instead, he is left with unrealized desires, half-baked projects, and the realization that tomorrow will begin with him running behind schedule.

Task Completion

A first cousin to the time boundary problem, task completion deals with "finishing well." Most of us have goals in the love and work areas of life. We may wish to be a veterinarian or a lawyer. We may wish to own our own business or own a home in the country. We may wish to start a Bible study program or an exercise regimen.

We all would like to say about our tasks, whether large or small, what Paul said: "I have fought the good fight, I have finished the race, I have kept the faith. Now there is in store for me the crown of righteousness" (2 Tim. 4:7–8). More eloquent in their simplicity are Jesus' words on the cross: "It is finished" (John 19:30).

Though they may be great starters, many Christians find themselves unable to be good finishers. For one reason or another, creative ideas don't pan out. A regular schedule of operations becomes bogged down. Success looms, then is suddenly snatched away.

The problem with many poor finishers lies in one of the following causes:

1. *Resistance to structure.* Poor finishers feel that submitting to the discipline of a plan is a putdown.

2. *Fear of success.* Poor finishers are overconcerned that success will cause others to envy and criticize them. Better to shoot themselves in the foot than to lose their buddies.

3. *Lack of follow-through.* Poor finishers have an aversion to the boring "nuts and bolts" of turning the crank on a project. They are much more excited about birthing the idea, then turning it over to other people to execute it.

4. *Distractibility.* Poor finishers are unable to focus on a project until it's done. They have often never developed competent concentration skills.

5. *Inability to delay gratification.* Poor finishers are unable to work through the pain of a project to experience the satifaction of a job well done. They want to go directly to the pleasure. They are like children who want to eat dessert before they eat the well-balanced meal.

6. *Inability to say no to other pressures.* Poor finishers are unable to say no to other people and projects. They don't have time to finish any job well.

Those with task completion problems often feel like two-year-olds in their favorite toy area. They'll bang a hammer for a bit, vroom with a toy car, talk to a puppet, and then pick up a book. All in two minutes or less. It's easy to see the boundary problems inherent in those with task completion problems. Their internal no hasn't been developed enough to keep them focused on finishing things.

The Tongue

In a therapy group I was leading, a man held the floor for some time. He'd go off on tangents, change the subject, and spend inordinate amounts of time on irrelevant details. He couldn't seem to get to the point. Other members were spacing out, dozing off, or becoming restless. Just as I was about to speak to the man's struggle with getting to the point, a woman in the group spoke up, saying bluntly, "Bill, talk net, willya?"

"Talking net," putting a net or boundary on their words, can be a struggle for many. How we use language can deeply affect the quality of our relationships. The tongue can be a source of both blessing and curse (James 3:9–10). It can be a blessing when we use our tongue to empathize, identify, encourage, confront, and exhort others. It can be a curse when we use it to:

- Talk nonstop to hide from intimacy
- Dominate conversations to control others
- Gossip
- Make sarcastic remarks, expressing indirect hostility
- Threaten someone, expressing direct hostility
- Flatter, instead of authentically praise
- Seduce

Many people who have difficulty setting verbal boundaries on themselves aren't really aware of their problem. They are often genuinely surprised when a friend says to them, "Sometimes it seems like you interpret my commas as periods."

I knew a woman who was desperately afraid that others would get to know her. She asked questions and talked quickly so that no one could turn the conversation toward her. She had only one problem: she had to take breaths to continue talking, and the breath created a space for someone else to say something. The woman resolved her problem, however, in an ingenious way; she drew her breaths in the middle of her sentences, rather than at the end. That kept people sufficiently off-balance so that she was rarely interrupted. An effective strategy, with only one problem: she had to keep finding new people to talk to. After a few rounds with her, people disappeared.

The Scriptures tell us to treat our words carefully: "When

words are many, sin is not absent, but he who holds his tongue is wise" (Prov. 10:19). "A man of knowledge uses words with restraint" (Prov. 17:27). According to *The Theological Wordbook of the Old Testament*, the Hebrew word for "restrain" refers to "the free action of holding back something or someone. The actor has the power over the object."[1] It's a boundary-laden term. We have the power to set boundaries on what comes out of our mouths.

When we can't hold back, or set boundaries, on what comes from our lips, our words are in charge—not us. But we are still responsible for those words. Our words do not come from somewhere outside of us, as if we were a ventriloquist's dummy. They are the product of our hearts. Our saying, "I didn't mean that," is probably better translated, "I didn't want you to know I thought that about you." We need to take responsibility for our words. "But I tell you that men will have to give account on the day of judgment for every careless word they have spoken" (Matt. 12:36).

Sexuality

As Christians are finding more safe places in the church to be honest about spiritual and emotional conflicts, sexual problems, especially for men, have emerged as a major issue. Such problems include compulsive masturbation, compulsive heterosexual or homosexual relationships, pornography, prostitution, exhibitionism, voyeurism, obscene phone calls, indecent liberties, child molestation, incest, and rape.

The individual caught up in an out-of-control sexual behavior generally feels deeply isolated and shameful. This keeps what is broken in the soul sequestered in the darkness—out of the light of relationship with God and others, where there can be neither help nor resolution. His sexuality takes on a life of its own, unreal and fantasy-driven. One man described it as a "not-me experience." It was, for him, as if the real him was watching his sexual actions from across the room. Others may feel so dead and detached that sexuality is the only way they feel alive.

The problem, however, is that, as in most internal boundary conflicts, sexual boundarylessness becomes a tyrant, demanding and insatiable. No matter how many orgasms are reached, the desire only deepens, and the inability to say no to one's lusts drives one deeper into despair and hopelessness.

Alcohol and Substance Abuse

Probably the clearest examples of internal boundary problems, alcohol and drug dependencies create devastation in the lives of addicts. Divorce, job loss, financial havoc, medical problems, and death are the fruits of the inability to set limits in these areas.

Most tragic are the increasingly younger children who are experimenting with drugs. Drug addiction is difficult for adults, who have some semblance of character and boundaries; for the child, whose boundaries are delicate and forming, the results are often lifelong and debilitating.

Why Doesn't My "No" Work?

"I'm throwing my no away," Burt told me. "It works fine for setting limits on other people, but every time I try to complete my tasks on time, it breaks down. Where can I trade it in?"

Where indeed? As you read about the out-of-control areas above, you may have felt defeated and frustrated with yourself. You probably could identify with one or more of the problem areas, and you probably are no stranger to the discouragement of not having mature boundaries in these internal areas. What's the problem? Why doesn't our no work on ourselves?

There are at least three reasons for this.

1. *We are our own worst enemies.* An external problem is easier to deal with than an internal one. When we switch our focus from setting limits on other people to setting limits on ourselves, we make a major shift in responsibility. Previously, we were only responsible to, not for, the other party. Now we have a great deal more involvement—we *are* the other party. We *are* responsible for ourselves.

When you are around a critical person, the kind who

finds fault with everything, you can set limits on your exposure to this person's constant criticism. You can change subjects, rooms, houses, or continents. You can leave. But what if this critical person is in your own head? What if you are the person with the problem? What if you have met the enemy, and he is you?

2. *We withdraw from relationship when we most need it.* Jessica came to me for treatment of an eating disorder. She was thirty years old, and she had been bingeing since she was a teenager. I asked her about her previous attempts to solve this internal boundary problem.

"I try to work out and eat right," she said. "But I always fall back."

"Who do you talk to about this?" I asked.

"What do you mean?" Jessica looked confused.

"Who do you tell about your eating problem when you can't take it anymore?"

Tears welled up in Jessica's eyes. "You're asking too much. This is a private problem. Can't I do this without anyone knowing?"

Since the Fall, our instincts have been to withdraw from relationship when we're in trouble, when we most need other people. (Remember how Adam and Eve hid from God after they ate the forbidden fruit?) Due to our lack of security, our loss of grace, our shame, and our pride, we turn inward, rather than outward, when we're in trouble. And that's a problem. As the Preacher in Ecclesiastes puts it: "Woe to one who is alone and falls and does not have another to help" (4:10 NRSV).

Such withdrawal happens in our hospital program time after time. Hurting people will begin to make attachments with staff or other patients. For the first time, they begin coming forth with their need for connection. Like a rose lifting its petals after a hard rain, they begin to relate and connect in the light of the grace of God and his people.

Then an unexpected difficulty will occur. Sometimes their depression will temporarily worsen as their pain inside is exposed. Sometimes traumatic memories will surface. Sometimes severe conflict will occur with family members. Instead of bringing these painful and frightening feelings and problems to their newfound relationships, these people will often retreat to their rooms to work out the problem. They'll spend several hours or a day doing everything possible to get back under control. They'll talk positively to themselves or read Scriptures compulsively to try to make themselves "feel better."

It is only when this attempt at a solution breaks down that they finally realize that these spiritual pains and burdens need to be brought out of themselves to the body of Christ. To the isolated person, nothing feels more frightening, unsafe, or unwise. Such a person needs to feel very secure before she will risk taking her spiritual and emotional problems to other people.

And yet the Bible doesn't recognize any other answer to our problems. Grace must come from the outside of ourselves to be useful and healing. Just as the branch withers without the vine (John 15:1–6), we can sustain neither life nor emotional repair without bonding to God and others. God and his people are the fuel, the energy source from which any problem is addressed. We need to be "joined and held together by every supporting ligament" (Eph. 4:16) of the body of Christ to heal and to grow up.

Whether our boundary issue is food, substances, sex, time, projects, the tongue, or money, we can't solve it in a vacuum. If we could, we would. But the more we isolate ourselves, the harder our struggle becomes. Just like an untreated cancer can become life-threatening in a short time, self-boundary problems will worsen with increased aloneness.

3. *We try to use willpower to solve our boundary problems.* "I've got it solved!" Pete was excited about his newfound victory over his overspending. A dedicated Christian and a leader in his church, he was intensely concerned about his out-of-control finances. "I made a vow to God and myself that I'll never spend beyond my budget again! It's so simple, but so true!"

Not wanting to burst Pete's bubble, I adopted a wait-and-see attitude. I didn't have to wait long. The next week he came in, feeling discouraged and hopeless.

"I just couldn't stop myself," he lamented. "I went out

and bought sports equipment; then my wife and I purchased new furniture. It was just what we needed. The price was right. The only problem was that we couldn't afford it. I guess I'm hopeless."

Pete wasn't hopeless, but his philosophy, popular among Christians, certainly was. He had been trying to use will-power to solve his boundary problems, probably the most common approach to out-of-control behavior.

The willpower approach is simple. Whatever the problem behavior is, just stop doing it. In other words, "just say no." Imperatives such as "Choose to stop," "Decide to say no," and "Make a commitment to never do it again" abound in this approach.

The problem with this approach is that it makes an idol out of the will, something God never intended. Just as our hearts and minds are distorted by the Fall, so is our power to make right decisions. Will is only strengthened by relationship; we can't make commitments alone. God told Moses to encourage and strengthen Joshua (Deut. 3:28); he didn't tell Moses to tell Joshua to "just say no."

If we depend on willpower alone, we are guaranteed to fail. We are denying the power of the relationship promised in the cross. If all we need is our will to overcome evil, we certainly don't need a Savior (1 Cor. 1:17). The truth is, willpower alone is useless against self-boundary struggles:

> Why do you submit to [the world's] rules: "Do not handle! Do not taste! Do not touch!"? These are all destined to perish with use, because they are based on human commands and teachings. Such regulations indeed have an appearance of wisdom, with their self-imposed worship, their false humility and their harsh treatment of the body, but they lack any value in restraining sensual indulgence. (Col. 2:20–23)

The King James Bible translates the Greek word for "self-imposed worship" as "will-worship." In other words, these self-denying practices that appear so spiritual don't stop out-of-control behavior. The boundaryless part of the soul simply becomes more resentful under the domination of the will—and it rebels. Especially after we make statements such as, "I will never" and "I will always," we act out with a vengeance. Jessica's indulgence in food, Pete's indulgence in money, someone else's indulgence in foolish or slanderous conversation, or still another's determination never to be late on a project again will not be healed by "white-knuckling it."

Establishing Boundaries with Yourself

Learning to be mature in self-boundaries is not easy. Many obstacles hinder our progress; however, God desires our maturity and self-control even more than we do. He's on our team as an exhorter, encourager, and implorer (1 Thess. 2:11–12). One way to begin developing limits on out-of-control behavior is to apply a modified version of the boundary checklist we used in Chapter 8:

1. *What are the symptoms?* Look at the destructive fruit you may be exhibiting by not being able to say no to yourself. You may be experiencing depression, anxiety, panic, phobias, rage, relationship struggles, isolation, work problems, or psychosomatic problems.

All of these symptoms can be related to a difficulty in setting limits on your own behavior. Use them as a road map to begin identifying the particular boundary problem you're having.

2. *What are the roots?* Identifying the causes of your self-boundary problems will assist you in understanding your own contribution to the problem (how you have sinned), your developmental injuries (how you have been sinned against), and the significant relationships that may have contributed to the problem.

Some possible roots of self-boundary conflicts include:

Lack of training. Some people never learned to accept limits, to pay the consequences of their actions, or to delay gratification when they were growing up. For example, they may never have experienced any consequences for dawdling as a child.

Rewarded destructiveness. People who come from families in which the mom or dad was an alcoholic may have learned that out-of-control behavior brings relationship. The family came together when the alcoholic member drank.

Distorted need. Some boundary problems are legitimate, God-given needs in disguise. God gave us sexual desire both to reproduce ourselves and to enjoy our spouses. The pornography addict has diverted this good desire; he feels real and alive only when acting out.

Fear of relationship. People really want to be loved but their out-of-control behavior (i.e., overeating, overworking) keeps others away. Some people use their tongues to keep other people at bay.

Unmet emotional hungers. We all need love during the first few years of life. If we don't receive this love, we hunger for it for the rest of our lives. This hunger for love is so powerful that when we don't find it in relationships with other people, we look for it in other places, such as in food, in work, in sexual activity, or in spending money.

Being under the law. Many Christians raised in legalistic environments were not permitted to make decisions for themselves. When they try to make their own decisions, they feel guilty. This guilt forces them to rebel in destructive ways. Food addictions and compulsive spending are often reactions against strict rules.

Covering emotional hurt. People who are injured emotionally, who were neglected or abused as children, disguise their pain by overeating, drinking too much, or working too much. They may abuse substances to distract from the real pain of being unloved, unwanted, and alone. If they were to stop using these disguises, their isolation would be intolerable.

3. *What is the boundary conflict?* Take a look at your particular self-boundary problems in relation to eating, money, time, task completion, the tongue, sexuality, or alcohol and substance abuse. These seven areas aren't exhaustive, though they cover a great deal of territory. Ask God for insight into what other areas of your life are out of control.

4. *Who needs to take ownership?* At this point, take the painful step of taking responsibility for your out-of-control behavior. The behavior pattern may be directly traceable to

family problems, neglect, abuse, or trauma. In other words, our boundary conflicts may not be all our fault. They are, however, our *responsibility*.

5. *What do you need?* It's useless to try to deal with your boundary conflicts with yourself until you're actively developing safe, trusting, grace-and-truth relationships with others. You are severely hampered in gaining either insight into or control over yourself when you are disconnected from God's source of spiritual and emotional fuel.

Plugging in to other people is often frustrating for "do-it-yourself" people who would like a how-to manual for solving out-of-control behaviors just as they would buy to teach themselves piano, plumbing, or golf. They wish to get this boundary-setting business over with quickly.

The problem is that many people with self-boundary struggles are also quite isolated from deep relationships. They have no "rootedness" in God or others (Eph. 3:17). Thus, they have to take what they think are steps backward to learn to connect with others. Connecting with people is a time-consuming, risky, and painful process. Finding the right people, group, or church is hard enough, but after joining up, admitting your need for others may be even more difficult.

Do-it-yourself people will often fall back into a cognitive or willpower approach, simply because it's not as slow or as risky. They'll often say things like, "Attachment is not what I want. I have an out-of-control behavior, and I need relief from the pain!" Though we can certainly understand their dilemma, they're heading toward another quick-fix dead end. Symptomatic relief—trying to solve a problem by only dealing with the symptoms—generally leads to more symptoms. Jesus described this process in a parable:

> When an evil spirit comes out of a man, it goes through arid places seeking rest and does not find it. Then it says, "I will return to the house I left." When it arrives, it finds the house swept clean and put in order. Then it goes and takes seven other spirits more wicked than itself, and they go in and live there. And the final condition of that man is worse than the first. (Luke 11:24–26)

Evil can take over the empty house of our souls. Even when our lives seem to be in order, isolation guarantees spiritual vulnerability. It's only when our house is full of the love of God and others that we can resist the wiles of the Devil. Plugging in is neither an option, nor a luxury; it is a spiritual and emotional life-and-death issue.

6. *How do I begin?* Once you have identified your boundary problem and owned it, you can do something about it. Here are some ways to begin practicing setting boundaries on yourself.

Address your real need. Often, out-of-control patterns disguise a need for something else. You need to address the underlying need before you can deal with the out-of-control behavior. For example, impulsive eaters may discover that food is a way to stay separate and safe from romantic and sexual intimacy. Their fear of being faced with those kinds of emotionally laden situations may cause them to use food as a boundary. As their internal boundaries with the opposite sex become firmer, they can give up their destructive food boundary. They learn to ask for help for the real problem— not just for the symptomatic problem.

Allow yourself to fail. Addressing your real need is no guarantee that your out-of-control behavior will disappear. Many people who address the real issue underneath a self-boundary problem are often disappointed that the problem keeps recurring. They think, "Well, I joined a support group at church, but I still have problems being on time, or viewing pornography, or spending money, or talking out of turn. Was all this for naught?"

No. The recurrence of destructive patterns is evidence of God's sanctifying, maturing, and preparing us for eternity. We need to continue to practice to learn things. The same process that we use to learn to drive a car, swim, or learn a foreign language is the one we use for learning better self-boundaries.

We need to embrace failure instead of trying to avoid it. Those people who spend their lives trying to avoid failure are also eluding maturity. We are drawn to Jesus because "he learned obedience from what he suffered" (Heb. 5:8). People who are growing up are also drawn to individuals who bear battle scars, worry furrows, and tear marks on their faces. Their lessons can be trusted, much more than the unlined faces of those who have never failed—and so have never truly lived.

Listen to empathic feedback from others. As you fail in setting boundaries on yourself, you need others who will let you know about it in a caring way. Many times, you are unaware of your own failures. Sometimes you may not truly understand the extent of the damage your lack of boundaries causes in the lives of those you care about. Other believers can provide perspective and support.

Keith had a difficult time returning money to others when they had loaned it to him. He wasn't broke. He wasn't selfish. He was just forgetful. He had little awareness of the discomfort he caused those who lent him money.

One afternoon a friend who had loaned him money several months before dropped by his office.

"Keith," his friend said, "Several times I've asked you about the money I lent you. I still haven't heard from you. I don't think you're intentionally ignoring my requests. At the same time I wanted to let you know that your forgetfulness has been hard on me. I had to cancel a vacation because I didn't have the money. Your forgetfulness is hurting me, and it's hurting our friendship."

Keith was astonished. He hadn't had a clue that such a little thing to him might mean so much to a close friend. Deeply remorseful over the loss his friend had suffered, he wrote a check immediately.

In a non-condemning, non-nagging manner, Keith's friend had helped him become more aware of his self-boundary problem. He used the empathy Keith felt for him as a close friend. True godly remorse for causing his friend pain was a powerful motivator for Keith to become more responsible. When others in our support system let us know how our lack of self-boundaries hurts them, we are motivated by love, not by fear.

Biblically based support groups, which provide empathy and clear feedback, keep people responsible by letting them see the effect their actions have on another. When one member tells another, "Your uncontrolled behavior makes

me want to stay away from you. I don't feel that I can trust
you when you act like that," the out-of-control person isn't
being parented or policed. He is hearing truth in love from a
peer. He's hearing how what he does helps or damages those
he loves. This kind of confrontation builds an empathy-based
morality, a love-based self-control.

Welcome consequences as a teacher. Learning about
sowing and reaping is valuable. It teaches us that we suffer
losses when we aren't responsible. The impulsive overeater
has medical and social difficulties. The overspender faces
bankruptcy court. The chronically late person misses plane
flights and important meetings, and loses friendships. The
procrastinator faces losses of promotions and bonuses. And
on and on.

We need to enter God's training school of learning to
suffer for our irresponsibility. Not all suffering should be
embraced;[2] however, when our own lack of love or responsibility causes the suffering, pain becomes our teacher.

Learning how to develop better self-boundaries is an
orderly process. First, we are confronted about the destructiveness of our behavior by others. Then consequences will
follow if we don't heed the feedback. Words precede actions
and give us a chance to turn from our destructiveness before
we have to suffer.

God doesn't glory in our suffering. Just as a loving
father's heart breaks when he sees his children in pain, God
wants to spare us pain. But when his words and the feedback
of his other children don't reach us, consequences are the
only way to keep us from further damage. God is like the
parent who warns his teenager that drinking will cause a loss
of car privileges. First, the warning: "Stop drinking now. It
will have bad consequences for you." Then, if it's not
heeded, car privileges are yanked. This painful consequence
prevents a possible serious catastrophe: a drunk-driving
accident.

*Surround yourself with people who are loving and
supportive.* As you hear feedback and suffer consequences,
maintain close contact with your support network. Your
difficulties are too much to bear alone. You need others who
will be loving and supportive, but who will not rescue.

Generally speaking, friends of people with self-boundary problems make one of two errors:

(1) They become critical and parental. When the person has failed, they adopt an "I told you so" attitude, or say things like, "Now, what did you learn from your experience?" This encourages the person to either look elsewhere for a friend (no one needs more than two parents), or simply avoid the criticism, instead of learning from consequences. "Brothers, if someone is caught in a sin, you who are spiritual should restore him gently" (Gal. 6:1).

Replace this parental position with gentle restoration, understanding that "there but for the grace of God go I."

(2) They become rescuers. They give in to their impulse to save the person from suffering. They call the boss and tell them their spouse was sick when he or she was drunk. They lend more money when they shouldn't. They hold up the entire dinner for the latecomer, instead of going ahead with the meal.

Rescuing someone is not loving them. God's love lets people experience consequences. Rescuers hope that by once again bailing out the out-of-control person, they'll reap a loving, responsible person. They hope to control the other person.

It's far better to be empathic, but at the same time refuse to be a safety net: "I'm sorry you lost another job this year, but I won't lend you any more money until you've paid back the other loan. However, I'm available to talk to for support." This approach will show people how serious you are about developing self-boundaries. The sincere searcher will value this approach and will take you up on your offer of support. The manipulator will resent the limits and quickly look for an easier touch somewhere else.

This five-point formula for developing self-boundaries is cyclical. That is, as you deal with real needs, fail, get empathic feedback, suffer consequences, and are restored, you build stronger internal boundaries each time. As you stay with your goal and with the right people, you will build a sense of self-restraint that can truly become part of your character for life.

If You Are a Victim

Establishing boundaries for yourself is always hard. It will be especially difficult if your boundaries were severely violated in childhood. No one who has avoided childhood victimization can truly understand what these individuals go through. Of all the injuries that can be endured, this type causes severe spiritual and emotional damage.

A victim is a person who has, while in a helpless state, been injured by the exploitation of another. Some victimization is verbal, some is physical, some is sexual, and some is satanically ritualistic. All cause extreme damage to the character structure of a child, who then grows up to adulthood with spiritual, emotional, and cognitive distortions. In each case, however, three factors remain constant: helplessness, injury, and exploitation.

Some results of victimization are these:

- depression
- compulsive disorders
- impulsive disorders
- isolation
- inability to trust others
- inability to form close attachments
- inability to set limits
- poor judgment in relationships
- further exploitation in relationships
- deep sense of pervasive badness
- shame
- guilt
- chaotic lifestyle
- sense of meaninglessness and purposelessness
- unexplainable terror and panic attacks
- phobias
- rage attacks
- suicidal feelings and thoughts

Victimization has long-lasting and far-reaching effects on the lives of adult survivors. Healing for victims is difficult because their developmental processes have been damaged or interrupted by abuse. The most primary damage done is that the victim loses a sense of trust. Trust, the ability to depend on ourselves and others in times of need, is a basic spiritual and emotional survival need. We need to be able to trust our own perceptions of reality and to be able to let significant people matter to us.

Our ability to trust ourselves is based on our experience of others as trustworthy. People who are "like a tree planted by streams of water" (Ps. 1:3) feel firm because of the streams of love coming from God and others in their life.

Victims often lose a sense of trust because the perpetrator was someone they knew as children, someone who was important to them. When the relationship became damaging to them, their sense of trust became broken.

Another damaging effect of abuse or molestation is the destruction of a sense of ownership over the victim's soul. In fact, victims often feel that they are public property—that their resources, body, and time should be available to others just for the asking.

Another injury due to victimization is a deep, pervasive sense of being "all-bad," wrong, dirty, or shameful. No matter how affirming others are of their loveableness and their attributes, victims are convinced that, underneath it all, there is no good inside themselves. Because of the severity of their injuries, many victims have overpermeable boundaries. They take on badness that isn't theirs. They begin believing that the way they were treated is the way they should be treated. Many victims think that, since they were told they were bad or evil thousands of times, it certainly must be true.

Boundaries as an Aid to the Victim

Boundary work as described in this book can be extremely helpful in moving victims toward restoration and healing. However, in many cases the severe nature of the need is such that the victim will be unable to set boundaries without professional help. We strongly urge abuse victims to seek out a counselor who can guide them in establishing and maintaining appropriate boundaries.

13

Boundaries and God

When some people read the Bible, they see a book of rules, do's and don'ts. When others read it, they see a philosophy of life, principles for the wise. Still others see mythology, stories about the nature of human existence and the human dilemma.

Certainly, the Bible contains rules, principles, and stories that explain what it is like to exist on this earth. But to us, the Bible is a living book about relationship. Relationship of God to people, people to God, and people to each other. It is about a God who created this world, placed people in it, related to people, lost that relationship, and continues to heal that relationship. It is about God as creator: this is his creation. It is about God as ruler: he ultimately controls his world and will govern it. And it is about God as redeemer: he finds, saves, and heals his loved ones who are lost and in bondage.

When a lawyer asked Jesus which was the greatest commandment in the Law, Jesus said to him, "'Love the Lord your God with all your heart and with all your soul and with all your mind.' This is the first and greatest commandment. And the second is like it: 'Love your neighbor as yourself.' All the Law and the Prophets hang on these two commandments" (Matt. 22:37–40). The entire Scripture communicates a message of love. "Love God, and love your neighbor as yourself."

But how do we do that? Well, that's why there are so many other passages! Loving God and our neighbor is difficult. One of the main reasons it's so difficult is because of boundary problems, which are essentially problems of responsibility. We do not know who is responsible for what, where we end and someone else begins, where God ends and we begin. The Bible clarifies those boundaries so that we can begin to see who should do what in this labor of love.

Respecting Boundaries

We have personal boundaries, personal property lines, in our relationship with God. God has designed the world so that boundaries are to be respected. He respects ours, and we need to respect his.

God respects our boundaries in many ways. First, *he leaves work for us to do that only we can do.* And he allows us to experience the painful consequences of our behavior so that we will change. He is not willing for any of us to perish and takes no pleasure in our destruction (2 Peter 3:9; Ezek. 18:23), but he wants us to change for our own good and his glory. It hurts him deeply when we don't. But at the same time, he does not rescue us; he wants us to work it out for our own good. He will not violate our wish to be left alone, although he will plead with us to come back to him.

Second, *he repects our no.* He tries neither to control nor nag us. He allows us to say no and go our way. Think of the parable of the prodigal son, the story of the rich young ruler, or the story of Joshua and his people. In all of these examples, God gives a choice and allows the people involved to make up their minds. When people say no, he allows it and keeps on loving them. He is a giver. And one of the things he always gives is a choice, but like a real giver, he also gives the consequences of those choices. He respects boundaries.

Many people are not as honest as these biblical characters were, however. The prodigal son was direct and honest: "I do not want to do it your way. I'm going to do it my way." We are more often like the second son in the parable of the two sons in the vineyard (Matt. 21:28–31). We say yes, but we act out no. God prefers honesty. "It is better not to vow than to make a vow and not fulfill it" (Eccl. 5:5). We would be much better off if we would say an honest no to whatever

God is asking, for the next step could be repentance. An honest no will lead us to the discovery of how destructive it is to say no to God and to a real hungering and thirsting for righteousness.

Jerry was a member of a support group I was leading. He was cheating on his wife, but he kept saying that he was sorry and that he really didn't want to be an adulterer. He really wanted to obey God; however, as much as he said that, he didn't change. He wanted to believe that he wanted to change without doing the work of change.

Tired of hearing how much he wanted to be different, I suggested that he tell God and the group the truth. He really did not want to change, he enjoyed his affairs, and his real wish was that God would take his rules and go somewhere else.

Jerry was taken aback, but gradually began to see how true this was. Finally, he told the truth about his lack of love for God and how he really wanted to do his own thing. At first this admission scared him. He was giving up the falsehood of seeing himself as a Christian who cared about holiness. But his honesty felt better to him than all the lies, and something began to happen.

In the safety of grace, which was allowing him to see himself as he really was, he began to regret who he was. He began to see the emptiness of his heart. When he owned who he really was from his heart, he did not like himself. He was developing godly sorrow, the kind that leads to repentance, and he began to change. He told his lover that he was not going to see her any more, and he made a new commitment to his wife. This time he meant it. Whereas for years he had been saying yes and acting out no, he finally owned his no to God directly and honestly. Only then was change possible.

Until we can own our boundaries with God, we can't ever change them or allow him to work with them. They are hidden and not communicated. They need to be honestly owned, exposed, and made a part of us. Then, we and God can face the problem.

Anger

In our deeper honesty and ownership of our true person, there is room for expressing anger at God. Many people who are cut off from God shut down emotionally because they feel that it is not safe to tell him how angry they are at him. Until they feel the anger, they cannot feel the loving feelings underneath the anger.

Job wanted to fully express his anger and disappointment with God to God (Job 13:3). But before he did this, he had to be sure of two things. He wanted God (1) to withdraw his hand of punishment and (2) to start communicating with him (v. 21). Job knew that if he were secure in the relationship, he could tell God what he really felt.

We often fear being honest because it was not safe to express honesty in our earthly relationships. With Job we fear both abandonment and retaliation. People abandoned us or attacked us when we told them how we really felt.

Rest assured, however, that God desires truth in our "inner parts" (Ps. 51:6). He is seeking people who will have a real relationship with him (John 4:23–24). He wants to hear it all, no matter how bad it seems to us. When we own what is within our boundaries, when we bring it into the light, God can transform it with his love.

Respecting His Boundaries

God expects his boundaries to be respected as well. When he makes choices, or says no to us, that is his right, his freedom. If we are to have a real relationship with him, we need to respect that freedom. When we try and put him into binds where he "has to do something," we are testing his freedom. When we are angry with him for what he does not do, we are not allowing him the freedom to be who he is.

The basic problem in human relationship is that of freedom. We call people bad because they do not do what we want them to do. We judge them for being themselves, for fulfilling their wishes. We withdraw love from them when they do what they feel is best for them, but it is not what we want them to do.

We do the same thing with God. We feel entitled to God's favor, as if he has to do what we want him to. How do you feel when someone asks you for a favor but does not give you a free choice? This childish entitlement gets many people dissatisfied with God the same way that they are dissatisfied with others in their lives. They hate the freedom of others.

God is free from us. When he does something for us, he does it out of choice. He is not "under compulsion" or guilt or manipulation. He does things, like dying for us, because he wants to. We can rest in his pure love; he has no hidden resentment in what he does. His freedom allows him to love.

Many Bible characters ran into God's freedom and learned to embrace it. Embracing his freedom and respecting his boundaries, they always deepened their relationship with God. Job had to come to accept the freedom of God to not rescue him when he wanted. Job expressed his anger and dissatisfaction with God, and God rewarded his honesty. But Job did not "make God bad," in his own mind. In all of his complaining, he did not end his relationship with God. He didn't understand God, but he allowed God to be himself and did not withdraw his love from him, even when he was very angry with him. This is a real relationship.

In the same way, Paul accepted the boundaries of God. When he planned trips that didn't work out, Paul accepted the sovereignty of God. He asked God repeatedly for a certain kind of healing that God would not give him. God said, "No. I do not choose to love you in the way that you want right now. I choose to love you with my presence." Paul did not reject God for setting that boundary.

Jesus was perfected through his suffering (Heb. 5:7–10). In the Garden of Gethsemane, he asked that his cup of suffering pass from him, but God said no. Jesus accepted God's wishes, submitted to them, and through that "became the source of eternal salvation for all who obey him" (Heb. 5:9). If Jesus had not respected God's boundaries and God's no, we would all be lost.

In the same way that we want others to respect our no, God wants us to respect his. He does not want us to make him the bad guy when he makes a choice. We do not like others trying to manipulate or control us with guilt, and neither does he.

"I Respectfully Disagree"

Then again, God does not want us to be passive in our relationship with him either. Sometimes, through dialogue, he changes his mind. We can influence him because ours is a real relationship of the kind Abraham had with God (Gen. 18:16–33). God said that he would destroy Sodom, yet Abraham talked him out of it if he could find ten righteous people.

When we make our feelings and wishes known, God responds. We do not often think of God this way, but the Bible is clear. It is as though God says, "If it really means that much to you, it's okay with me." One of the most astounding teachings of the Bible is that we can influence God. It wouldn't be a real relationship if we couldn't. " 'Come now, let us reason together,' says the LORD" (Isa. 1:18). Like a real friend, or a real father, he says, "Let me hear your side of things and I will consider them. They matter to me. Maybe you can convince me to change my mind."

Consider Jesus' parables about prayer. In one story a judge who "neither feared God nor cared about men," for some time refused to grant a widow her request for justice. But because the widow kept bothering him, he changed his mind and granted her wish (Luke 18:1–8). Jesus told them this parable so "that they should always pray and not give up" (v.1). In another story, a neighbor who persistently asks for bread is granted the request because of his continuing boldness (Luke 11:5–9). Other people Jesus decided to heal after they persisted in asking for healing.

God wants us to respect his boundaries; he doesn't want us to withdraw our love when he says no. But he has nothing at all against our trying to persuade him to change his mind. In fact, he asks for us to be tenacious. Often he says, "Wait," seeing how much we really want something. Other times, it seems he changes his mind as a result of our relationship with him. Either way, we respect his wishes and stay in relationship.

Respecting His Own

In addition to our respecting God's boundaries and his respecting ours, he is a good model for how we should respect our own property.

God is the ultimate responsibility taker. If someone else causes him pain, he takes responsibility for it. If we continue to abuse him, he is not masochistic; he will take care of himself. And for our own sakes, we do not want to suffer the consequences of his boundaries.

The parable of the wedding banquet shows us God taking responsibility (Matt. 22:1–14). A king who was planning a banquet invited many people to come. When they said no, he pleaded with them. They continued to say no and went about their own business. Finally, the king had had enough. Taking responsibility for the situation, he said to his servants, "The wedding banquet is ready, but those I invited did not deserve to come. Go to the street corners and invite to the banquet anyone you find" (vv. 8–9).

Whenever God decides that "enough is enough," and he has suffered long enough, he respects his own property, his heart, enough to do something to make it better. He takes responsibility for the pain and makes moves to make his life different. He lets go of the rejecting people and reaches out to some new friends.

God is a good model. When we are hurting, we need to take responsibility for the hurt and make some appropriate moves to make things better. This may mean letting go of someone and finding new friends. It may mean forgiving someone and letting them off the hook so we can feel better.

A Real Relationship

We started this chapter talking about relationship. Relationship is what the gospel is about. It is a gospel of "reconciliation" (Rom. 5:11; Col. 1:19–20). This gospel brings hostile parties together (Col. 1:21) and heals relationships between God and humanity, and between people.

The gospel brings things back to their created order, the truth and order of God. In terms of relationships, we think that God's order of relationship is himself and the way he works. And that is why we think boundaries are so important, because he has them and we are to be redeemed into his image.

Boundaries are inherent in any relationship God has created, for they define the two parties who are loving each other. In this sense, boundaries between us and God are very important. They are not to do away with the fundamental oneness or unity that we have with him (John 17:20–23), but they are to define the two parties in unity. There is no unity without distinct identities, and boundaries define the distinct identities involved.

We need to know these boundaries between us and him. Boundaries help us to be the best we can be—in God's image. They let us see God as he really is. They enable us to negotiate life, fulfilling our responsibilities and requirements. If we are trying to do his work for him, we will fail. If we are wishing for him to do our work for us, he will refuse. But if we do our work, and God does his, we will find strength in a real relationship with our Creator.

PART THREE

———

DEVELOPING
HEALTHY BOUNDARIES

14

Resistance to Boundaries

We have talked about the necessity of boundaries and their wonderful value in our lives. In fact, we have all but said that life without boundaries is no life at all. But establishing and maintaining boundaries takes a lot of work, discipline, and, most of all, desire.

The driving force behind boundaries has to be desire. We usually know what is the right thing to do in life, but we are rarely motivated to do it unless there's a good reason. That we should be obedient to God, who tells us to set and maintain boundaries, is certainly the best reason. But sometimes we need a more compelling reason than obedience. We need to see that what is right is also good for us. And we usually only see these good reasons when we're in pain. Our pain motivates us to act.

Even with the desire for a better life, we can be reluctant to do the work of boundaries for another reason: it will be a war. There will be skirmishes and battles. There will be disputes. There will be losses.

The idea of spiritual warfare is not new. For thousands of years, God has given people the choice of living lives of ruin, or possessing what he has secured for them. And it has always involved battles. When he led the Israelites out of Egypt toward the promised land, they had to fight many battles and learn numerous lessons before they could possess the land.

We have to fight for our healing as well. God has secured our salvation and our sanctification. In position and principle he has healed us. But we have to work out his image in us.

Part of this process of healing is regaining our boundaries. As we become like him, he is redeeming our boundaries and our limits. He has defined who we are and what our limits are so that he can bless us: "LORD, you have assigned me my portion and my cup; you have made my lot secure. The boundary lines have fallen for me in pleasant places; surely I have a delightful inheritance" (Ps. 16:5–6).

But we are the ones who have to do battle. The battles fall into two categories: outside resistance and inside resistance—the resistance we get from others and the resistance we get from ourselves.

Outside Resistance

Julie had had a difficult time with boundaries most of her life. As a child, she had a domineering father and a mother who controlled her with guilt. She had been afraid to set boundaries with some people because of their anger and with others because of the guilt she would feel for "hurting them." When she wanted to make a decision for herself, she would listen to other people's anger or pouting and let their reactions affect her decision.

Coming out of this family, she married a very self-centered man who controlled her with his anger. Throughout her adult life, she alternated between being controlled by her husband's anger and by her mother's guilt trips. She was unable to set limits on anyone. After many years, depression caught up with her, and she ended up in one of our hospitals.

After a number of weeks of therapy, she was beginning to understand that she was miserable because she lacked boundaries. She finally decided to take a risk and set some limits with her husband.

One day in a joint session with her therapist and her husband, she confronted him. She returned to her support group in tears.

"How did it go?" one group member asked.

"Terrible. This boundary stuff doesn't work," she said.

"What do you mean?" the group therapist asked her.

"I told my husband that I was tired of being treated that way and that I was not going to put up with it any more. He got angry and started yelling at me. If the therapist had not been there, I don't know what I would have done. He's never going to change."

She was right. It was a good thing that the therapist was there and that she was in the hospital. She needed a lot of support in learning to set boundaries, for she would encounter a lot of resistance from both her husband and herself.

She learned through the next few weeks that others were going to fight hard against her limits and that she needed to plan how she was going to fight back. If she did that, the chances of their changing were pretty good. In fact, that is exactly what happened. Her husband finally learned that he could no longer "have it his way" all the time and that he needed to consider other people's needs as well as his own.

Angry Reactions

The most common resistance one gets from the outside is anger. People who get angry at others for setting boundaries have a character problem. Self-centered, they think the world exists for them and their comfort. They see others as extensions of themselves.

When they hear no, they have the same reaction a two-year-old has when deprived of something: "Bad Mommy!" They feel as though the one who deprives them of their wishes is "bad," and they become angry. They are not righteously angry at a real offense. Nothing has been done "to them" at all. Someone will not do something "for them." Their wish is being frustrated, and they get angry because they have not learned to delay gratification or to respect others' freedom (Prov. 19:19).

The angry person has a character problem. If you reinforce this character problem, it will return tomorrow and the next day in other situations. It is not the situation that's making the person angry, but the feeling that they are entitled to things from others. They want to control others and, as a result, they have no control over themselves. So, when they lose their wished-for control over someone, they "lose it." They get angry.

The first thing you need to learn is that the person who is

angry at you for setting boundaries is the one with the problem. If you do not realize this, you may think you have a problem. Maintaining your boundaries is good for other people; it will help them learn what their families of origin did not teach them: to respect other people.

Second, you must view anger realistically. Anger is only a feeling inside the other person. It cannot jump across the room and hurt you. It cannot "get inside" you unless you allow it. Staying separate from another's anger is vitally important. Let the anger be in the other person. He will have to feel his anger to get better. If you either rescue him from it, or take it on yourself, the angry person will not get better and you will be in bondage.

Third, do not let anger be a cue for you to do something. People without boundaries respond automatically to the anger of others. They rescue, seek approval, or get angry themselves. There is great power in inactivity. Do not let an out-of-control person be the cue for you to change your course. Just allow him to be angry and decide for yourself what you need to do.

Fourth, make sure you have your support system in place. If you are going to set some limits with a person who has controlled you with anger, talk to the people in your support system first and make a plan. Know what you will say. Anticipate what the angry person will say, and plan your reaction. You may even want to role-play the situation with your group. Then, make sure your support group will be available to you right after the confrontation. Perhaps some members of your support group can go with you. But certainly you will need them afterward to keep you from crumbling under the pressure.

Fifth, do not allow the angry person to get you angry. Keep a loving stance while "speaking the truth in love." When we get caught up in the "eye for eye" mentality of the law, or the "returning evil for evil" mentality of the world, we will be in bondage. If we have boundaries, we will be separate enough to love.

Sixth, be prepared to use physical distance and other limits that enforce consequences. One woman's life was changed when she realized that she could say, "I will not allow myself to be yelled at. I will go into the other room until you decide you can talk about this without attacking me. When you can do that, I will talk to you."

These serious steps do not need to be taken with anger. You can empathize lovingly and stay in the conversation, without giving in or being controlled. "I understand that you are upset that I will not do that for you. I am sorry you feel that way. How can I help?" Just remember that when you empathize, changing your no will not help. Offer other options.

If you keep your boundaries, those who are angry at you will have to learn self-control for the first time, instead of "other control," which has been destructive to them anyway. When they no longer have control over you, they will find a different way to relate. But, as long as they can control you with their anger, they will not change.

Sometimes, the hard truth is that they will not talk to you anymore, or they will leave the relationship if they can no longer control you. This is a true risk. God takes this risk every day. He says that he will only do things the right way and that he will not participate in evil. And when people choose their own ways, he lets them go. Sometimes we have to do the same.

Guilt Messages

A man telephoned his mother, and she answered the phone very weakly, with hardly any voice at all. Concerned, thinking she was sick, he asked her, "Mother, what's wrong?"

"I guess my voice doesn't work very well anymore," she replied. "No one ever calls me since you children left home."

No weapon in the arsenal of the controlling person is as strong as the guilt message. People with poor boundaries almost always internalize guilt messages leveled at them; they obey guilt-inducing statements that try to make them feel bad. Consider these:

- "How could you do this to me after all I've done for you?"
- "It seems that you could think about someone other than yourself for once."
- "If you really loved me, you would make this telephone call for me."
- "It seems like you would care enough about the family to do this one thing."
- "How can you abandon the family like this?"
- "You know how it's turned out in the past when you haven't listened to me."
- "After all, you never had to lift a finger around here. It seems like it's time you did."
- "You know that if I had it, I would give it to you."
- "You have no idea how much we sacrificed for you."
- "Maybe after I'm dead and gone, you'll be sorry."

Sometimes guilt manipulation comes dressed up in God talk:

- "How can you call yourself a Christian?"
- "Doesn't the Bible say 'Honor your parents'?"
- "You're not being very submissive. I'm sure that grieves the Lord."
- "I thought Christians were supposed to think of others."
- "What kind of religion would teach you to abandon your own family?"
- "You must really have a spiritual problem to be acting this way."

People who say these things are trying to make you feel guilty about your choices. They are trying to make you feel bad about deciding how you will spend your own time or resources, about growing up and separating from your parents, or about having a life separate from a friend or spiritual leader. Remember the landowner's words in the parable of the workers in the vineyard: "Don't I have the right to do what I want with my own money?" (Matt. 20:15). The Bible says that we are to give and not be self-centered.

It does not say that we have to give whatever anyone wants from us. We are in control of our giving.

Probably everyone is able to some degree to recognize guilt messages when they hear them. But if you feel bad about your boundaries, maybe you have not looked specifically at the ones your family or other people are using. Here are a few tips about dealing with these external messages:

1. *Recognize guilt messages.* Some people swallow guilt messages without seeing how controlling they are. Be open to rebuke and feedback; you need to know when you are being self-centered. But guilt messages are not given for your growth and good. They are given to manipulate and control.

2. *Guilt messages are really anger in disguise.* The guilt senders are failing to openly admit their anger at you for what you are doing, probably because that would expose how controlling they really are. They would rather focus on you and your behavior than on how they feel. Focusing on their feelings would get them too close to responsibility.

3. *Guilt messages hide sadness and hurt.* Instead of expressing and owning these feelings, people try to steer the focus onto you and what you are doing. Recognize that guilt messages are sometimes an expression of a person's sadness, hurt, or need.

4. *If guilt works on you, recognize that this is* your *problem and not theirs.* Realize where the real problem is: inside. Then you will be able to deal with the outside correctly, with love and limits. If you continue to blame other people for "making" you feel guilty, they still have power over you, and you are saying that you will only feel good when they stop doing that. You are giving them control over your life. Stop blaming other people.

5. *Do not explain or justify.* Only guilty children do that. This is only playing into their message. You do not owe guilt senders an explanation. Just tell what you have chosen. If you want to tell them why you made a certain decision to help them understand, this is okay. If you wish to get them to not make you feel bad or to resolve your guilt, you are playing into their guilt trap.

6. *Be assertive and interpret their messages as being about their feelings.* "It sounds like you are angry that I chose to . . ." "It sounds like you are sad that I will not . . ." "I understand you are very unhappy about what I have decided to do. I'm sorry you feel that way." "I realize this is disappointing to you. How can I help?" "It's hard for you when I have other things to do, isn't it?"

The main principle is this: Empathize with the distress people are feeling, but make it clear that it is *their* distress.

Remember, love and limits are the only clear boundaries. If you react, you have lost your boundaries. "Like a city whose walls are broken down is a man without self-control" (Prov. 25:28). If other people have the power to get you to react, they are inside your walls, inside your boundaries. Stop reacting. Be proactive. Give empathy. "Sounds like life is hard right now. Tell me about it." Sometimes people who give guilt messages just want to tell someone how hard it is. Be a listener, but don't take the blame.

Remember the mother who tried to make her son feel guilty. A man with good boundaries would emphathize with his mother: "Sounds like you are feeling lonely, Mom." He would make sure she hears that he hears the feeling beneath the guilt message.

Consequences and Countermoves

Brian was having difficulty with his father, a wealthy man who had always used his money to control other people, even his family. He had taught his children to obey by threatening to cut off his financial support or cut them out of his will.

As Brian got older, he wanted more freedom from his father, but he found himself addicted to the family money and the pleasures it afforded him. He liked being able to take his wife on vacations to the family summer home. He liked the tickets to the Big Ten basketball games and the membership in the country club.

But Brian didn't like what his father's control was costing him emotionally and spiritually. He decided to make some changes. He started saying no to some of his father's requests that were disruptive to him and his immediate family. He declined to go on some of the holiday trips when his children wanted to do other things. His father did not like that.

Predictably, he started to cut Brian off from the resources that he had had access to. He used him as an example to the siblings. He began to lavish more privileges onto Brian's brothers and sister to show Brian his mistake. Lastly, he changed his will.

This was hard for Brian. He had to cut down on his lifestyle and do without some of the things he was used to. He had to make different plans for the future as he had always planned on inheriting his father's money. In short, he had to deal with the consequences of his choice to free himself from his father's control. But, for the first time in his life, he was free.

This scenario is common. It is not always a family fortune that's at stake, but it may be parents' financial support for college. Or it may be a mother's availability to be babysitter. Or a father's help in business. Or it may be as serious as the loss of the relationship. The consequences of setting boundaries will be countermoves by controlling people. They will react to your act of boundary setting.

First, figure out what it is that you are getting for your lack of boundaries and what you stand to lose by setting boundaries. In Brian's case it was money. For others, it may be a relationship. Some people are so controlling that if someone starts to stand up to them, they will not relate to them any more. Many people are cut off by the family they grew up in when they stop playing the family's dysfunctional games. Their parents or their "friends" will no longer speak to them.

You face a risk in setting boundaries and gaining control of your life. In most instances, the results are not drastic, for as soon as the other person finds out that you are serious, they start to change. They find the limit setting to be something good for them. As Jesus says, you have "won them." The rebuke of a friend turns out to be good medicine.

Good, honest people need discipline, and they respond, however reluctantly, to limits. Others have what psychologists call "character disorders"; they don't want to take responsibility for their own actions and lives. When their friends and spouses refuse to take responsibility for them, they move on.

When you count the cost of the consequences, as difficult or as costly as they seem, they hardly compare to the loss of your "very self." The message of the Bible is clear: Know the risk and prepare.

Second, decide if you are willing to risk loss. Is the "cross you must pick up" worth it to you for your "very self?" For some, the price is too high. They would rather continue to give in to a controlling parent or friend than to risk the relationship. Intervention specialists caution the family to think hard about whether they are ready to enforce the consequences they agreed on if the alcoholic does not get treatment. Boundaries without consequences are not boundaries. You must decide if you are willing to enforce the consequences before you set the boundaries.

Third, be diligent about making up for what you have lost. In Brian's case, he had to plan to find a way to make more money. Others may need to find new child care arrangements, make new friends, or learn to deal with loneliness.

Fourth, do it. There is no way of dealing with the power moves of others and the consequences of our boundaries other than setting the boundaries and going through with your plan. When you have a plan, do like Peter: Get out of the boat and make your way toward Jesus. Fix your eyes on Jesus, "the author and perfecter" of your faith (Heb. 12:2). The first step will be the hardest. Go out and do it, and look for his help. Remember, "he trains my hands for battle; my arms can bend a bow of bronze" (Ps. 18:34).

Fifth, realize that the hard part is just beginning. Setting the limit is not the end of the battle. It is the beginning. Now is the time to go back to your support group and use them to spiritually nourish you so that you will be able to keep your stand. Keep working the program that got you ready to set your boundaries.

Countermoves to your boundary setting are tough to

battle. But God will be there to match your efforts as you "work out your salvation."

Physical Resistance

It is sad that we have to include this section, but some people can't maintain their boundaries with another person because they are physically overpowered. Abusive spouses and boyfriends will not take no for an answer; often women who try to set limits are physically abused.

These abused individuals need help. They are often afraid to tell anyone about what has happened, or what is continuing to happen, for many reasons. They are trying to protect their spouse's reputation with friends or the church. They are afraid to admit that they allow this treatment. They are often afraid that they will get beaten worse if they tell. They must realize the seriousness of the problem and get outside help. The problem will not go away, and it could get a lot worse.

If you are in this situation, find other people to help you set limits on the abuse. Find a counselor who has dealt with abusive spouses before. Arrange to call people in your church if your spouse or friend gets violent. Arrange for a place to stay overnight if you are threatened, no matter what the hour. Call the police and an attorney. Get a restraining order on such an individual if he will respect no other limit. Do it for yourself and for your children. Do not allow this to go on. Seek help.

Pain of Others

When we begin to set boundaries with people we love, a really hard thing happens: they hurt. They may feel a hole where you used to plug up their aloneness, their disorganization, or their financial irresponsibility. Whatever it is, they will feel a loss.

If you love them, this will be difficult for you to watch. But, when you are dealing with someone who is hurting, remember that your boundaries are both necessary for you and helpful for them. If you have been enabling them to be irresponsible, your limit setting may nudge them toward responsibility.

Blamers

· Blamers will act as though your saying no is killing them, and they will react with a "How could you do this to me?" message. They are likely to cry, pout, or get angry. Remember that blamers have a character problem. If they make it sound as though their misery is because of your not giving something to them, they are blaming and demanding what is yours. This is very different from a humble person asking out of need. Listen to the nature of other people's complaints; if they are trying to blame you for something they should take responsibility for, confront them.

Susan had to confront her brother, who wanted her to lend him money to get a new car. They were both adults. She was responsible and worked hard; he was irresponsible and never saved enough of what he made. For years he hit her up for loans; for years, she forked over the money. He seldom paid her back.

Finally, after attending a workshop on boundaries, she saw the light and said no to his latest request. He responded as though she had ruined his life. He said that he would not be able to advance in his career "because of her," because he could never attract business unless he had a new car. He said that he would not be able to get dates "because of her" with his old car.

Having learned to hear the blame, she confronted him. She said that she was sorry his career was not going well but his career was his problem. These responses were good for her and good for him.

Real Needs

You may need to set boundaries on people in real need. If you are a loving person, it will break your heart to say no to someone you love who is in need. But there are limits to what you can and can't give; you need to say no appropriately. These are not cases of giving "reluctantly or under compulsion" (2 Cor. 9:7). These are the instances in which your broken heart wants to give, but you would burn out if you did.

Remember the story of Moses' impending burnout in Exodus 18. Moses' father-in-law, Jethro, saw all that he was doing for the people and told Moses to delegate some of the work so that he could better meet the needs of the people.

Learn what your limits are, give what you have "decided in your heart" to give, and send other people in need to those who can help them. Empathize with these people's situations. They often need to know that you see their needs as valid and that they really do need help. And pray for them. This is the most loving thing you can do for the pain and needs around you that you can't meet.

Forgiveness and Reconciliation

Many people have a problem determining the difference between forgiveness and reconciliation. They fail to deal with external resistance because they feel that they have to give in to the other person again or they are not being forgiving. In fact, many people are afraid to forgive because they equate that with letting down their boundaries one more time and giving the other person the power to hurt them again.

The Bible is clear about two principles: (1) We always need to forgive, but (2) we don't always achieve reconciliation. Forgiveness is something that we do in our hearts; we release someone from a debt that they owe us. We write off the person's debt, and she no longer owes us. We no longer condemn her. She is clean. Only one party is needed for forgiveness: me. The person who owes me a debt does not have to ask my forgiveness. It is a work of grace in my heart.

This brings us to the second principle: we do not always achieve reconciliation. God forgave the world, but the whole world is not reconciled to him. Although he may have forgiven all people, all people have not owned their sin and appropriated his forgiveness. That would be reconciliation. Forgiveness takes one; reconciliation takes two.

We do not open ourselves up to the other party until we

have seen that she has truly owned her part of the problem. So many times Scripture talks about keeping boundaries with someone until she owns what she has done and produces "fruit in keeping with repentance" (Matt. 3:8). True repentance is much more than saying "I'm sorry"; it is changing direction.

You need to clearly communicate that, while you have forgiven her, you do not trust her yet, for she has not proven herself trustworthy. There has not been enough time to see if she really is going to change.

Remember, God is your model. He did not wait for people to change their behavior before he stopped condemning them. He is finished condemning, but that does not mean that he has a relationship with all people. People must choose to own up to their sin and repent, then God will open himself to them. Reconciliation involves two. Do not think that because you have forgiven that you have to reconcile. You can offer reconciliation, but it must be contingent upon the other person owning her behavior and bringing forth trustworthy fruits.

Internal Resistances

We have to have good boundaries, not only externally, as we have seen in the last section, but also internally, to say no to the flesh as it wants to have dominion over us. Let's look at boundaries in regard to our internal resistance to growth.

Human Need

Jane was in therapy because of her pattern of picking destructive men. She quickly fell in love with men who were very smooth and charming. In the beginning it was always "great." They would seem to be "what she always wanted" and to fulfill some missing part within her.

She would coast along for a while in this state, then she would slowly "lose herself" in the relationship and find herself giving in to things she did not want to give in to, doing things she did not want to do, and giving things she did not want to give. The men she had fallen for would turn out to be very self-centered and unable to see her needs and respect her boundaries. Before long she would be miserable.

She would talk with friends, who would tell her what she already knew: the guy is a jerk, and you should tell him to take a hike. But she would not act on this knowledge, and she would be in bondage to the relationship, unable to leave. She lacked boundaries. She could not say no.

As we began to look at this pattern in Jane's life, we discovered that the drive to stay with these men was motivated by Jane's desire to ward off the depression she would feel if she separated. We further discovered that the depression was rooted in a very empty place inside Jane that had never been filled by her father. Jane's father had been very much like the men she would pick, unavailable to her emotionally and unwilling to show love to her. She was trying to fill the space her father should have filled with destructive people who would never fulfill this need. Jane's internal resistance to setting the boundaries was this unmet developmental need from childhood.

God has designed us with very specific needs from the family we grew up in. We have talked about these before and have written extensively about them elsewhere.[1] When we have unmet needs, we need to take inventory of these broken places inside and begin to have those needs met in the body of Christ so that we will be strong enough to fight the boundary fights of adult life.

These unmet developmental needs are responsible for much of our resistance to setting boundaries. God has designed us to grow up in godly families where parents do the things he has commanded. They nurture us, they have good boundaries, they forgive and help us resolve the split between good and bad, and they empower us to become responsible adults. But many people have not had this experience. They are psychological orphans who need to be adopted and cared for by the body of Christ; to differing extents, this is true of all of us.

Unresolved Grief and Loss

If the "unmet needs" resistance has to do with getting the "good," grief has to do with letting go of the "bad." Many times when someone is unable to set boundaries, it is because they cannot let go of the person with whom they are fused. Jane kept trying to get her need for a caring and loving father met. But to get this need met, Jane was going to have to let go of what she could never have: her father's love. This was going to be a huge loss to her.

The Bible is full of examples of God asking people to "leave behind" the people and lives that are not good for them. He asked the Israelites to leave Egypt to have a better life, but many of them kept looking back, holding on to what they thought was better. When Lot and his wife left Sodom, the warning was to not look back, yet she did, and turned to salt.

The basic rule in biblical recovery is that the life before God is not worth holding on to; we must lose it, grieve it, and let go so that he can give us good things. We tend to hold on to the hope that "someday they will love me" and continue to try to get someone who is unable to love us to change. This wish must be mourned and let go so that our hearts can be opened to the new things that God wants for us.

Many times to set boundaries with someone is to risk losing the love that you have craved for a long time. To start to say no to a controlling parent is to get in touch with the sadness of what you do not have with them, instead of still working hard to get it. This working hard keeps you away from the grief and keeps you stuck. But accepting the reality of who they are and letting go of the wish for them to be different is the essence of grief. And that is sad indeed.

We play the "if onlys," instead of having boundaries. We say to ourselves, unconsciously, "if only I would try harder instead of confronting his perfectionistic demands, he will like me." Or, "if only I would give in to her wishes and not make her angry, she will love me." Giving up boundaries to get love postpones the inevitable: the realization of the truth about the person, the embracing of the sadness of that truth, and the letting go and moving on with life.

Let's look at the steps you need to take to face this internal resistance:

1. *Own your boundarylessness.* Admit that you have a problem. Own the fact that if you are being controlled,

manipulated, or abused, the problem is not that you are with a bad person and your misery is their fault. The problem is that you lack boundaries. Don't blame someone else. You are the one with the problem.

2. *Realize the resistance.* You may think, "Oh, I just need to set some limits," and that you are then on the road to getting better. If it were this easy, you would have done it years earlier. Confess that you do not want to set boundaries because you are afraid. You sabotage your freedom because of inside resistance (Rom. 7:15, 19).

3. *Seek grace and truth.* As in every other step in the process, you cannot face these hard truths in a vacuum. You need the support of others to help you own up to your internal resistance and also to empower you to do the work of grief. Good grief can only take place in relationship. We need grace from God and others.

4. *Identify the wish.* Behind the failure to set limits is the fear of loss. Identify whose love you are going to have to give up if you choose to live. Place a name to it. Who are you going to have to place on the altar and give to God? Your strong tie to that person is keeping you stuck. "You are not restrained by us, but you are restrained in your own affections" (2 Cor. 6:12 NASB). Like the Corinthians who could not open up to Paul's love, you get stuck in your "affections," your ties to people you need to let go of.

5. *Let go.* In the safety of your supportive relationships, face what you will never have from this person, or who this person symbolizes. This will be like a funeral. You will go through the stages of grief: denial, bargaining, anger, sadness, acceptance. You may not necessarily go through these stages in this order, but you will probably feel all these emotions. This is normal.

Get with your supportive people and talk about your losses. These wishes run very deep and may be very painful to face; you may need to see a professional counselor. To let go of what you never had is difficult. But in the end you will save your life by losing it. Only God can fill the empty place with the love of his people and himself.

6. *Move on.* The last step in grieving has to do with finding what you want. "Seek and you will find." God has a

real life out there for you if you are willing to let go of the old one. He can only steer a moving ship, though. You have got to get active and begin to seek his good for you.

You will be amazed how much can change in your life when you finally begin to let go of what you can never have. All of your attempts to preserve the old life were taking a lot of energy and opening you up to a lot of abuse and control. Letting go is the way to serenity. Grief is the path.

Internal Fears of Anger

Three partners of a management team of one company were working on a big project with another company. In the course of negotiations, the president of the other company got very angry with the trio because they wouldn't do something he wanted them to do.

Two of the three partners lost sleep, worried, and fretted about the breakdown of negotiations; they wondered what they would do if the president of the other company no longer liked them. They finally called a meeting with the third partner to talk about a strategy. They were prepared to change all of their plans to appease the angry man. When the two told their third partner of their plans to "give away the store," he just looked at them and said, "What's the big deal? So he's angry. What else is on the agenda?"

They all began to laugh as they saw how silly they were being. They were acting like children with an angry parent, as if their psychological survival depended on this president's being happy.

Each of the two partners who had feared the anger of the other man came from homes where anger was used to control; the third partner had never been exposed to that tactic. As a result, the latter had good boundaries. They elected him to meet with the president of the other company. He confronted the man, saying that if he was able to get over his anger and wanted to work with them, fine. But if not, they would go somewhere else.

It was a good lesson. The first two looked at the man from a dependent child's perspective. They acted like he was the only person in the world that they could depend on, and so his anger frightened them. The other one saw it from an adult's eyes and knew that if this man could not get his act together, they could move on.

The problem was internal for two of the three partners. The same angry man got two different responses. The first two resisted setting limits; the third did not. The determining factor was inside the man with the boundary skills, not with the angry man.

If angry people can make you lose your boundaries, you probably have an angry person in your head that you still fear. You will need to work through some of the hurt you experienced in that angry past. A hurt, frightened part of you needs to be exposed to the light and the healing of God and his people. You need love to allow you to let go of that angry parent and stand up to the adults you now face.

Here are the steps you need to take:

1. Realize it is a problem.

2. Go talk to someone about your paralysis. You will not work this out alone.

3. In your support relationships, find the source of your fear and begin to recognize the person in your head that the angry person represents.

4. Talk out your hurts and feelings regarding these past issues.

5. Practice the boundary-setting skills in this book.

6. Don't go into automatic pilot and give up your boundaries either by fighting or by being passive. Give yourself time and space until you can respond. If you need physical distance, get it. But don't give up your boundaries.

7. When you are ready, respond. Stick to self-control statements. Stick to your decisions. Just reiterate what you will do or not do, and let them be angry. Tell them that you care for them; maybe ask if you can do anything else to help. But your no still stands.

8. Regroup. Talk to your support people about the interaction and see if you kept your ground, lost ground, or were attacking. Many times you will feel mean when you were not, and you may need a reality check on that. You may

have thought that you kept your boundaries when you gave away the farm. Get feedback.

9. Keep practicing. Role play, continue to gain insight and understanding about the past, and grieve your losses. Continue to gain skills in the present. After a while, you will think, "I remember when angry people could control me. But I've dealt with the things inside that allowed that. It's nice to be free." Remember, God does not want angry people to control you. He wants to be your master, and does not want to share you with anyone. He is on your side.

Fear of the Unknown

Another powerful internal resistance to setting boundaries is the fear of the unknown. Being controlled by others is a safe prison. We know where all the rooms are. As one woman said, "I didn't want to move out of hell. I knew the names of all the streets!"

Setting boundaries and being more independent is scary because it is a step into the unknown. The Bible has many stories about people called by God out of the familiar to an unknown land. And he promises them if they will step out on faith and live his way, he will lead them to a better land. "By faith Abraham, when called to go to a place he would later receive as his inheritance, obeyed and went, even though he did not know where he was going" (Heb. 11:8).

Change is frightening. It may comfort you to know, that if you are afraid, you are possibly on the right road—the road to change and growth. One businessman I know says that if he is not totally frightened at some point in every day, he is not stretching himself far enough. He is very successful at what he does.

Boundaries separate you from what you have known and what you do not want. They open up all sorts of new options for you. You will have mixed emotions as you let go of the old and familiar and venture out into the new.

Think for a moment about the new and frightening developmental boundary steps that have opened up bigger and better worlds for you. As a two-year-old you stepped away from your mom and dad to explore the world. As a five-year-old you left home to go to school, opening up possibilities of socialization and learning. As an adolescent, you stepped further away from your parents as new competencies and possibilities emerged. As a high school graduate, you left for college or got a job and learned to live on your own.

These steps are scary indeed. But, along with the fear, you stretched to new heights, possibilities, and realizations of God, yourself, and the world. This is the two-sided nature of boundaries. You may lose something, but you gain a new life of peacefulness and self-control.

Here are some ideas that may prove helpful:

1. *Pray.* No better antidote to anxiety about the future exists than faith, hope, and the realization of the one who loves us. Prayer gets us in touch with the one in whom our security lies. Lean on God and ask him to lead your future steps.

2. *Read the Bible.* God continually tells us in the Bible that he has our future in his hands and that he promises to lead us. The Bible is full of stories about how he has proven himself faithful to others as he led them into the unknown. When I was a college student faced with the uncertainty of the future, my favorite verse was "Trust in the LORD with all your heart and lean not on your own understanding; in all your ways acknowledge him, and he will make your paths straight" (Prov. 3:5–6).

Memorizing Scripture verses will give you comfort when you face the unknown. It will remind you that God is trustworthy.

3. *Develop your gifts.* Boundaries create independence of functioning. We cannot feel good about our independence if we are not developing skills and competencies. Take classes. Gain information. Get counseling. Get more training and education. And practice, practice, practice. As your skills develop, you will have less fear of the future.

4. *Lean on your support group.* Just as the child who is learning boundaries needs to look back and check in with mother for refueling, so do adults. You need your support group to help comfort you in the changes you are going through. Lean on them, gain strength from them. "Two are

better than one, because they have a good return for their work: If one falls down, his friend can help him up" (Eccl. 4:9–10). Remember, as the disciples were about to embark on the unknown, Jesus prayed for their unity, oneness, and love for each other and God (John 17).

5. *Learn from the witness of others.* Research and experience has shown that it is very helpful to get with other people who are struggling and who have gone through what you have gone through. This is more than support. It is being able to hear the stories of people who have been there, who have been scared, but who can witness to the fact that you can make it. Listen to their trials, how they have been in your shoes, and how God was faithful to them (2 Cor. 1:4).

6. *Have confidence in your ability to learn.* There is nothing that you are presently doing that you did not have to learn. At one time the things you are now able to do were unfamiliar and frightening. This is the nature of life. But the important thing to remember is that *you can learn.* Once you realize that you are able to learn new things and handle new situations, you cease fearing the future. People who have strong fears about the unknown have a strong need to "know everything" beforehand, and no one ever knows how to do something before they do it. They go and learn it. Some people have confidence in their ability to learn, and others don't. If you can begin to *learn that you can learn,* future unknowns look totally different.

Many depressed people suffer from a syndrome called "learned helplessness," in which they have been taught that whatever they do will make no difference on the outcome. Many dysfunctional families caught in destructive cycles reinforce this in their children. But when you grow up and see other options that will make a difference, you do not have to stay stuck in the helplessness you learned at home. You can learn new patterns of relating and functioning; this is the essence of the personal power God wants you to have.

7. *Rework past separations.* Often when you have to make a change or go through a loss, you find that your fear or sadness seems greater than the situation warrants. Some of these heightened emotions may come from past separations or memories of change.

If you had some serious losses in the past, such as losses of friends through frequent moves, you may be tapping into what was not resolved in the past.

Make sure that you find someone with wisdom and begin to see if the fear and pain you are feeling as you face the present is coming from something unresolved in the past. This will help you get into perspective what you feel and perceive. You may be seeing the world through the eyes of a six-year-old, instead of the thirty-five-year-old that you are. Rework the past and do not let it become the future.

8. *Structure.* For many people life changes are unbearable because of the loss of structure they entail. In such changes, we often lose both internal and external structures. Things we used to depend on inside are no longer there, and people, places, and schedules that made us secure on the outside have disappeared. This can leave us in a state of chaos.

Creating internal as well as external structure will help in these times of reorganization. Internal structure will come from creating boundaries, following the steps in this book. In addition, gaining new values and beliefs, learning new spiritual principles and information, having new disciplines and plans and sticking to them, and having others listen to your pain are all structure building. But while you are doing this, you may also need some strong external structure.

Set a certain time every day to call a friend, schedule weekly meeting times with your support group, or join a regular Bible study or a twelve-step support group. In chaotic times, you may need some structure around which to orient your new changes. As you grow, and the change is not overwhelming, you can begin to give up some structure.

9. *Remember what God has done.* The Bible is full of God's reminding his people of the things he has done in the past to give them faith for the future. Hope is rooted in memory. We remember getting help in the past and that gives us hope for the future. Some people feel so hopeless because they have no memory of being helped in the past.

Remind yourself of what God has done and who he is. If you have been a Christian for a long time, look back into your life and remember how he has intervened, the situations from which he has delivered you, the ways that he has come through for you. Listen to others. Remember the grace he has shown us in his Son. He did not do that for nothing; he did it for our redemption and future.

If he has let you down or it seems that he has never done anything for you, allow him to start now. Many times God allowed terrible things for a long time before delivering his people. We do not know God's timing, but if you have started in recovery now, he is moving in your life. The time of your deliverance is near. Hang on and let God do for you what he has done for so many. "So do not throw away your confidence; it will be richly rewarded. You need to persevere so that when you have done the will of God, you will receive what he has promised" (Heb. 10:35–36).

Unforgiveness

"To err is human, to forgive is divine." And to not forgive is the most stupid thing we can do.

Forgiveness is very hard. It means letting go of something that someone "owes" you. Forgiveness is freedom from the past; it is freedom from the abusive person who hurt you.

The Bible compares forgiving people to releasing them from a legal debt. When a debt is incurred, when people trespass on your personal property, real "owing" occurs. You have on the "books" of your soul an accounting of who owes you what. Your mother controlled you and owes you to make it right. Your father dominated you and owes you to make it right. If you are "under the law," you are motivated to collect these debts from them.

Attempts at collection may take many forms. You may try to please them to help them pay you back. You think that if you do a little something more, they will pay their bill and give you the love they owe. Or you may think that if you confront them enough, they will see their wrong and make it right. Or you may feel that if you convince enough people of how bad you've had it and how bad your parents were, that will somehow clear the account. Or you could "take it out" on someone else, repeating the sin they did to you on someone else—or on them—to even the score. Or you could continue to try and convince them of how bad they are. You think that if they just understood, they would make it better. They would pay what they owe.

Nothing is wrong with wanting things to be resolved. The problem is that things will get resolved in only one way: with grace and forgiveness. An eye for an eye and a tooth for a tooth does not work. The wrong can never be undone. But it can be forgiven and thereby rendered powerless.

To forgive means to write it off. Let it go. Tear up the account. It is to render the account "canceled." "Having canceled the written code, with its regulations, that was against us and that stood opposed to us; he took it away, nailing it to the cross" (Col. 2:14).

To forgive means we will never get from that person what was owed us. And that is what we do not like, because that involves grieving for what will never be: The past will not be different.

For some, this means grieving the childhood that never was. For others it means other things, but to hang on to the demand is to stay in unforgiveness, and that is the most destructive thing we can do to ourselves.

Warning: *Forgiveness and opening up to more abuse are not the same thing.* Forgiveness has to do with the past. Reconciliation and boundaries have to do with the future. Limits guard my property until someone has repented and can be trusted to visit again. And if they sin, I will forgive again, seventy times seven. But I want to be around people who honestly fail me, not dishonestly deny that they have hurt me and have no intent to do better. That is destructive for me and for them. If people are owning their sin, they are learning through failure. We can ride that out. They want to be better, and forgiveness will help. But if someone is in denial, or only giving lip service to getting better, without trying to make changes, or seeking help, I need to keep my boundaries, even though I have forgiven them.

Forgiveness gives me boundaries because it unhooks me from the hurtful person, and then I can act responsibly, wisely. If I am not forgiving them, I am still in a destructive relationship with them.

Gain grace from God, and let others' debts go. Do not keep seeking a bad account. Let it go, and go and get what you need from God and people who can give. That is a better life. Unforgiveness destroys boundaries. Forgiveness creates them, for it gets bad debt off of your property.

Remember one last thing. Forgiveness is not denial. You must name the sin against you to forgive it. God did not deny what we did to him. He worked through it. He named it. He expressed his feelings about it. He cried and was angry. And then he let it go. And he did this in the context of relationship. Within the Trinity, he was never alone. Go and do the same. And watch out for the resistance that will want you to stay in the past, trying to collect what will never be.

External Focus

People tend to look outside of themselves for the problem. This external perspective keeps you a victim. It says that you can never be okay until someone else changes. This is the essence of powerless blame. It may make you morally superior to that person (in your own thinking, never in reality), but it will never fix the problem.

Face squarely the resistance to looking at yourself as the one who has to change. It is crucial that you face yourself, for that is the beginning of boundaries. Responsibility begins with an internal focus of confession and repentance. You must confess the truth about the ways you are keeping your boundarylessness going, and you must turn from those ways. You must look at yourself and face the internal resistance of wanting the problem to be on the outside of you.

Guilt

Guilt is a difficult emotion, for it is really not a true feeling, such as sadness, anger, or fear. It is a state of internal condemnation. It is the punitive nature of our fallen conscience saying, "You are bad." It is the state Jesus died for, to put us into a state of "no condemnation." Biblically, it is something legal, not emotional.

Scripture teaches that we are to be out from under

condemnation and that guilt should not be a motivator of our behavior. We are to be motivated by love, and the resulting emotion that comes out of love when we fail is "godly sorrow" (2 Cor. 7:10). This is contrasted with "worldly sorrow," which is guilt, and "brings death."

This guilt comes mainly from how we have been taught in our early socialization process. Therefore, our guilt feelings are not inerrant. They can appear when we have not done anything wrong at all, but have violated some internal standard that we have been taught. We have to be careful about listening to guilt feelings to tell us when we are wrong, for often, *the guilt feelings themselves* are wrong. In addition, guilt feelings are not good motivators anyway. It is hard to love from a condemned place. We need to feel not condemned, so that we can feel "godly sorrow" that looks at the hurt we have caused someone else, instead of how "bad" we are. Guilt distorts reality, gets us away from the truth, and away from doing what is best for the other person.

This is particularly true when it comes to boundaries. We have seen over and over in this book how the Bible tells us to have good boundaries, to enforce consequences, to set limits, to grow up and separate from families of origin, and to say no. When we do these things, we are doing right. These boundaries are loving actions to take. Even though they are painful, they are helpful to others.

But our fallen consciences can tell us that we are bad or doing something mean when we set boundaries. The people with whom we are setting boundaries will often say things to reinforce our guilty consciences. If you have been raised in a family that said implicitly or explicitly that your boundaries are bad, you know what I am talking about. When you say no to a request, you feel guilty. When you do not allow someone to take advantage of you, you feel guilty. When you separate from the family to create a life of your own, you feel guilty. If you do not rescue someone who is irresponsible, you feel guilty. The list goes on.

Guilt will keep you from doing what is right and will keep you stuck. Many people do not have good boundaries because they are afraid of disobeying the internal parent inside their heads. There are several steps you can take to avoid this guilt, but you must begin with one realization: the guilt is your problem. Many people without boundaries complain about how "so and so makes me feel guilty when I say no," as if the other person had some sort of power over them. This fantasy comes from childhood, when your parents seemed so powerful.

No one has the power to "make you feel guilty." A part of you agrees with the message because it taps into strong parental messages in your emotional brain. And that is your problem; it is on your property, and you must gain control over it. See that being manipulated is your problem, and you will be able to master it.

1. Own the guilt.
2. Get into your support system.
3. Begin to examine where the guilt messages come from.
4. Become aware of your anger.
5. Forgive the controller.
6. Set boundaries in practice situations with your supportive friends, then gradually set them in more difficult situations. This will help you to gain strength as well as gain the supportive "voices" you need to rework your conscience.
7. Learn new information for your conscience. This is where reading books like this and reading what God says about your boundaries will give you new information that will become the new guiding structures in your head instead of the old voices. Learning God's ways can restore your soul and make your heart rejoice instead of feeling that controlling, parental guilt.
8. Acquire guilt. That may sound funny, but you are going to have to disobey your parental conscience to get well. You are going to have to do some things that are right but make you feel guilty. Do not let the guilt be your master any longer. Set the boundaries, and then get with your new supporters to let them help you with the guilt.
9. Stay in your support group. Guilt is not resolved by just retraining your mind. You need the new connections to internalize new voices in your head.
10. Do not be surprised by grief. This will be sad, but let others love you in that process. Mourners can be comforted.

Abandonment Fears: Taking a Stand in a Vacuum

Remember from the developmental section in Chapter 4 that boundaries come after bonding. God designed the learning process this way. Babies must be secure before they learn boundaries so that learning separateness will not be frightening, but new and exciting. Children who have good connections naturally begin to set boundaries and move away from others. They have enough love inside to risk setting boundaries and gaining independence.

But if one does not have secure bonding, setting boundaries is too frightening. Many people stay in destructive relationships because they fear abandonment. They fear that if they stand up for themselves, they will be all alone in the world. They would rather have no boundaries and some connection than have boundaries and be all alone.

Boundaries are not built in a vacuum. They must be undergirded by strong bonding to safe people, or they will fail. If you have a good support group to go to after setting boundaries with someone you love, you will not be alone.

Being "rooted and grounded" in love in the body of Christ and with God will be the developmental fuel you need to risk boundary setting. People often vacillate between compliance and isolation. Neither is healthy or sustainable for very long.

Over and over in our hospital program we have seen people in destructive patterns unable to set limits because they were working in a vacuum. They repeatedly say that the understanding support they received in the program fueled them to do the hard things they had never been able to do.

If It Were Easy, You Would Have Done It By Now

This chapter is about trouble, the kind Jesus warned about. "In this world you will have trouble. But take heart! I have overcome the world" (John 16:33). When you begin to do things Jesus' way, you will encounter troubles—from both outside *and* inside. The world, the Devil, and even your own flesh will resist you and pressure you to do it the wrong way.

But the wrong way is not working. To do it right will be difficult, but he warned us about that. "Narrow [is] the road that leads to life" (Matt. 7:14). To hammer out a godly identity takes a lot of courage and a lot of work. And a lot of battles.

Running into resistance is a good sign that you are doing what you need to do. It will be worth it. Remember the clear message of the Scriptures: when you encounter resistances, persevering to the end will bring great reward, "receiving the goal of your faith, the salvation of your souls" (1 Peter 1:9). As James puts it, "Consider it pure joy, my brothers, whenever you face trials of many kinds, because you know that the testing of your faith develops perseverence. Perseverence must finish its work so that you may be mature and complete, not lacking anything" (James 1:2–4).

These resistances will surely come. I promise you. If they didn't come, you would have established boundaries a long time ago. But as they come, see them in their biblical perspective. They are part of a long history of your sisters and brothers—people who have encountered many trials as they ventured out on the road of faith, seeking a better land. This journey is always riddled with trouble, but also with the promises of our Shepherd to carry us through if we do our part. Go for it.

15

How to Measure Success with Boundaries

J ean sat at her kitchen table, teacup in hand, amazed. It was an unfamiliar sensation, but a pleasant one. Her mind wandered back to the events of the morning.

Her eight-year-old son Bryan had begun the day with his usual waking-up shenanigans. He sulked and pouted his way to the breakfast table, announcing, "I'm not going to school—and no one's going to make me!"

Normally Jean would have either tried to talk Bryan into attending school, or blown up at him in frustration. However, this morning was different. Jean simply said, "You're right, Honey. No one can make you go to school. That has to be something you choose to do. However, if you don't choose to go to school, you *are* choosing to stay in your room all day with no TV. But that's something you'll have to decide for yourself, like you did last week."

Bryan hesitated in his tantrum. He was thinking about when Mom had made him stay in his room and miss dinner when he had refused to set the table. Finally, he said, "Well, I'll go—but I don't have to like it!"

"Absolutely," Jean agreed. "You don't have to like a lot of things like school. But I'm sure you've made the right choice." She helped Bryan on with his jacket and watched him walk to the carpool ride outside.

Not ten minutes later, Jean had received a call from her husband, Jerry, who had driven to work early. "Honey," he said. "I just found out I have a meeting after work. The last time I showed up late for dinner, there wasn't any. Think you could save some this time?"

Jean laughed. "Last time, you never called me to let me know. I really appreciate your telling me in advance. I'll feed the kids, and you and I'll eat together later."

My son makes it to school, even with a cranky attitude. My husband calls me to inform me about schedule changes. I'm dreaming, aren't I, Lord?

Jean wasn't dreaming. She was, for the first time in her life, experiencing the rewards of setting and maintaining clear boundaries in her life. A great deal of hard work and risk-taking had gone into them. But it was worth it. She rose up from the table and began to ready herself for work.

Jean saw visible, demonstrable proof that her boundary work was bearing fruit in her life. Things were different. But how did she get from Point A (boundarylessness) to Point B (mature boundaries)? Can we measure our boundary development?

Yes. Specific, orderly changes herald the emerging of mature boundaries. It's helpful to be aware of them. The following eleven steps allow you to measure your growth—to see where you are in your development. Use this chapter as a guide to the next step in your growth.

Step #1: Resentment—Our Early-Warning Signal

Randy had never before felt irritated at his best friend Will's sarcastic digs. Resentment was a new sensation for him. Being the butt of the jokes had always been easy for him. "Good-natured Randy" could roll with the punches.

But when Will came up to him at church and said in front of several observers, "Are you buying smaller clothes—or putting on weight?" Randy didn't laugh it off. He said nothing to his friend, but the remark stuck inside him. He was embarrassed and hurt. He couldn't shake it off as he had for so many years.

This never got to me before, Randy thought to himself. *Why is it getting to me this time? Maybe I'm getting too sensitive.*

One of the first signs that you're beginning to develop boundaries is a sense of resentment, frustration, or anger at the subtle and not-so-subtle violations in your life. Just as radar signals the approach of a foreign missile, your anger can alert you to boundary violations in your life.

Randy had come from a family who largely avoided conflict and disagreement. Arguments were replaced by compliance. When Randy was in his thirties, he sought therapy for a long-standing eating disorder. To his surprise, instead of discussing diet and exercise plans, the therapist had asked him about how he reacted to controlling people in his life.

At first, Randy couldn't think of a controlling person. But after some consideration, he thought of Will. Will teasing Randy. Will humiliating Randy in front of friends. Will taking Randy for granted. Will taking advantage of Randy.

Those memories were not simply intellectual pictures in Randy's mind. They carried hurt, anger, and resentment. They were the seeds of boundaries in Randy's life.

People who can't get angry when they are being violated, manipulated, or controlled have a genuine handicap. No "warning light" alerts them to boundary problems. This light, when functioning properly, should turn on quickly when you are being attacked. The Bible describes anger in terms of heat: "Then the LORD's anger burned against Moses" (Exod. 4:14); "Therefore the LORD's anger burned against this land" (Deut. 29:27). Anger is like a fire that shoots up within your heart, letting you know there's a problem to confront.

Our inability to get angry is generally a sign that we are afraid of the separateness that comes with telling the truth. We fear that saying the truth about our unhappiness with someone will damage the relationship. But when we acknowledge that truth is always our friend, we often give ourselves permission to be angry.

So before you say anything confrontive, even before you set that first boundary, examine your heart. Ask yourself, "Do I have permission to feel angry when I'm controlled by others? Am I aware when I'm being violated? Can I hear my early-warning signal?" If so, you're on the right track. If not, this is a good time to work on finding a safe place to tell the truth. As you are better able to be honest about differences and disagreements, you will be better able to allow your anger to help you.

Step #2: A Change of Tastes—Becoming Drawn to Boundary-Lovers

It had been a full twelve months since Tammy and Scott had changed churches. They were reflecting back on the last year.

They had attended their former church since their marriage several years ago. It was a doctrinally correct and active fellowship. But one problem that didn't go away was the church members' attitude toward attendance at church functions. They placed a great premium on being present at each and every gathering, from choir specials to night-time services to weekly Bible studies.

When Scott and Tammy had to miss meetings, conflicts arose. They recalled the night old friends from out-of-town came to visit them. Tammy had called Janice, her Bible study leader, to tell her they'd be missing that evening's meeting.

"I think there's a problem in commitment here, Tammy," Janice had replied. "If we really meant something to you, you'd be here. But you just go and do what you have to do."

Tammy was furious—and hurt. Janice had shamed her for wanting to have a night off with her friends. It was this inability of her group to understand the word *no* that subsequently fueled the couple's move to another church.

Now, a year later, she and Scott were pleased with their decision. Though their present fellowship was also conservative and active, stressing lots of involvement, they didn't become critical or judgmental when members needed time off for some reason or another.

"How's this for a contrast?" Scott said to Tammy. "I called Mark, our men's prayer breakfast leader yesterday— I'd just flown in on a red-eye flight from L.A. I told him I'd be shot if I went to the breakfast. What do you think he told me? 'What are you doing on the phone with me?' he said. 'Get yourself in bed and catch some Z's!' That sort of understanding makes me want to be there next time."

At one time both Scott and Tammy thought their first church's attitude was correct. They weren't even aware that others could understand their no. Now, a year later, they couldn't conceive of returning to that situation.

People with immature limit-setting abilities often find themselves involved with "boundary-busters." These may be family members, colleagues, spouses, church members, or friends. The boundary confusion seems normal to them— so they aren't very aware of the destruction it causes for themselves and others.

As boundary-injured individuals begin developing their own boundaries, however, a change occurs. They become attracted to people who can hear their no without being critical. Without getting hurt. Without personalizing it. Without running over their boundaries in a manipulative or controlling fashion. People who will simply say, "Okay— we'll miss you. See you next time."

The reason for this shift is hidden in the way we have been constructed by God. We were created free for one basic purpose: to love, to be meaningfully close to God and to others: "And over all these virtues put on love, which binds them all together in perfect unity" (Col. 3:14). This fundamental truth underscores the deepest parts of our hearts. And when we find relationships in which we have freedom to set limits, something wonderful happens. In addition to the freedom to say no, we find the freedom to say a wholehearted, unconflicted, gratitude-driven yes to others. We become attracted to boundary lovers, because in them, we find permission to be honest, authentic, loving individuals.

To a boundary-injured person, people who can say a clear no sometimes seem curt and cold. But as the boundaries become more firm, curt and cold people change into caring, refreshingly honest people.

We need to join with boundary lovers in deep, meaningful attachments. Boundaries can't develop in a vacuum. As we make connections involving asking for support and understanding with these people, God gives us, through them, the grace and power to do the hard work of limit setting. This drawing to boundaried individuals extends to God. Some people will begin finding out that the holy, just

God about whom they read in the Old Testament isn't so bad or scary. He just has very clear boundaries: "As the heavens are higher than the earth, so are my ways higher than your ways and my thoughts than your thoughts" (Isa. 55:9).

Step #3: Joining the Family

As we find our tastes changing, from boundary-muddied relationships to more clearly defined people, we begin developing close and meaningful connections with people who have clear boundaries. We begin either growing in boundaries in our present relationships, or finding new attachments in which to invest, or both. This is a crucial phase in boundary development.

Why is it so important to join the boundaried family? Mainly because as with any spiritual discipline, boundaries can't be worked on in a vacuum. We need others with the same biblical values of limit setting and responsibility to encourage us, practice with us, and stay with us. That's what Wayne discovered.

Wayne couldn't believe the change. Over the past few months, he'd become aware of his lack of boundaries at work. While other employees went home on time, he was frequently asked to stay later. He wanted to stand up to his boss and let him know that his work limits were going to become tighter and more realistic. But every time he approached his superior, his anxiety kept him tongue-tied and silent.

Wayne despaired of ever developing mature work boundaries. About this time, he joined a support group at church. His relationships in the group deepened, and he began to trust the members. Finally, he was able to emotionally "take them with him" to work the day he sat down with his boss and worked out the overtime conflict. It was the safety and support of the group that gave Wayne the strength he needed to tell the truth at work.

Jesus defined fellowship as two or three people gathered in his name, saying that he would be there in their midst (Matt. 18:20). It is this very combination of his Spirit and the emotional memories of those who believe in us that helps us keep firm boundaries. Why? Because we know we have a spiritual and emotional home somewhere. No matter how caustic the criticism, or how severe the rejection of the one we're in conflict with, we aren't alone. And that makes all the difference in the world in boundary setting.

Step #4: Treasuring Our Treasures

After you feel safe being around people who believe that grace and truth are good (John 1:17), your values will start to change. You will begin to see that taking responsibility for yourself is healthy, and you will begin to understand that taking responsibility for other adults is destructive.

When people are treated as objects for long enough, they see themselves as someone else's property. They don't value self-stewardship because they relate to themselves the same way that significant others have related to them. Many people are told over and over again that nurturing and maintaining their souls is selfish and wrong. After a while, they develop a deep conviction that this is true. And at that point, they place little value on taking care of the feelings, talents, thoughts, attitudes, behavior, body, and resources God entrusted to them.

This principle is taught in Scripture: "We love because he first loved us" (1 John 4:19). In other words, we learn to be loving because we are loved. Grace must come from the outside for us to be able to develop it inside. The opposite side of this truth is that we can't love when we aren't loved. And, taking the thinking further, we can't value or treasure our souls when they haven't been valued or treasured.

This is a key principle. Our basic sense of ourselves, of what is real and true about us, comes from our significant, primary relationships. That's why many people who were unloved in childhood can be inundated by caring people in their adult years, yet not be able to shake a deep sense of being worthless and unloveable, no matter how much people try to show them their loveability.

Helen's father sexually abused her in her early years. She was terribly traumatized by the molestation, but tried to keep the secret and protect the family from being upset. By her teenage years, however, Helen inadvertently began to "tell the truth" about her family problem, in nonverbal ways. She became sexually promiscuous at a very early age. As an adult, Helen reflected in therapy on her tumultuous teen years. "I can't even remember the boys' faces. All I knew was that someone wanted something from me, and I felt it was my duty to give it to them—for no other reason than that they wanted it! I felt that I had no say-so in the matter."

Helen had not been treasured by one of the people who should have treasured and cherished her most. As a result, she did not treasure herself. She provided sexual services to just about anyone who requested them. She had no sense that her body and feelings were a "pearl of great value" (Matt. 13:46), given to her by God, which she was to protect and develop.

When Christians begin to value getting well, recovering, and developing themselves into the image of God (all of which are different ways of saying the same thing), a shift occurs. They begin desiring a return on God's investment (remember the parable of the talents in Matthew 25:14–30). Taking care of themselves becomes important.

Steve walked up to me excitedly one day. As he wasn't given to emotional outbursts, I knew something important was going on. He showed me his Bible, where he had been reading 1 Corinthians 8:11: "So this weak brother, for whom Christ died, is destroyed by your knowledge."

"Something is happening inside of me," he said. "For years, I felt guilty about reading that passage. I thought it was condemning me for leading weaker Christians into sin."

"Well, it does say that," I replied. "But you've noticed something else."

"I have," said Steve. "I'm seeing that I'm also a 'brother for whom Christ died.' That means I need to be as careful and concerned about myself as I am about others. There's no difference between what God thinks of him and what God thinks of me."

Steve had realized an important theological point. For years, Christians have been taught that protecting their spiritual and emotional property is selfish. Yet God is interested in people loving others, and you can't love others unless you have received love inside yourself.

Have you had Steve's experience? Is getting help and learning self-protection and biblical boundaries important to you? If it isn't, it will be difficult, if not impossible, to go through the hard work of developing good limits. You may need to spend some time around people who have a mature understanding of healthy boundaries and learn from their modeling.

This principle is illustrated when the psalmist says, "Above all else, guard your heart, for it is the wellspring of life" (Prov. 4:23). When we "watch over" our hearts (the home of our treasures), we guard them. We are to value our treasures so much that we keep them protected. Whatever we don't value, we don't guard. The security around a bank is significantly tighter than that around a junkyard!

Begin a list of your "treasures": your time, money, feelings, and beliefs. How do you want others to treat them? How do you want others to not treat them?

Step #5: Practicing Baby No's

The group was silent. After many sessions of considering the prospect, Shareen was about to set a limit with another group member for the first time in her life. Praying silently, the group waited to see if she could become a truthteller.

I had asked Shareen to mention to a group member one thing that had rubbed her the wrong way in the past few sessions. Though she was terrified, she agreed to try. At first she said nothing, obviously gathering up courage. Then, slowly, she turned to a woman sitting next to her and said, "Carolyn, I don't know how to say this, but here goes. It bothers me when you always take the good chair at group." Quickly, she ducked her head, waiting for the rebuttal.

There was none, at least not what Shareen had expected.

"I've been waiting for you to say something," Carolyn explained. "I knew you were acting distant toward me, but I didn't know why. It helps to know, and I feel closer to you now. You took a risk to confront me. Who knows—I may even arm wrestle you for the chair!"

Does this sound trivial? It isn't. Given her family background of a mother who made her feel guilty for setting limits and a father who had rage attacks when she dared disagree, Shareen was taking a genuine plunge. For her, boundaries were out of the question until her anxiety and depression wrenched her life out of control. That's why the best possible place for Shareen to begin her boundary work was in her therapy group.

Growth in setting emotional boundaries must always be at a rate that takes into account your past injuries. Otherwise, you could fail massively before you have solid enough boundaries.

"This boundary teaching doesn't work," complained Frank in a therapy session.

"Why not?" I asked.

"Well, as soon as I understood that I don't set good limits with people, I called my father the same day and gave him what for. Can you believe what he did? He hung up on me! This is great, just great. Boundaries have made things worse for me, instead of better."

Frank is like the overeager child who is too impatient for training wheels on his new bicycle. It's only several falls and skinned knees later that he begins to entertain the possibility that he skipped some steps in his training.

Here's an idea to help you navigate this step. Ask your support group or your good friends if you could work on boundaries with them. They will show you their true value in their response to your truthtelling. Either they'll warmly cheer you on in being able to disagree with and confront them, or they'll resist you. Either way, you'll learn something. A good supportive relationship cherishes the no of all parties involved. The members know that true intimacy is only built around the freedom to disagree: "He who conceals his hatred has lying lips" (Prov. 10:18). Begin practicing your no with people who will honor it and love you for it.

Step #6: Rejoicing in the Guilty Feelings

As strange as it may seem, a sign that you're becoming a boundaried person is often a sense of self-condemnation, a sense that you've transgressed some important rules in your limit setting. Many people experience intense critical self-judgment when they begin telling the truth about what is and isn't their biblical responsibility. Why is that? Let's look at the answer in terms of slavery and freedom.

Boundary-injured individuals are slaves. They struggle to make value-based decisions on their own, but they most often reflect the wishes of those around them. And even though they can be surrounded by supportive boundary lovers, they still experience trouble setting limits.

The culprit here is a weak conscience, or an overactive and unbiblically harsh internal judge. Though we need our internal "evaluator" to help us know right from wrong, many people carry around an extremely self-critical—and inaccurate—conscience. They feel that they are transgressing when they aren't.

Because of this overactive judge, the boundary-injured individual often has great difficulty setting limits. Questions such as, "Aren't you being too harsh?" and "How can you not attend the party? What a selfish thought!" are raised.

You can imagine the havoc when the struggler actually sets a limit or two, even a small one. The conscience moves into overdrive, as its unrealistic demands are being disobeyed. This rebellion against honest boundaries is a threat to the parental control of the conscience. It attacks the soul with vigor, hoping to beat the person into submitting again to its untruthful do's and don'ts.

In a funny way, then, activating the hostile conscience is a sign of spiritual growth. A signal that you may be protesting unbiblical restraints. If the conscience were silent and providing no "how could you?" guilt-inducing messages, it might mean that you were remaining enslaved to the internal parent. That's why we encourage you to rejoice in the guilt. It means you are moving ahead.

Step #7: Practicing Grownup No's

Think for a minute about this question: Who is your number-one "boundary buster"? Who is the foremost person in your life with whom it's difficult to set limits? More than one person may come to mind. This step deals with those extremely complicated, conflictual, frightening relationships. Straightening out these relationships is a major goal in becoming a boundaried person.

The fact that this is the seventh, and not the second, step underscores the importance of making sure we've done our painstaking homework and practice before now. Setting important limits with signficant people is the fruit of much work and maturing.

It's important not to confuse our goals here. Often, Christians who have been boundary injured think that the objective is to set limits on those important areas, and get life stabilized again. They may be living for the day when "I can tell Mom no." Or when "I can set limits on my husband's drinking." While these sorts of confrontations are very important (Jesus spoke of them in Matthew 18:15–20), they aren't the ultimate target of learning boundaries.

Our real target is maturity—the ability to love successfully and work successfully, the way God does. This is the goal of becoming more like Christ:

> Dear friends, now we are children of God, and what we will be has not yet been made known. But we know that when he appears, we shall be like him, for we shall see him as he is. (1 John 3:2)

Boundary setting is a large part of maturing. We can't really love until we have boundaries—otherwise we love out of compliance or guilt. And we can't really be productive at work without boundaries; otherwise we're so busy following others' agendas that we're doubleminded and unstable (James 1:8). The goal is to have a character structure that has boundaries and that can set limits on self and others at the appropriate times. Having internal boundaries results in having boundaries in the world: "For as he thinks within himself, so he is" (Prov. 23:7 NASB).

Developing a well-defined, honest, and goal-oriented character structure produces this step. By this time, those frightening major no's have been prepared for over time, with lots of work and practice.

Sometimes the large no will precipitate a crisis. Someone

important to you will be angry. Or hurt. Or abusive. The truth will expose the divisions in relationships. The conflicts and disagreements already exist. Boundaries simply bring them out to the surface.

Prayerfully make a list of your significant relationships. Now add to that what specific treasures are being violated in these relationships. What specific boundaries need to be set to protect these treasures?

Step #8: Rejoicing in the Absence of Guilty Feelings

Step #6 involved understanding that your first steps into a boundaried existence will most likely be met by the harsh resistance of an overactive and weak conscience. With consistent work and good support, however, the guilt diminishes. We become more able to "keep hold of the deep truths of the faith with a clear conscience" (1 Tim. 3:9).

You can take this step now that you have shifted allegiance spiritually and emotionally. You have changed from listening to your internal parent to responding to the biblical values of love, responsibility, and forgiveness. And these values have been internalized in the heart by many, many relational experiences with people who understand these values. The heart has somewhere to go for self-evaluation besides a critical conscience. The heart rests in the emotional memories of loving, truthful people.

Evelyn knew something was different inside when she confronted her husband on his critical tirades. "That's it, Paul," she said, without raising her voice. "If you're not using a civil voice with me in ten seconds, I'll be spending the evening at my friend Nan's house. Make your choice, because I'm not bluffing."

Paul, ready to launch another verbal attack, closed his mouth. He, too, sensed that Evelyn was serious this time. He sat down on the couch and waited for her next move.

What surprised Evelyn was the absence of her self-recriminations after setting limits. Usually, she would say to herself, "You didn't give Paul enough chances," or, "You've just got to stop being so thin-skinned," or "But he works hard and he's good with the kids."

Her group had worked. Her practicing had paid off. And her conscience had begun growing up.

Step #9: Loving the Boundaries of Others

A client once asked me, "Is there any way I can set boundaries with my wife—but not have her set limits with me?" Though I admired his candor, the answer, obviously, was no. If we expect others to respect our boundaries, we need to respect theirs for several reasons.

Loving others' boundaries confronts our selfishness and omnipotence. When we are concerned about protecting the treasures of others, we work against the self-centeredness that is part of our fallen nature. We become more other-centered.

Loving others' boundaries increases our capacity to care about others. It isn't difficult to love the agreeable aspects of others. It's another story, however, when we encounter another's resistance, confrontation, or separateness. We may find ourselves in conflict, or not getting something we might want from the other.

When we can love and respect the boundaries of others, we accomplish two things. First, we genuinely care for another person because we gain nothing by helping someone tell us no. It just helps him or her deprive us better!

The second advantage in loving others' boundaries is that it teaches us empathy. It shows us that we need to treat others as we would like to be treated: "The entire law is summed up in a single command: 'Love your neighbor as yourself'" (Gal. 5:14). We should fight for the no of others just as we should fight for our own no—even if it costs us something.

Step #10: Freeing Our No and Our Yes

"I love you, Peter," said Sylvia to her boyfriend as they sat over dinner. It was an important moment. Peter had just proposed marriage to Sylvia. And she was attracted to him; they seemed to be compatible in so many ways. There was only one problem: they had only been dating a few weeks.

Peter's impulsive proposal was pushing it a little for Sylvia's tastes.

"And though I love you," she continued, "I need more time for us to be together before we get engaged. So, because I can't say yes to you, I'm saying no."

Sylvia shows the fruit of maturing boundaries. She wasn't sure, so she said no. People with undeveloped limit-setting abilities do the opposite. They say yes when they are unsure. Then, when they have committed themselves to someone else's schedule, they realize that they don't want to be in that particular situation anymore. But, by then, it's too late.

I worked as a house parent in a children's home for a time. In our training for the job of living in the same cottage with several active adolescents, one experienced professional told us, "There are two ways you can start off with kids: first, you can say yes to everything. Then, when you start putting limits on them, they'll resent you and rebel. Or you can begin with clear and strict limits. After they get used to your style, you can loosen up a little. They'll love you forever."

Obviously, the second method worked better. Not only did it clarify my boundaries for the kids, it taught me to free up my own no. This principle is at the heart of this yardstick: our no becomes as free as our yes. In other words, when you are as free to say no to a request as you are to say yes, you are well on the way to boundary maturity. There's no conflict, no second thoughts, no hesitation in using either word.

Think for a second about the last time you were asked for something from someone. Perhaps it was for some of your time that you weren't sure you had to give. Suppose the person asking is not selfish, manipulative, or controlling. Reasonable people can make reasonable requests sometimes.

So you were asked for something you weren't sure you had left over to give. You weren't sure you could do it with a "cheerful heart" (2 Cor. 9:7). What happened next is what this particular boundary yardstick is all about. You probably did one of two things:

1. Since you were unsure, you said yes.

2. Since you were unsure, you said no.

Which is the more mature of these? In most cases, the second. Why? Because it is more responsible to give out of our resources than to promise that which we might not be able to deliver. Jesus said that we are to "calculate the cost" of our endeavors.

> Suppose one of you wants to build a tower. Will he not first sit down and estimate the cost to see if he has enough money to complete it? For if he lays the foundation and is not able to finish it, everyone who sees it will ridicule him. (Luke 14:28–30)

Boundary-injured individuals make promises and then do one of two things: (1) They resentfully make good, or (2) they fail on the promise. Boundary-developed people, however, make good freely and gladly. Or they don't promise at all.

Following up on guilt-ridden or compliant responsibilities can be quite costly, painful, and inconvenient. The lesson you need to learn is not to promise too much before you have done your spiritual and emotional calculations.

Step #11: Mature Boundaries— Value-Driven Goal Setting

Ben placed his pen down on the desk and looked over at his wife, Jan, satisfied. They had just spent a day together reviewing the last year and planning for the next one. This annual tradition had been developed over the past several years. It was a way for them to feel that their lives had some direction, some purpose.

Before they had begun setting goals together, life had been chaotic. Ben had been controlling and impulsive. They hadn't been able to save much money because of his spending habits. Though she was good with money, Jan had been compliant and nonconfrontive. So the more Ben spent, the more she withdrew and busied herself outside the house in volunteer missions.

Finally, after a great deal boundary work with a marriage

therapist, Jan began setting limits on Ben's out-of-control behavior. She became more honest, less blaming, and much less resentful. Ben, in his turn, began developing more of a sense of responsibility toward the family. He even felt more tender toward his wife—even after she nailed him to the wall several times about his irresponsibility!

Ben smiled. "Honey," he said to her, "this last year has been a one-hundred-eighty degree change from the one before. We saved some money. We achieved some financial goals. We're more honest with each other. We like each other better. And you're not running off helping every committee in town who needs a volunteer!"

Jan responded, "Well, I don't need to anymore. I've got what I want here, with you, the kids, our church support group, and the ministries we work in. Tell you what. Let's plan what we want to do—with ourselves, with the Lord, with our money, and with our friends—and make next year even better!"

Ben and Jan were reaping the fruit of years of work. Their maturing boundary-setting abilities were paying off in all sorts of ways. After all, the ultimate goal of learning boundaries is to free us up to protect, nurture, and develop the lives God has given us stewardship over. Setting boundaries is mature, proactive, initiative-taking. It's being in control of our lives.

Individuals with mature boundaries aren't frantic, in a hurry, or out of control. They have a direction in their lives, a steady moving toward their personal goals. They plan ahead.

The reward for their wise boundaries is the joy of desires fulfilled in life. Their investments in the years God has given pay off for them. It's a lot like Paul reflected at the end of his life:

> The time has come for my departure. I have fought the good fight, I have finished the race, I have kept the faith. (2 Tim. 4:6–7)

But does life interrupt the process of the person with mature boundaries? Won't there be trials, complications, and people wanting me on their track and not God's? Absolutely.

The days truly are evil. There will be all sorts of resistances to our boundaries and goals.

But the person with mature limits understands that, makes room for that, allows for that. And he or she knows that, should it be needed, a no is waiting inside the heart— ready to use. Not for an attack. Not to punish another. But to protect and develop the time, talents, and treasures that God has allocated to us during our threescore and ten years on this planet (Ps. 90:10).

16

A Day in a Life
with Boundaries

Remember Sherrie from chapter one? She stumbled through the day in a haphazard, out-of-control fashion. Imagine, now, that Sherrie has read this book. She's decided to restructure her life within the clear boundaries we've outlined. Her day is now characterized by freedom, self-control, and intimacy. Let's take a peek in on her life with boundaries:

6:00 A.M.

The alarm sounded. Sherrie reached over and turned it off. *I'll bet I can do without this alarm,* she thought to herself. *I've been awake for five minutes already.* Getting seven or eight hours of sleep had long been a fantasy of Sherrie's—one which she'd always felt was unrealistic with a family.

Yet, it had begun to happen. The kids went to bed earlier now that she and Walt had begun setting better time limits with them. She and Walt even got a few minutes to relax together before bed.

The sleep goal didn't come without its price, however. Like the other night when Sherrie's mother had once again made her unexpected surprise visit. This time, she showed up at a time when Sherrie had to work on a science fair project with her son, Todd.

It had been one of the hardest things Sherrie ever had to say. "Mom, I want to visit with you. But this is a really bad time. I'm helping Todd finish up his solar system project,

287

and he needs my full attention. You could come in and watch if you'd like, or I could call you tomorrow and plan a time for us to get together."

Sherrie's mother hadn't reacted well. The martyr syndrome had kicked in full force: "It's just as I've always known, Dear. Who'd want to spend time with a lonely old lady? Well, I'll just go home and be by myself. Like every other night."

At one time Sherrie would have folded under such a masterful onslaught of the "guilties." But Sherrie had, after lots of practice with her support group, decided how to handle her mom's unexpected visits. And she didn't feel so guilty anymore. Mom would be fine the next morning—and Sherrie would have had a good evening.

6:45 A.M.

Sherrie slipped into her new dress. It fit perfectly—two sizes smaller than she had worn a few months ago. *Thanks, God for my new self-boundaries,* she prayed. Her diet and exercise program had finally worked, not because she learned any new secrets about food and working out, but because she saw taking care of herself not as selfishness, but stewardship. She'd stopped feeling guilty about taking the time away from other things to work on her body. Getting in shape made her a better wife, mom, and friend. And she liked herself better.

7:15 A.M.

Amy and Todd were finished with breakfast and were taking their plates to the sink to rinse them and place them into the dishwasher. Sharing household tasks had become a comfortable habit for all members of the family. Sure, the kids and Walt had resisted, but then Sherrie stopped preparing breakfast until she got help with cleaning up. A miracle had happened with the kids and Walt. A light had gone on inside, saying, "If I don't work, I don't eat."

Even more satisfying was watching the kids get to their

school rides on time, with a couple of minutes to spare. Beds made. Homework done. Lunches packed. Incredible.

Of course, the path to that place had been rocky. In the beginning, Sherrie had called the carpool parents and told them to wait a maximum of sixty seconds for her kids, then leave for school. And they did. When Amy and Todd missed their ride, they had accused Sherrie of betraying and humiliating them. "You just don't care about our feelings!" Tough words for a loving mother trying to learn boundaries.

Yet, with a fervent prayer life and a good support group, Sherrie held to her boundaries. After a few days of having to walk and being several hours late to school, the kids had begun setting their own alarms.

7:30 A.M.

Sherrie put her makeup on in front of her dresser. She was still not used to this after all those years of applying eyeliner in the car's rearview mirror. But she enjoyed the peacefulness—and left for work with a few minutes to spare.

8:45 A.M.

Walking into the conference room of McAllister Enterprises where she worked as a fashion consultant supervisor (the promotion had been for "leadership effectiveness"), Sherrie glanced at her watch. The meeting was about to start—with herself as chairperson.

Glancing around the room she noted that three key people weren't here yet. She made a note to chat with those colleagues. Maybe they were having boundary problems she could assist them with.

Sherrie smiled. She remembered the days—not too long ago—when she would have been grateful for someone at work to help her with the same problems. *Thank you, God, for a church that teaches a biblical view of boundaries*, she prayed. And began the meeting. On time.

Sherrie's extension rang. She picked it up: "Sherrie Phillips," she said, waiting for the answer.

"Sherrie, thank goodness you're there! I don't know what I'd have done if you'd been at lunch!"

There was no mistaking that voice. It belonged to Lois Thompson. It was unusual for Lois to call these days. She didn't call much at all since Sherrie had begun addressing the imbalances in the relationship. She had confronted Lois over coffee:

"Lois, it seems as though you always want to talk to me when you're hurting. And that's fine. But when I'm struggling, you're either unavailable, distracted, or uninterested."

Lois had protested that this wasn't at all true. "I'm a true friend, Sherrie," she said.

"I guess we'll find out. I need to know if our friendship is based on what I do for you—or on true friendship. And I want you to be aware of some boundaries I'm setting with us. First, I won't always be able to drop everything for you, Lois. I love you, but I simply can't take that kind of responsibility for your pain. And second, there will be times when I'm really hurting—and I'm going to call you and ask for support. I actually don't know if you know me and my pain at all. So we both need to find out."

Over the next few months, Sherrie had found out a great deal about this friendship. She found out that when she couldn't console Lois during her chronic emergencies, Lois would withdraw, hurt. She found out that when Lois was doing all right, she would ignore Sherrie. Lois never called just to see how Sherrie was doing. And she found out that when Sherrie herself called Lois with problems, Lois could only talk about herself.

It was sad to find out that a childhood connection had never really flourished into a mutual attachment. Lois simply couldn't come out of her self-centeredness enough to want to understand Sherrie's world.

But back to the phone call. Sherrie answered, "Lois. I'm glad you called. But I'm out the door. Can I call you back later?"

"But I need to talk to you now," came the sullen response.

"Lois, call back if you want to. Here are some better times."

They said their good-bys and hung up. Maybe Lois would call back, maybe not. More likely Lois's other friends were all busy, and Sherrie's name had come up next on the call list. *Well, I'm sad that Lois isn't happy with me,* Sherrie thought to herself. *But people probably weren't too happy with Jesus when he withdrew from them to be with his Father. Trying to take responsibility for Lois's feelings was trying to own something God never gave me.* With that thought, she went to lunch.

4:00 P.M.

Sherrie's afternoon passed fairly uneventfully. She was on the way out of the office when her assistant, Jeff Moreland, flagged her down.

Without stopping her pace, Sherrie said to him, "Hi, Jeff—can you leave me a message? I need to be on the road in thirty seconds." Frustrated, Jeff left to write the message.

What a shift in the last few months. For Sherrie's boss to be her assistant wasn't something she had expected. Yet, when she had begun setting limits in her job and not covering Jeff's bases for him, Jeff's productivity had dropped dramatically. Jeff's irresponsibility and lack of follow-through emerged. His own superiors had, for the first time, become aware that he was the problem.

They had discovered that Sherrie was the driving force behind the design department. She was the one who made things happen. While Jeff took credit for all the work, he let her do it while he talked to friends on the phone all day.

Sherrie's boundaries had done their job: they had exposed his irresponsibility. They had clarified where the actual hole in the wall was. And Jeff had begun changing.

At first, he had been angry and hurt. He'd threatened to leave. But finally things had settled down a bit. And Jeff had actually begun being more punctual. He'd buckled down.

The demotion had woken him up—let him see that he'd been riding on the coattails of others.

Sherrie and Jeff still had their problems. He had a hard time hearing no from her. And it was difficult for Sherrie to tolerate the resentment. But there was no way she'd trade problems with the Sherrie who'd had no boundaries.

4:30 P.M.

The session with Todd's fourth-grade teacher went well. For one thing, Walt had attended with Sherrie. Knowing he was supportive made a lot of difference. But more important, the hard boundary work that Sherrie and Walt were doing at home with Todd was beginning to pay off.

"Mrs. Phillips," said the teacher, "I'll admit, I took Todd with some reservations after consulting with Mrs. Russell, his third-grade teacher. But there is a significant improvement in your son's ability to respond to limits."

Walt and Sherrie smiled at each other. "Believe me," Walt said, "there was no magic formula. Todd hated doing homework, minding us, and taking responsibility for household chores. But consistent praise and consequences seem to have helped."

The teacher agreed. "They really have. Not that Todd's a compliant angel—he'll always speak his mind—and I think that's good in a child. But there's no major struggle in getting him to behave. It's been a good year so far. Thank you for your support as parents."

5:15 P.M.

As Sherrie fought the afternoon rush-hour traffic, she felt strangely grateful for it. *I can use this time to thank God for my family and friends—and plan a fun weekend for us.*

6:30 P.M.

Amy walked into the family room right on time. "Mother-daughter time, Mom," she said. "C'mon outside."

Leaving the house, they started on their pre-dinner walk

around the block. It mainly consisted of Sherrie's listening to Amy chatter about school, books, and friends. All the things she'd yearned to be able to discuss with her daughter. The walk was always too short.

It hadn't always been like that. After a Christian therapist had seen Amy and the family about her withdrawal, he'd noticed that Todd's misbehavior monopolized the family's attention. Amy wasn't a squeaky wheel, so she received less time with Sherrie and Walt.

Gradually, she'd withdrawn into herself. There just wasn't anyone in the house to give her anything. Her world had become her bedroom.

Noting the problem, Sherrie and Walt had made special attempts to make sure Amy was encouraged to talk about her issues—even if they weren't the crises Todd was in.

Over time, like a flower opening up to the light, Amy began interacting with her parents once again. She was beginning to connect like a normal little girl would. The boundary work that Sherrie and Walt did with Todd was part of Amy's healing process, too.

7:00 P.M.

Halfway through dinner, the phone rang. After the third ring, the answering machine screened the caller. "Sherrie, this is Phyllis, from church. Can you pitch in for the retreat next month?"

The answering machine was the answer to dinner's disruptions. The family's boundary was "no phone conversations until dinner is through." And the family time at the table was richer for it.

Sherrie made a mental note to call Phyllis later that evening and regretfully decline. She and Walt were having a couple's weekend during those days. It helped keep them honeymooning.

Interestingly enough, when Sherrie's boundary work had first begun, she'd started backing off from church commitments to sort out her chaotic life. Now, however, she was sensing more of a desire to be involved in a couple of ministries to which she felt called. *It's like comforting as*

I've been comforted, she thought to herself. But she realized
that she'd probably never be as available to Phyllis as Phyllis
wanted. But that was between Phyllis and God. Sherrie was
out of that particular loop.

7:45 P.M.

The kids and Walt cleared the table. They didn't want to
miss the next night's dinner any more than they had
breakfast!

9:30 P.M.

The kids were in bed with their homework assignments
done. They had even had some play time before bed. Walt
and Sherrie sat down together with a cup of coffee. They
talked quietly about each other's day. They laughed over the
goofups, commiserated over the failures, planned the weekend, and talked about the kids. They looked into each others'
eyes—glad the other one was there.

A miracle of miracles. And a hard-won one. Sherrie had
had to go to therapy herself, along with joining a church
support group. It had taken a long time to move out of her
"Loving Walt Out of His Anger" modality. Her boundaries
had needed much practice with safe people before she was
ready to confront her husband.

And it had been a scary time. Walt hadn't known what to
do with a wife who could set limits, who would say to him,
"Just so you'll know in advance. It hurts me and distances
me from you when you cruelly criticize me in public. If you
continue, I'll confront you on it immediately. And I'll take a
cab home. I won't live a lie anymore. And I will protect
myself from now on."

Here was a wife who would no longer take responsibility
for Walt's tantrums and withdrawal, who would say, "If you
won't talk to me about your unhappiness, I'll back off. I'll be
with a couple of my friends if you want to talk." This was a
difficult adjustment, for Walt was used to Sherrie's drawing
him out, soothing his ruffled feathers, and apologizing for
being imperfect.

Here was a wife who confronted his emotional distance with, "You're my first choice for intimacy. I love you, and want to make you first in my heart. But if you won't spend time being close, I'll spend that time in support groups, at church, and with the kids. But I won't be in the den, watching you watching TV anymore. You'll have to micro-wave your own popcorn from now on."

He'd threatened. He'd sulked. He'd withdrawn.

But Sherrie stuck to her guns. With help from God, her friends, her therapist, and her church support group, she'd withstood Walt's blusterings. He began to experience what it was like not to have her around and underfoot all the time.

And he missed her.

For the first time, Walt actually experienced his dependency on Sherrie. How much he needed her. How much fun she was when she was around. He began to slowly, gradually, fall in love with his wife again—this time a wife with boundaries.

She changed, too. Sherrie stopped playing the victim with Walt. She found herself blaming him less. She was less resentful. Her boundaries helped her develop a full life that didn't need Walt to be as perfect as she'd wished.

No, it wasn't an ideal marriage. But it felt more solid now, like an anchor in the storms. They were more like a team, with mutual love and mutual responsibility. They were not afraid of conflict, they forgave each other's mistakes, and respected each other's boundaries.

10:15 P.M.

Lying in bed, snuggled next to Walt, Sherrie reflected over the past months of boundary work. She felt warm and grateful for the second chance God had given her.

A passage of Scripture came to her mind, one which she had read many times and knew well. It was the words of Christ from the Sermon on the Mount:

> "Blessed are the poor in spirit, for theirs is the kingdom of heaven. Blessed are those who mourn, for they will be

comforted. Blessed are the meek, for they will inherit the earth." (Matt. 5:3–5)

I'll always be poor in spirit, she thought. But by boundaries help me find the time to recieve the kingdom of heaven. I'll always mourn the losses I suffer in this lifetime. But setting limits helps me find the comfort I need from God and others. I'll always be meek and gentle. But being a separate person helps me take the intitiative to inherit the earth. Thanks, God. Thank you for the hope you gave me. And for taking me—and those I love—along your path.

It's our prayer that your biblical boundaries will lead you to a life of love, freedom, responsiblity, and serivce.

> Henry Cloud, Ph.D.
> John Townsend, Ph.D.
> Newport Beach, California 1992

For other resources, and for dates of seminars and workshops
by Dr. Cloud and Dr. Townsend, visit:
www.cloudtownsend.com

For other information **Call (800) 676-HOPE (4673)**

Or write to:
Cloud-Townsend Resources
3176 Pullman Street, Suite 105
Costa Mesa, CA

Notes

Chapter 3: Boundary Problems

1. An introduction to the four categories can be found in *Secrets of Your Family Tree*, by Dave Carder, Earl Henslin, John Townsend, Henry Cloud, and Alice Brawand (Chicago: Moody Press, 1991), 176–79.

Chapter 4: How Boundaries Are Developed

1. The following structure was developed by Margaret Mahler, and described in *The Psychological Birth of the Human Infant* by Margaret Mahler, Fred Pine, and Anni Bergman (New York: Basic Books, 1975). A researcher, Mahler observed the operationalizing of these biblical concepts in general revelation.
2. For more information on a biblical perspective on bonding and attachment, see chapters 3–5 of *Changes That Heal* by Henry Cloud (Grand Rapids: Zondervan, 1992) and chapters 4 and 13 of *Hiding from Love* by John Townsend (Colorado Springs: NavPress, 1991).

Chapter 6: Common Boundary Myths

1. Francis Brown, S. R. Driver, and Charles A. Briggs, *A Hebrew and English Lexicon of the Old Testament* (Oxford: Clarendon Press, 1977), 60; Merrill C. Tenney, ed., *The Zondervan Pictorial Encyclopedia of the Bible*, Vol. 1 (Grand Rapids: Zondervan, 1977), 166–68.
2. James Dobson, *Love Must Be Tough* (Waco, Texas: Word, 1983).

Chapter 11: Boundaries and Work

1. James Bramlett, *How to Get a Job* (Grand Rapids: Zondervan, 1991).

Chapter 12: Boundaries and Your Self

1. R. Laird Harris, Gleason L. Archer, and Bruce K. Waltke, eds., *Theological Wordbook of the Old Testament* (Chicago: Moody, 1980), 329.
2. See chapter 8, "Helpful Hiding: Dealing with Suffering," from John Townsend, *Hiding from Love: How to Change the Withdrawal Patterns That Isolate and Imprison You* (Colorado Springs: NavPress, 1991).

Chapter 14: Expect Resistance
1. See Henry Cloud, *Changes That Heal: Understanding Your Past to Ensure a Healthier Future* (Grand Rapids: Zondervan, 1992); and John Townsend, *Hiding from Love: How to Change the Withdrawal Patterns That Isolate and Imprison You* (Colorado Springs: NavPress, 1991).

Index